FOREWORD

s lead-based paint training manual is to be used by training providers to certify and to re-certify
rkers and supervisors performing lead abatement work in accordance with the recommendations of the
velopment of Urban Development (HUD), the US Environmental Protection Agency (EPA), the
cupational Safety and Health Administration (OSHA), and other local and state agencies.

e Worker section of this manual, Chapters 1 through 13, is a reprint from materials developed by the
EPA. Chapters 14 through 17 are materials developed from OSHA, HUD, and EPA materials to
mplete the Supervisor section of the book.

anges have been made to these materials to reflect changes in federal regulations. However, students
st become familiar with the regulations and stay informed of these changes. Contact your state
ency and federal agencies for up-to-date lead-based paint regulations. Your training provider may
pplement this book with additional materials.

r additional information concerning lead, health, and safety or other environmental courses please
ntact your training provider.

is manual is published with the permission of the US Department of Housing and Urban Development
UD), the US Environmental Protection Agency (EPA) and the Occupational Health Safety and Health
ministration (OSHA).

keep up to date with new information, do the following:

Go to refresher training classes

Keep in contact with your training provider and others in the field

· Talk with your local, state, and federal officials at least every 6 months

Read trade magazines

Use the resources listed in this manual

Printed by

ehsMaterials.com INC

Box 447, DuQuoin, IL 62832

800-530-1161; Fax: 888-494-6140

D1319248

In this chapter you will learn about:

- **What lead is**

- **Why lead was used**

- **Where lead is found today**

- **How you can be exposed to lead**

- **What jobs and hobbies can expose you to lead**

- **The lead paint problem in the United States**

True / False Quiz

This is an exercise to see how much you already know about lead.
It is not a test. Please take a few minutes to read the statements, then circle T for "True" or F for "False." Your instructor will go over the answers when everyone in the class is done.

1. Lead is dangerous only to children age 6 or younger.   T   F

2. We have known for thousands of years that lead
    is dangerous.   T   F

3. Experts can identify lead paint just by looking at it.   T   F

4. Lead can affect a man's ability to have children.   T   F

5. Lead is so dangerous that there is no way you
    can protect yourself from it.   T   F

6. The law says that if you find lead-based paint in a
    building, you must remove it as soon as possible.   T   F

What is lead?

Lead is a heavy, gray metal. It is also soft and pliable. Lead dust and particles stick to surfaces. The chemical symbol for lead is Pb. People used lead even before history was recorded. The Egyptians used it in solder, cosmetics, and building materials. The Greeks and Romans used lead in plumbing. The Romans used it in food containers. They added lead to wine because it tastes sweet and prevents spoiling.

Why was lead used?

Lead has been put in products for many reasons:

- **Prevents corrosion.** Lead will not crack easily with wear, weather, or temperature change.
- **Kills mold and mildew.** Lead is used in areas with lots of moisture.
- **Is easy to shape.** Lead is a soft metal and melts at a low temperature (620 F).
- **Is strong.** Lead has a lot of mechanical strength.
- **Blocks radiation.** Lead is used in products designed to block radiation, such as the lead aprons used when X-rays are taken.
- **Blocks sound.** Lead was sometimes used for sound-proofing.
- **Helps paint dry.** Lead was added to paint to quicken the drying process.

Lead is dangerous

LEAD = POISON!

Lead is a dangerous poison. You can't see or feel the lead that can make you sick. Lead is most dangerous when it is in the form of dust or fumes.

Lead dust particles can be very small. Sometimes they are so small you can't see them. They are easy to breathe if they are in the air. They are easy to swallow if they are on anything you put in your mouth-like food, cigarettes, or fingers. Lead dust settles on flat surfaces. When you touch those surfaces, you get lead on your hands. If you put your hands to your mouth, you will swallow lead dust. Young children put their hands in their mouths a lot. They are at a high risk for lead poisoning.

Lead causes health problems

Lead has caused sickness for a very long time. Ancient Egyptians knew that lead could kill people if they swallowed too much of it. In the Middle Ages, doctors realized that the health problems of painters, miners, and artists were caused by exposure to lead on the job.

In 1786, Ben Franklin wrote to a friend about work-related lead poisoning cases.

Chapter 1 - What is Lead?

In the early 1900's, doctors found that lead-based paint caused reproductive problems for workers and their families. Doctors from all over the world began to study lead-based paint as a cause of childhood diseases. Many doctors in the United States studied and wrote articles about childhood lead poisoning. In 1913, Dr. Alice Hamilton-an American occupational health doctor-wrote about painters and the hazards of their work. She documented their exposure to lead and their health problems.

Where is lead found?

Lead can be found almost anywhere today. Let's look at some places where we find lead:

Paint. "Lead-based paint" is defined in the Residential Lead-Based Paint Hazard Reduction Act (also known as Title X) as "paint, varnish, shellac, or other coatings on surfaces that contain more than 1.0 mg/cm^2 of lead or more than 0.5 % lead by weight." You will learn about identifying lead-based paint in Chapter 3.

Lead was used in paints for color and durability. Lead-based paint made a coating that stood up to wear and tear and weather changes. In addition, lead was added to paints to help them dry faster.

Lead paint becomes a health hazard when lead dust is created.

Lead-based paint **seems** like a good product. But when lead-based paint gets old or damaged, it creates lead dust and chips. Sometimes children put lead paint chips in their mouths and swallow lead. When lead-based paint turns into lead dust, it is easy to breathe and swallow. If you breathe or swallow lead, it becomes a poison to the body.

Lead dust pollutes the air, soil, household dust, and any surface it lands on. Lead dust contaminates floors, counter tops, furniture, toys, shelves, books, pets and people. Lead dust can get on children when they play on the floor. (Even when the floor looks clean, there may be harmful amounts of lead dust). Children put their dusty hands and toys in their mouth and swallow lead dust. Pets can pick up lead from dust and soil. When children play with pets, they can get lead dust on their hands. They swallow the lead dust when they put their hands in their mouth. This is called **"hand-to-mouth contact"**. **Most lead-poisoned children are poisoned by lead dust.**

House paint. Lead-based paint in the home is a major source of lead poisoning.

Any home built before 1978 may contain lead-paint. Homes built before 1960 are more likely to contain higher levels of lead.

Lead-based paint was used inside homes on woodwork, walls, floors, windows, doors, and stairs because it stood up to wear and tear. It was also used on the outside of homes, porches, windows, and doors because it stood up to weather changes.

Lead-based paint kills mold and mildew. Mold and mildew grow in moisture. So, lead-based paint was often used in places where moisture is found, like kitchen and bathroom walls and on windows and doors.

Industrial use of lead-based paint.
Lead-based paint is still used on bridges and on the inside and outside of steel structures to prevent rust and corrosion. This is called "industrial use."

Lead-based paint is still allowed for industrial use today. It is used in shipbuilding and repair. About 90,000 bridges in the United States are coated with lead-based paint. Blasting or grinding lead-based paint off steel structures creates huge amounts of lead dust. Workers can be exposed to this lead dust. The community may be exposed to this lead dust. The lead dust gets into the air and nearby soil, plants, and water.

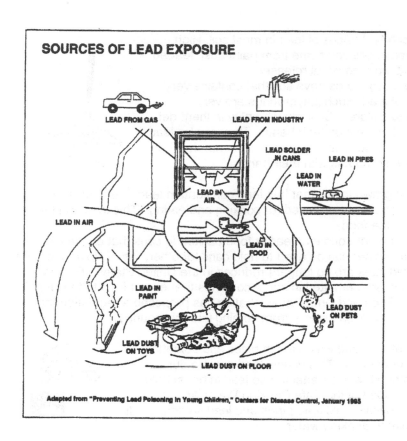

SOURCES OF LEAD EXPOSURE

LEAD FROM GAS

LEAD FROM INDUSTRY

LEAD SOLDER IN CANS

LEAD IN PIPES

LEAD IN WATER

LEAD IN AIR

LEAD IN AIR

LEAD IN FOOD

LEAD IN PAINT

LEAD DUST ON PETS

LEAD DUST ON TOYS

LEAD DUST ON FLOOR

Adapted from "Preventing Lead Poisoning in Young Children," Centers for Disease Control, January 1985

Leaded gasoline. In the past, lead was added to gasoline as an anti-knock agent. The lead was released into the air through car exhaust. This lead polluted the air and soil.

In 1978, the Environmental Protection Agency reduced the amount of lead that could be added to gasoline. By 1982, the U.S. national average level of lead found in people's blood dropped by 37%. Use of leaded gasoline should continue to decline in the USA. A higher amount of lead is allowed for farm vehicles and equipment. Leaded gas is still used in some other countries such as Mexico.

Industrial releases. Many industries use lead. Lead is used in many different types of products. It is used to make batteries, ceramics, lead crystal, bullets, and plastics. When these products are made, lead can be released into the air. Lead in the air can pollute anything it lands on. The use of these products can pollute soil, water, and air.

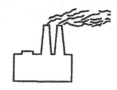

Soil. You can find traces of lead in most soil. High levels of lead in soil can come from paint dust, leaded gas exhaust, and industrial releases.

Some playgrounds have soil that contains very high levels of lead. Such playgrounds are very dangerous to children. Children who play in them get dirt that has lead in it on their hands. They can be lead poisoned if they swallow the lead on their hands when they touch their mouths with their hands.

Food. Food grown in soil that has lead can contain lead. Lead ceramic ware, pottery and glassware are used for cooking and eating. This lead can be released into the food.

Another source of lead is food packed in cans that contain lead solder. Lead solder can be used to hold cans together. As of November 1991, lead-soldered cans are no longer produced in the United States. But lead-soldered cans are permitted in some countries that export food to the United States. The Food and Drug Administration has proposed a regulation that would stop any cans with lead solder from coming into this country.

Drinking water. Lead was used in pipes and soldering - even in water coolers! This is how lead got into our drinking water. Now it is illegal to use lead in household plumbing because of the Safe Drinking Water Act (1986 and 1988). However, old lead pipes and lead soldering still can contaminate drinking water.

Hobbies. Many people can be exposed to lead in their hobbies. Hobbies that may expose you to lead are:

- Home remodeling
- Glazed pottery making
- Target shooting at firing ranges
- Electronics
- Car and boat repair
- Refinishing furniture
- Painting-some art paints have lead pigments
- Making lead fishing sinkers or lures
- Stained-glass window making

Occupational exposure. Many jobs or occupations can expose people to lead. These workers are in danger of getting lead poisoned. They may also contaminate their cars and homes by bringing home lead dust on their clothes, shoes, hair, or skin. If they do this, they could poison their own families.

Some jobs that have a high risk of lead exposure include:

Construction trades
- Lead abatement workers
- Carpenters
- Remodelers
- Renovators
- Demolition workers
- Iron workers
- Steel welders and cutters
- Sheet metal workers
- Painters
- Plumbers and pipe fitters
- Cable splicers

Industry
- Lead miners
- Lead smelter workers
- Lead refinery workers
- Lead crystal makers
- Ceramic glazers
- Plastic manufacturers
- Wire and cable manufacturers
- Electronics makers

Others
- Firing range employees
- Police officers
- Artists
- Radiator repair workers
- Car mechanics
- Printers
- Scrap yard workers and Recyclers

The lead paint problem in the United States

Lead is a known poison. Other countries limited the use of lead-based paint as early as 1840. The United States did not act until the 1970's. The U.S. Government banned the use of lead-based paint in houses, hospitals, schools, parks, playgrounds, and public buildings in 1978. Lead-based paint has been found in homes built before 1980.

Lead-based paint can still be used on cars, boats, metal furniture, industrial steel, farm equipment, and on roads as traffic paint. This lead-based paint sometimes has been used for the wrong purpose.

Today about 57 million U.S. homes contain lead-based paint. This number includes houses and apartments in the cities, in suburbs, and in the country. It includes the homes of rich people, as well as the homes of middle class and poor people. Older homes are more likely to have lead-based paint than newer homes.

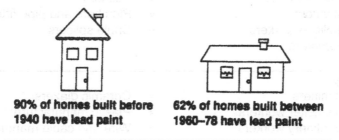

90% of homes built before 1940 have lead paint   **62% of homes built between 1960–78 have lead paint**

Renovation in a home where lead-based paint is found is one of the greatest causes of childhood lead poisoning. Many homes with lead-based paint are occupied by families with children under age 6. Children under 6 are most easily damaged by lead because their nervous systems are still developing. **Millions of children in the United States are at risk for lead poisoning.**

Damaged and deteriorating lead-based paint is in many of our homes, day care centers, schools, hospitals, and other buildings. Lead-based paint is also on many bridges and steel structures. When lead-based paint deteriorates or is disturbed, it creates lead dust. Lead dust from paint removal on steel structures can pollute a whole community if it is not removed properly.

Doing lead abatement safely is very important. When you work safely with lead, you prevent lead poisoning. Removing lead-based paint from buildings and structures in our communities helps prevent serious lead exposures and lead poisoning.

Chapter 1 - What is Lead?

Key facts for Chapter 1

⇒ **What is lead?**
Lead is a heavy metal.
Lead has been used for thousands of years. It prevents corrosion and kills mold and mildew. It is durable and easy to shape.
Lead is a poison. It can make you sick if you breathe or swallow it.

⇒ **Lead-based paint is "paint, varnish, shellac, or other coatings on surfaces that contain more than 1.0 mg/cm^2 of lead or more than 0.5% lead by weight"**

⇒ **Sources of lead exposure**
Lead-based paint
Leaded gasoline
Industrial releases
Soil, food, and water
Pottery, crystal, and glassware
Different jobs and hobbies

⇒ **Lead dust**
Lead paint is a health hazard when it chips, or becomes dust or fumes.
Lead dust is created when:
  Lead-based paint gets old and deteriorates.
  Lead-painted surfaces are broken, damaged, or disturbed.
  Lead-painted surfaces are sanded or scraped.
  Lead dust and particles tend to stick to surfaces.
Lead dust particles can be so small, you can't see them.

⇒ **Lead-based paint in the home**
Lead paint in the home is a major cause of childhood lead poisoning.
Renovation of these homes is the greatest cause of childhood lead poisoning.
The United States banned the use of lead paint in homes in 1978.

TRAINING FACT SHEET

Federal agencies with rules on lead

In 1992, The U.S. Congress passed a law called the Residential Lead-Based Paint Hazard Reduction Act, also known as Title X (Title 10). Title X requires federal agencies to establish rules about working with lead. Title X changes the way people work with lead. There are several Federal agencies with rules on working with lead.

1. Environmental Protection Agency (EPA)
2. Occupational Safety and Health Administration (OSHA)
3. Department of Housing and Urban Development (HUD)
4. Centers for Disease Control & Prevention (CDC)
5. Consumer Product Safety Commission (CPSC)
6. National Institute for Occupational Safety and Health (NIOSH)

You will hear about each of these agencies during your training. The first three above are briefly described as follows.

## 1.	Environmental Protection Agency (EPA)

This agency is in charge of protecting the air, water, and land from pollution. EPA also has some responsibility for the health of the public. Under Title X, EPA must:
- Develop a plan to train and certify people who work with lead.
- Develop specific regulations about how people work with lead.
- Determine exactly what a lead paint hazard is.
- Determine how to dispose of lead paint waste.

## 2.	Occupational Safety and Health Administration (OSHA)

This agency covers worker safety and health. OSHA makes and enforces standards to protect workers. OSHA has standards about:

Lead	Asbestos
Ladders	Scaffolds
Respirators	Electrical Safety
Chemical safety	Other workplace hazards

Under Title X, OSHA had to develop a standard about lead exposure on construction jobs. In May 1993, OSHA published an Interim Final Lead in Construction Standard. This OSHA standard is important for you when you work with lead. In this manual we refer to the OSHA Interim Final Lead in Construction Standard as the **OSHA Lead Standard.**

## 3.	Department of Housing and Urban Development (HUD)

This agency is responsible for mortgage insurance, housing assistance, housing rehabilitation programs, public housing, federally supported private housing, and Indian housing. HUD has guidelines for how people should work with lead. HUD also has guidelines for what buildings should be inspected for lead. These guidelines must be followed in public housing. HUD'S guidelines were considered the most protective methods of lead abatement for workers and the general public. Title X required that the regulations EPA and OSHA wrote be as protective as the HUD guidelines.

State and local laws about lead

Some states, cities, and other local areas have laws, regulations, and standards about how people should work with lead. You must become familiar with the law in the state where you will be working.

Measuring lead in the air

Airborne lead is measured in micrograms per cubic meter of air.

A **cubic meter** is a measure of volume. It is equal to about the size of a street corner U.S. Post Office box. The abbreviation for cubic meter is **m3.**

A **microgram** is a measure of weight. The abbreviation for microgram is **ug.**

There are one million micrograms in a gram. A penny weighs about two grams. Imagine cutting a penny into 2 million pieces. A microgram would weigh the same as one of those 2 million pieces.

Another common unit of weight is the milligram. 1,000 micrograms make up one milligram. 1,000 milligrams make up one gram. The abbreviation for gram is **g.**

The abbreviation for milligram is **mg.**

1 gram (g) = 1,000,000 micrograms (ug)
1 gram (g) = 1,000 milligrams (mg)
1 milligram (mg) = 1,000 micrograms (ug)

Why are these measurements important to you?

When lead is in the air, you can breathe it. Your employer is responsible for dotormining how much lead is in the work air.

OSHA sets limits on the amount of lead you can breathe when you are working. There are two limits you need to know: 1) Action Level and 2) Permissible Exposure Limit (PEL).

Both EPA and HUD issued Lead Renovation, Repair & Painting Training Requirements in April 2008

Action Level

The Action Level is like a yellow light. It means caution. The Action Level for lead is **30 ug/m3.**

The Action Level is an **average** of the amount of lead in the air over an 8-hour period. If you are exposed to this much lead, your employer must measure the amount of lead in the air at least every six months, **or any time you change the activity or work environment.** You also must be trained about the hazards of lead and visit a doctor for blood testing.

Permissible Exposure Limit

The Permissible Exposure Limit (PEL) is like a red light. It means stop. The PEL for lead is **50 ug/m3.**

The PEL is the highest average amount of lead that you are allowed o be exposed to. It is the average amount of lead you are allowed to breathe over an 8-hour period.

The PEL (50 ug/m^3) is a very small amount of lead. Imagine a single rain drop in a three story building ---that's how much lead 50 ug/m^3 is. Even this amount of lead can damage your health.

When you work in an area where the amount of lead goes above the PEL, the OSHA Lead Standard says you must stop until you have:

Respirators	Protective equipment
Protective clothing	Change areas
Washing facilities	Showers, when feasible
Medical surveillance	Training

If you are exposed to lead above the PEL (averaged over an 8-hour time period), your employer must monitor lead in the air every three months, or **any time you change the activity or the work environment.**

Tasks that produce high levels of lead in the air

There are lead abatement tasks that produce lead in the air above the PEL. Whenever you do these tasks, OSHA says your employer must provide you with:

Respirators	Protective equipment
Protective clothing	Clean change area
Washing facilities	Medical surveillance
Training	

Chapter 1 - What is Lead?

Class 1 Tasks

Your employer must assume your lead exposure **is above the PEL.**

- Manual demolition of structures
- Manual scraping or sanding
- Using a heat gun
- Power tool cleaning with dust collection systems
- Spray painting with lead paint

Class 2 Tasks

Your employer must assume your lead exposure **is 10 times the PEL.**

- Using lead-containing mortar
- Burning lead
- Rivet busting lead-paint surfaces
- Power tool cleaning with**out** dust collection systems
- Cleaning up with dry abrasives
- Moving and removing enclosure used for abrasive blasting

Class 3 Tasks

Your employer must assume your lead exposure is **50 times the PEL.**

- Abrasive blasting
- Welding
- Cutting
- Torch burning

Measuring lead in blood

The OSHA Lead Standard says you need a blood test when you first work with lead. The level of lead in your blood is measured in **micrograms** of lead per **deciliter** of blood.

A **microgram** is a unit of weight. It is equal to one millionth of a gram (that means there are 1 million micrograms in 1 gram). The abbreviation for microgram is **ug.**

A **deciliter** is a measure of volume. It is equal to one tenth of a liter (that means there are 10 deciliters in 1 liter). A deciliter is a little less than half a cup. A person weighing 165 pounds has about 60 deciliters of blood. The abbreviation for deciliter is **dl.**

The OSHA Lead Standard says that if you have two blood lead levels above 50 ug/dl two weeks apart, your employer must give you work to do that does not expose you to lead. Referred to as **TMRP (Temporary Medical Removal Protection)**

Measuring lead in paint

Lead in paint is measured in **milligrams per square centimeter.** Any surface coating that contains more than 1 milligram of lead per square centimeter is considered **"lead-based paint."**

A **milligram** is a unit of weight. It is equal to one thousandth of a gram (that means there are 1,000 milligrams in 1 gram.) The abbreviation for milligram is mg.

A **square centimeter** is a measure of area. It is about the same size as your thumbnail. The abbreviation for square centimeter is **cm².**

Lead in paint is also measured by **weight.** If lead is 0.5% of weight of the paint, the paint is considered **"lead-based paint."**

Measuring lead dust on surfaces

Lead dust on surfaces is measured with dust wipe tests. Results from these tests are measured in **micrograms per square foot.**

A microgram is a unit of weight. It is equal to one millionth of a gram (that means there are 1 million micrograms in 1 gram). The abbreviation for microgram is **ug.**

A square foot is a measure of area. The abbreviation for square foot is **ft².** To imagine a square foot, think of drawing a square around the edges of a normal size dinner plate. The square you draw would be about a square foot.

Measuring lead in soil

Lead in soil is measured in parts of lead per million parts of soil. You must have special training and special tools to test for lead in soil. Samples are taken from all sides of a building.

Current Federal standards for lead in bare residential soil are:

400 ppm -- play areas and high contact areas for children
1,200 ppm -- areas where contact with children is not likely

Respirators

Respirators are used to protect you from breathing in lead. There are three terms that you need to know:

1. Maximum Use Concentration (MUC) = highest amount of lead a respirator can handle under the OSHA Lead Standard.
2. Assigned Protection Factor (APF) = degree of protection a respirator gives you.
3. Permissible Exposure Limit (PEL) = amount of lead that requires the use of a respirator (50 ug/m³).

When you understand these terms, you can use them in a formula to make sure you have a respirator that protects you enough:

PEL x APF = MUC

An example of how to use this formula:
A half-mask, air-purifying respirator has a Protection Factor of 10.
This means that for every 10 micrograms (ug) of lead on the outside of the mask, one leaks in. What is the MUC for this respirator?

$$PEL \times APF = MUC$$
$$50 \text{ ug/m}^3 \times 10 = 500 \text{ ug/m}^3$$
The Maximum Use Concentration is 500 ug/m³.

This means that:

1. If there is less than 500 ug/m³ lead in the air, a half-face, air-purifying respirator is legal.
2. If there is more lead in the air than 500 ug/m³, a half-face, air-purifying respirator is not allowed. You need to use a respirator with a higher Protection Factor.

Lead-related tasks

The OSHA Lead Standard requires you to wear certain respirators when you do certain tasks. The type of respirator you wear depends on the task you are doing, and how much lead dust gets in the air.

Class 1 Tasks (up to 500 ug/m³)

- Manual demolition of structures
- Manual scraping or sanding
- Using a heat gun
- Power tool cleaning with dust collection systems
- Spray painting with lead paint

Respirators: half-face; full-face (optional)

Class 2 Tasks (up to 2,500 ug/m³)

- Using lead-based mortar
- Burning lead
- Rivet busting lead-paint surfaces
- Power tool cleaning without dust collection systems
- Cleaning up with dry abrasives
- Moving and tearing down enclosures used for abrasive blasting

Respirators: full face; papr (optional)

Class 3 Tasks (over 2,500 ug/m³)

- Abrasive blasting
- Welding
- Cutting
- Torch burning

Respirators: pressure-demand; supplied-air

PART 1: HOW LEAD AFFECTS THE BODY

In this part of Chapter 2 you will learn about:

- **How lead enters and affects the body**

- **Lead poisoning and children**

- **How lead levels in the body are measured**

- **How lead poisoning can be prevented**

Lead poisoning affects you

Lead is poisoning many children and adults around the country. You can prevent lead poisoning by working with lead-based paint safely. Your job is very important. But lead can also poison you. Lead can make you very sick and can cause death. At low levels of exposure, you can feel fine, but lead is still harming you. When you work with lead, you must work carefully. You are in this class to learn how to protect yourself, others, and the environment from lead poisoning.

As a construction worker-especially if you do remodeling, demolition, or lead-based paint abatement work-you are exposed to lead. Without proper protection, lead in the workplace can make you sick. You will wear a respirator and protective clothing when you work with lead. Clean up, shower, and put on clean street clothes before going home. If you forget to shower before leaving the job site or you wear dirty work clothes home, you could expose your family to lead.

How much lead is dangerous?

Even a small amount of lead can make you sick or damage you. Lead can stay in the body for a long time. It stays in the blood for several months, and can be stored in the bones for 30 years or more.

The more lead you are exposed to, the more likely you are to get lead poisoned. Many small doses of lead over a long time can make you lead poisoned. One large dose of lead in less than a day can also make you lead poisoned. A low dose of lead can make you feel tired and irritable. A high dose of lead can cause permanent damage to your brain, nervous system, and kidneys. A very high dose of lead can cause death.

How does lead get into your body?

Lead can make you sick if you breathe or swallow it.

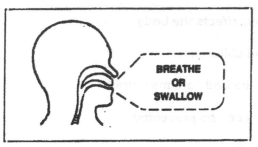

Breathing lead

When lead is in the air, you breathe tiny lead particles into your lungs. The lead particles travel quickly from your lungs as they are absorbed into your bloodstream.

Swallowing lead

If you swallow lead particles, the lead eventually goes through your digestive system and then slowly gets into your blood. You can swallow lead particles if you eat, drink, smoke, or chew your fingernails without washing your hands after working with lead.

Up to 50% of the lead that children and pregnant women swallow is absorbed into their bodies. About 10 to 15% of the lead that adults swallow is absorbed into their bodies. Your body will hold more lead if you don't have enough calcium or iron in your diet.

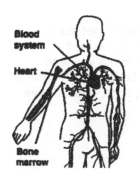

How can lead harm your body?
Heart and blood system

When lead reaches your blood, it attaches to red blood cells in the area where iron and oxygen are. If your body does not get enough iron, lead will attach to the red blood cells more quickly. Then, red blood cells cannot carry oxygen.

You cannot get enough oxygen to the rest of your body. When there is not enough iron or red blood cells in your blood, you have anemia. Anemia is a condition that makes you very tired.

Lead damages red blood cells. It makes red blood cells die earlier than they are supposed to. Lead also reduces your body's ability to make more red blood cells in the bone marrow. Lead poisoning may cause high blood pressure. When you have high blood pressure, your heart muscles cannot relax. This increases your risk of heart attack, stroke, and kidney disease.

Kidneys

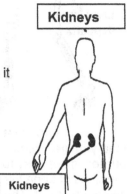

Kidneys

Kidneys

Your blood is cleaned and filtered in the kidneys, where it can cause damage. Kidney damage can be very serious. Often this damage cannot be detected until much of the kidney's function is lost. This damage requires serious medical treatment. Lead poisoning can make your kidneys fail. Kidney failure can cause death.

Nervous system

The nervous system is the system in your body most affected by lead. The nervous system includes your brain, spinal cord, and nerves. The damage lead causes to the nervous system can be permanent.

Nervous system

Brain

Spinal cord

Nerves

Lead damages the brain. It can even kill brain cells. Lead damage to your brain can make you depressed, irritable, forgetful, clumsy, and even less smart. At very high doses, lead poisoning can cause hallucinations, swelling of the brain, coma, and even death.

Lead damages the ability of your nerves to give and take messages. Lead can damage the nerves that go to your hands and feet. This nerve damage can cause your hands to shake. It can also cause your hand or foot to drop. If you get wrist drop or foot drop, you may never have full use of your hand or foot again.

The nervous system of a fetus, infant, or child is affected by even small amounts of lead. Lead poisoning can decrease the intelligence of children. Lead can cause behavior problems in children.

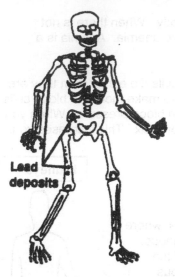

Lead
deposits

Bone tissue

As blood travels through the bones, lead from the blood is deposited into the bone tissue. Lead blocks your body's natural process of making new blood cells. Lead also competes with calcium in the bone. Calcium is released from bone tissue as our bodies need it. If lead is there, instead of calcium, then lead is released into the blood.

The bones and teeth store 95% of the lead in the body. **Lead can be stored in bone tissue for more than 30 years.** When the body is under stress, lead is released from the bone tissue into the blood. Your body is under stress whenever you get sick, are overactive, become pregnant, or are under a lot of pressure. **If the lead goes from the bone back into the blood, it causes problems all over again.**

Lead that stays in your body is called a **"body burden."** The more lead you are exposed to, the higher your lead body burden is. The lead body burden is not easy to measure because it is mostly found in your bone tissue. Samples of bone tissue are difficult to get. A child's tooth can be tested for lead when it falls out. The tested tooth can tell you how much lead is in the child's bones; that is, the child's lead body burden. A special X-ray machine can measure body burden. But, there are very few of these machines available.

Female reproductive health and pregnancy

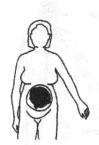

Lead poisoning is very dangerous to the female reproductive system. It can make women less fertile. It can cause abnormal menstrual cycles and affect menopause.

When a woman is pregnant, her body must take in nutrients for herself and for the developing fetus. Her body works hard to do this. If she is exposed to lead, her body will take it in very quickly. A pregnant woman's body absorbs 50% of the lead that she takes in. (A non-pregnant woman's body absorbs only 10%.) This lead will stay in her body. Lead stored in her bones will be released into her blood. Even if her exposure to lead was 20 years before this pregnancy, that lead could be released from her bones into her blood now. This is dangerous. Very small amounts of lead can make a pregnant woman sick.

The fetus gets blood and calcium to make bone from the mother. If the mother has lead in her blood or bones, it will go to the fetus. Very small amounts of lead can hurt the fetus. The cells of the fetus are developing rapidly. Lead can cause brain damage and even death to the fetus. It can cause miscarriages and premature (early) births.

Male reproductive system

Lead is very dangerous to the male reproductive system. Lead can make men lose interest in sex. It can cause men to have problems having an erection. Lead can cause infertility. It damages sperm. Lead causes the sperm to have an odd shape. It makes sperm move slowly. Wives of lead-poisoned workers have more miscarriages and premature births. Their children have more birth defects.

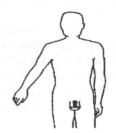

REPRODUCTIVE HEALTH EFFECTS OF LEAD

Men

. Decreased sex drive

. Problems having an erection

. Decreased fertility

. Miscarriages in female partner

.

Women

. Decreased sex drive

. Decreased fertility

. Abnormal menstrual cycles

. Premature births

   Miscarriages

Their children

. Birth defects

. Lower birth weight

. Learning problems

. Behavioral problems

Fetal protection policies

   In the past, many companies developed policies with the stated purpose of protecting the fetus. They were called **fetal protection policies.** Fetal protection policies may really have been developed to protect companies against lawsuits.

   Women were forced to prove they could not have children to keep their jobs. Women who wanted to have children in their lifetime were fired. In some cases, women had to be sterilized to keep their jobs.

   In 1991, the Supreme Court decided fetal protection policies discriminated against women. Fetal protection policies are now illegal. Lead affects both male and female reproductive systems. Both men and women need to be protected from harmful levels of lead to have healthy babies. The employer must provide a safe workplace for both male and female workers.

Children are at high risk

Children can get lead poisoned very quickly. Even a small dose of lead can poison a young child. A child's rapidly developing brain, nervous system, and entire body are affected by lead. Toddlers (age 1 to 3) are at a very high risk of lead poisoning. Toddlers are always crawling on the floor and putting everything in their mouths. Therefore, they can swallow a lot of lead dust. Children absorb up to 50% of the lead that they take in.

Recent medical research shows that lead may affect a child's intelligence, even at blood lead levels as low as 10 to 15 micrograms per deciliter. Lead poisoned children have a higher high school dropout rate than non-poisoned children. Lead poisoning can cause children to be less smart than they could have been. It can also cause:

- Poor muscle and bone growth
- Poor hearing
- Speech and language problems
- Coordination problems

Lead is the most significant environmental health hazard for children in the United States. Lead interferes with the development of a child's nervous system. It can make a child hyperactive. Lead can also make a child react very slowly. Lead can make it hard for a child to pay attention. It can make a child very clumsy. Lead kills brain cells and blood cells. The effects of childhood lead poisoning can last a lifetime.

Protect yourself and your family from lead poisoning!

Julia's husband Mike is an auto mechanic and machinist. He is exposed to lead on the job. Julia was exposed to lead on the job for three months while she worked in a shipyard as a burner. Two years later, Julia became pregnant with their son. The parents' lead exposure may have affected their son's health.

"As my son grew up," says Julia, "he developed learning disabilities. He had a lot of trouble paying attention and following directions. He has really poor organization skills. We had to send him to a special education program for several years. My son is 14 years old now. He's doing better, but he still needs help organizing. He still needs special care."

From interview with a worker. (The names have been changed.)

Health effects of lead poisoning

Lead poisoning can affect you in many different ways. A large amount of lead can make you sick right away. A small amount of lead, day after day, can make you sick over a long period of time.

The health effects of lead poisoning are often difficult to recognize. There are many different signs and symptoms of lead poisoning. Signs and symptoms are things you see and feel when you are sick. The signs and symptoms for lead poisoning can also be caused by a number of other things, like the flu or a cold. Lead poisoning can easily be mistaken for a cold or the flu.

Signs and symptoms of lead poisoning

- Tiredness (fatigue)
- Sleep problems (insomnia)
- Dizziness
- Irritability
- Nervousness
- Headaches
- Difficulty concentrating
- Depression
- Forgetfulness
- Hyperactivity (children)
- Numbness

- Wrist or food drop
- Weakness
- Clumsiness
- Joint and muscle pain
- Vomiting
- Loss of appetite
- Stomach aches
- Constipation
- Metal taste in the mouth
- Problems having healthy children

Sometimes the signs of lead poisoning come and go. You have them one day and then they disappear. Then the signs come back again. This can happen for several months.

Lead can cause damage without symptoms. You may not know you have lead poisoning. Lead poisoning often goes unnoticed. A child with lead poisoning may seem healthy, while damage is being done to their bodies. Signs and symptoms of the damage usually don't develop until the condition is serious.

Some health effects of lead poisoning

- Anemia
- High blood pressure
- Damage to blood cell formation
- Kidney disease

- Brain damage
- Nerve damage
- Decreased fertility
- Premature births
- Miscarriages

Short-term or long-term effects

Sometimes the effects of lead poisoning are short term. This means they don't last a long time-maybe a few weeks or months. Sometimes the symptoms of lead poisoning are long term. This means the symptoms stay with you a long time-sometimes for years or even permanently. Long-term effects can be caused by repeated small doses of lead, or by a very high dose at one time.

Reversible or permanent damage

Some effects of lead poisoning can be reversed. This means the effects may go away. High blood pressure is an effect of lead poisoning that is reversible. High blood pressure can return to normal when the lead in your body decreases.

Lead poisoning can cause **permanent damage.** This means that the damage is always there. An example of permanent damage caused by lead is wrist drop. Wrist drop is when your wrist hangs limp at the end of your arm. You may never be able to use that hand again. Wrist drop is caused when lead damages your nervous system.

Lead can cause permanent damage to your

- Brain
- Learning ability
- Coordination
- Hearing
- Nerves

- Digestive system
- Heart
- Blood cell formation
- Kidneys
- Reproductive system

Testing for lead in your body

The only way to tell for sure that you are lead poisoned is to get a blood test. When lead enters your body, it gets into your blood. A blood test is the only way to find out how much lead is in your blood. The amount of lead in your blood is called your **blood lead level.**

There are two kinds of tests to monitor blood lead levels. Both tests can be done from blood taken from either your arm or your finger. Both can be taken from the same sample of blood.

1. Blood lead level test

This test measures the amount of lead in your blood. It shows how much lead you have been exposed to in the **last 6 to 8 weeks.** The blood lead test is the most accurate test. Your blood lead level is measured in micrograms of lead per **deciliter** of blood.

2. ZPP test (Zinc Protoporphyrin)

ZPP is a chemical in your body. Your ZPP level becomes abnormal when a lot of lead has entered your body over the last **few months** It tells how much lead your body has absorbed by looking at some of your body proteins. It does not measure the amount of lead in your blood. Results are measured in **micrograms per deciliter**. Normal results for the ZPP test are 35-50 ug/dl. The ZPP test is not as accurate as the blood lead level test for early or low level lead exposures. ZPP results can vary because of diet, anemia, and other factors.

A **microgram** is a measure of weight. There are I million micrograms in a gram. The abbreviation for microgram is ug.

A penny weighs about two grams. Imagine cutting a penny into 2 million pieces. A microgram would weigh the same as **one** of those 2 million pieces.

A deciliter is a measure of volume. It is equal to a little less than half a cup. A person weighing 165 pounds has about 60 deciliters of blood. The abbreviation for deciliter is dl.

Blood lead levels

Lead is a poison to your body. Recent studies say lead can harm health at blood levels as low as 10 to15 ug/dl. Imagine that a penny broken into 2 million pieces again. Now picture 15 of those pieces dissolved in a half cup of liquid. That tiny amount of lead in your blood can cause health problems!

Lead is dangerous because it builds up in your body. It can stay there for years. It is difficult to say exactly what happens to your body with specific lead levels because we are all so different. Different people have different reactions to lead in their bodies. Some people do not even know that they are having problems with lead poisoning when their blood levels are 60 ug/dl. You may not know that lead is harming your body. Other people suffer obvious signs of lead poisoning at 30 ug/dl. This box is a very rough estimate of an adult's reaction to different levels of lead.

ADULT REACTION TO LEAD

Blood Lead Level	Possible Health Effects
15ug/dl	Increase in blood pressure; harmful effects on fetus; joint and muscle aches
20 ug/dl	Reproductive problems
40 ug/dl	Kidney damage; damage to blood formation
60 ug/dl	Anemia; nerve damage; constipation; stomach pains; irritability and fatigue; memory and concentration problems; clumsiness; drowsiness and sleep problems
80 ug/dl	Blue line on gums; uncontrollable shaking hands; wrists and foot drop; hallucinations; brain damage; coma death.

Every child is also different in his or her reactions to lead. The following chart is a very rough scale of children's reactions to different levels of lead. A lead poisoned child may not look or act sick, but his or her body is being damaged. The health effects of lead sometimes may not be seen.

Researchers have known for a long time that children are especially sensitive to lead exposures. Scientists have discovered that even very low exposures to lead can cause serious health effects in children.

In 1991, the Centers for Disease Control and Prevention lowered the level of concern for children's blood lead levels from 25 ug/dl to 10 ug/dl. About 10 to 15% of all preschool children (3 to 4 million children) are estimated to have blood lead levels above 10 ug/dl. The major source of lead exposure for children is lead-based paint and lead dust in their homes.

CHILD'S REACTION TO LEAD

Blood Lead Level	Possible Health Effects
10 ug/dl	Slight loss in IQ (not as smart as they should be); hearing and growth problems
20 ug/dl	Moderate loss in IQ; hyperactivity; poor attention span; difficulty learning; language and speech problems; slower reflexes
40 ug/dl	Poor bone and muscle development; clumsiness-lack of coordination; early anemia; fewer red blood cells to carry oxygen and iron; tiredness; drowsiness
50 ug/dl	Stomach aches and cramps; anemia; destruction of red blood cells; brain damage
100 ug/dl and above	Swelling of the brain; seizures; coma; death

Preventing lead poisoning

Lead-based paint in the homes of lead poisoned children should be abated. Lead-based paint abatement is any set of actions that removes the lead hazard permanently. Abatement often cannot happen right away. While the family waits, you can use interim controls to control the lead hazard until it is abated. "Interim" means "in between time." Interim controls are actions that

Lessen the amount of lead dust. When lead dust is reduced, the source of lead poisoning is reduced. Interim controls do not take the place of abatement. By doing lead abatement and interim controls, you are helping prevent lead poisoning.

Make sure that you do not get sick.

When you work with lead, you have a higher risk of getting lead poisoned. You need to do as much as possible to reduce that risk. Here are some things that you can do:

- Make sure your employer provides a safe workplace.
- Know your rights as a worker.
- Wear protective gear.
- Use safe work practices.
- Use good personal hygiene.
- Don't take lead home on your clothes or in your car.
- Get the medical exams that your employer provides.
- Inform your employer if you develop any signs of lead poisoning.
- Do non lead work if your blood lead level is too high.

In this class, you will learn how to make your workplace safer. You will learn what your rights are as a lead abatement worker. You will learn about the protective gear that you need to wear and the safe work practices that you will need to use. You will learn how important good personal hygiene is. The OSHA Lead Standard says your employer must provide this training for you. The standard also says your employer must make special medical exams available to you.

Good nutrition

Good nutrition is important. A diet with enough iron and calcium prevents worse lead poisoning. When you eat a diet high in iron and calcium, it can reduce lead absorption. People with low amounts of iron and calcium have increased lead absorption. If you have enough iron and calcium in your body, lead will be absorbed less quickly. Vitamin C, zinc, and protein-found in a well-balanced diet-appear to decrease lead absorption as well. Stay away from foods high in fat. Foods with a lot of fat, such as fried foods, appear to increase lead absorption.

Eat foods high in iron - cheese, fish, seafood, meat (especially liver), eggs, spinach, beans, raisins, apricots, seeds (pumpkin, squash, sunflower), black walnuts, almonds, barley, wheat germ

Eat foods high in calcium - milk, cheese, ice cream, yogurt, bread, fish, seafood, meat, beans, broccoli, leafy green vegetables (spinach, etc.), cherries, blackberries, raisins, fruit juice (orange, prune, grapefruit, pineapple), peaches, apricots, dates, sunflower seeds, almonds, hazelnuts, pecans.

Key facts for Chapter 2, Part 1

Lead can poison you and make you very sick.
Even a small amount of lead can make you sick.
Lead is dangerous when you breathe or swallow it.
Lead can cause permanent damage.
Children's developing brains and bodies are easily damaged by lead
Even low levels of lead can cause permanent damage to a child.
Pregnant women and children are most easily lead poisoned.

Lead in your body
Lead can damage your body without your feeling any symptoms.
Lead poisoning can easily be mistaken for the *flu*.
Lead attaches to your red blood cells and travels through your body.
Lead can be stored in your body for more than 30 years.
Body burden is the amount of lead stored in your body.
Lead can be released from your bones and poison you.
Lead can harm many parts of your body----blood cells, heart, kidneys, nervous system, bone tissue, and reproductive organs.
Lead can cause men to have problems having an erection.
Lead can cause women to have stillbirths or miscarriage

Blood tests find out how much lead is in your blood.
The tests used are: blood lead level test and zinc protoporphyrin (ZPP) test. The blood lead level test is the more accurate test.
Blood lead levels are measured in micrograms of lead per deciliter (ug/dl) of blood. People can have different reactions to the same blood lead level.

Lead poisoning can be prevented.
Your work as a lead abatement worker will prevent future lead poisoning.

PART 2: MEDICAL EXAMS & MONITORING
In this part of Chapter 2 you will learn about:

- What medical tests lead workers must have

- What happens if you can't work with lead

- Medical treatment for lead poisoning

- Your right to your medical records

Medical exams
    When you work with lead, you need special kinds of medical exams called medical surveillance. There are two types of medical surveillance for workers exposed to lead:

1. **Initial medical surveillance**
2. **On-going medical surveillance program**

    The medical exams must be given or supervised by a licensed doctor. By law, your employer must pay for the blood tests and exams. The exams must be scheduled at a reasonable time and place for you.
    The doctor will send all test results and exam results to your employer. Your employer must then notify you in writing of the results within 5 working days. When you work with **lead you need special** medical exams.

1. Initial medical surveillance
    Initial medical surveillance is a set of special blood tests. The blood tests check how much lead is in your blood. The two blood tests used are the blood lead level test and the zinc protoporphyrin (ZPP) test. Checking your blood for lead is called biological monitoring.
    If you are going to do any of the lead-related tasks, you will need the initial medical exam. **If you are exposed to lead on the job** at or above the Action Level for any one day, you need the initial medical surveillance.

    Your employer must make these tests available to you and pay for them. The tests must be available and easy for you to get during work time.

**YOU WILL NEED
BLOOD TESTS**

2. On-going medical surveillance program

The medical surveillance program is a special program of medical exams. You need a medical surveillance program if you are or may be exposed to lead on the job at or above the Action Level for more than 30 days in a year.

If you are a lead abatement worker, you may be exposed to lead above the Action Level for 30 or more days in a year. When you expect to do lead abatement work for at least 30 days, you should take part in a medical surveillance program.

The medical surveillance program has three types of exams. The doctor must follow the OSHA Lead Standard.

Medical surveillance program include
A. Blood tests for biological monitoring
B. Six-part medical exam
C. Medical exam and consultation

A. Blood tests for biological monitoring
OSHA requires the blood lead level test and the ZPP test

1. When you begin working with lead and every 2 months for the first 6 months and then every 6 months as long as you work with lead at or above the Action Level for 30 or more days in a year.

2. When your blood lead level results are at or above 40 ug/dl, you must be tested at least every 2 months until your blood lead level drops below 40 ug/dl.

3. When your blood lead level results are at or above 50 ug/dl, you must be tested again within two weeks. If the second test result is at or above 50 ug/dl, you must be medically removed and tested at least every month until your blood lead level is 40 ug/dl less on two separate testing dates. The tests should be taken at least 30 days apart. This is referred to as TMRP – Temporary Medical Removal Protection.

This schedule is required under the OSHA Lead Standard. It is the required minimum amount of blood lead testing. **Many doctors recommend that construction workers get blood lead tests every month.**

Remember, a blood test is the only way to find out if lead is poisoning your body. The most accurate blood test is the blood lead level test. It shows how much lead you have been exposed to in the last 6 to 8 weeks. When you feel any of the symptoms of lead poisoning, you need to have your blood tested.

If your blood lead level rises more than 6 ug/dl, you need more protection when you work. You may need to change the work method, wear a better respirator, wash your hands and face more often, and shower before you go home at the end of the day.

B. Annual Six-part medical exam
(If your blood lead level is 40+ ug/dl)

Your employer must make the required six-part medical exam in the medical surveillance program available to you whenever you will be working with lead at or above the Action Level for 30 or more days in a year, and your blood lead level results are 40 ug/dl or above.

The six-part medical exam consists of the following:

1. An interview about your work and medical history to evaluate your
   -- Past lead exposures
   -- Personal habits (like smoking and hygiene)
   -- Previous medical problems with the kidneys, heart, nerves, blood, stomach, intestines, and reproductive organs

2. A complete physical exam to check your

Blood	Nerves	Teeth
Brain	Stomach	Intestines
Heart	Kidneys	Lungs

3. A blood pressure check

4. Blood tests which will show
   - Blood lead level
   - ZPP
   - Hemoglobin and hematocrit (anemia test)
   - Blood ureanitrogen
   - Serum creatinine (kidney test)

5. Urinalysis (kidney protein check)—ordered if protein indicates kidney disease has already started

6. Any additional test that the doctor needs to do to determine how lead has affected you or could affect you. Pregnancy testing and male fertility testing must be provided if you request them.

Medical Evaluation and Consultation

You have the right to a medical exam and consultation whenever you will be working with lead at or above the Action Level for 30 days or more in a year and:

- You feel sick with any of the symptoms of lead poisoning.
- When you have a blood lead level at or above 40 ug/dl.
- Whenever you are concerned about having a healthy baby.
- You have difficulty breathing while wearing a respirator.

You need to notify your employer that you want the medical exam and consultation. The content of this medical exam and consultation is determined by the doctor. Your employer must pay for the exam.

After your exam and blood tests, the doctor will send your blood test results and a written opinion of your fitness for work to your employer. Your employer must notify you in writing of the results within 5 working days.

Medical removal

Medical removal means that you are removed from the lead exposure on your job. The law states you must be removed if your blood lead levels get too high.

Medical removal can prevent you from getting severe lead poisoning. Removing you from the lead exposure gives your body time to get rid of the lead. Sometimes this is enough to bring your blood lead level down.

You must be medically removed if:

1. You have a high blood lead level
2. A doctor gives you a final medical determination

---

1. You have a high blood lead level

If your blood lead level is 50 ug/dl or higher, you must get a follow-up test within two weeks. If your blood lead level is still 50 ug/dl or higher, you must be removed from exposure to lead. This means that you cannot work in an area that is above the Action Level. You cannot do any of the lead-related tasks.

It is dangerous for you to work with lead when your blood lead level is too high. Your lead poisoning could become worse.

2. A doctor gives you a final medical determination

You can be medically removed if a doctor states that you have a medical condition that will be affected by lead exposure. The doctor believes that the risk to your health is too high. **The doctor must recommend to your employer that you not work with lead. The** doctor does not tell the employer what your medical problem is, but that your health is at risk if you continue to work with lead. The doctor will give a written medical opinion to remove you from lead exposure. This written opinion is called a final medical determination.

There are several reasons why a doctor might use a final medical determination: kidney problems, high blood pressure, and other conditions that lead could make worse. If you decide you want to have children, your doctor should make sure your blood lead level is below 30 ug/dl. If your blood lead level is at or above *30* ug/dl, your doctor should recommend that you be removed from doing lead work. OSHA recommends that men **and women who want to have children keep** their blood lead level below 30 ug/dl.

Medical removal protection

When you are medically removed, you are protected by the OSHA Lead Standard. While you are unable to work with lead, your **employer must give you another job where you are not exposed to lead above the Action level. , If another job** is not available, your employer must pay your wages and benefits, and maintain your seniority, for as long as your job exists or up to 18 months. This is **"medical removal protection."**

If you get medically removed because of a high blood lead level, you may return to work with lead when your blood lead level is down to 40 ug/dl or lower on two separate tests.

If you get medically removed because of a final medical determination, you may return to working with lead when the doctor determines that your health is no longer at high risk from lead exposure. The doctor must put the medical opinion in writing that you can return to working with lead. Then you can return to your lead job.

When should you be medically removed?

Many doctors believe that medical removal should happen before your blood lead level reaches 50 ug/dl They can use the final medical determination to protect you. You will then have medical removal protection.

Some professional groups, including the Society for Occupational and Environmental Health, support medical removal at 30 ug/dl.

The National Institute for Occupational Safety and Health recommends removal at 25 ug/dl.

Your right to a second medical opinion

Your employer must make medical surveillance available to you. You can request a second exam by a doctor of your choice. You can request a second opinion if you do not agree with the first doctor's findings. You must request a second exam in writing within 15 days after getting a copy of the first exam results. Your employer must pay for the second exam.

If the two doctors do not agree, they are asked to talk with each other. If they cannot agree, they will pick a third doctor to provide an opinion. The third doctor's opinion stands unless you and your employer agree to one of the initial two opinions. The right to a second medical opinion is for your protection. It is your right under the OSHA Lead Standard.

Medical treatment for lead poisoning

The best treatment is prevention. Medical treatment includes medical removal, observation, and follow up exams, as well as drug treatment.

Medical drug treatment for lead poisoning is called **chelation**. Most chelating drugs are given by a needle into your muscle or vein. Chelating chemicals hook onto the lead in your body and carry it out through the kidneys. It is then passed through the urine. There are also chelating drugs that can be swallowed. These chelating drugs are now being studied. They are mainly used to chelate children.

Chelation is the medical treatment for severe lead poisoning. It can be a painful and risky treatment. You can receive the treatment in the hospital.

Consider getting a second doctor's opinion.

If a doctor says you need chelation, consider getting a second doctor's opinion. If you are **feeling very sick or have a very high** blood lead level, do **not delay your medical treatment.** If your blood lead level is 100 ug/dl or higher, you do not want to wait for a second opinion.

The second doctor should be a doctor that you know and trust. Chelation is a serious medical treatment. It would be best to know that at least two doctors think it is necessary for you to have it. The OSHA Lead Standard requires your employer to pay for this second opinion. Make sure you put your request in writing. This request must be received by your employer within 15 days of your receiving the first doctor's opinion.

Prophylactic chelation is illegal

"Prophylactic" means "to prevent." Prophylactic chelation means to take chelating drugs to prevent lead poisoning. Prophylactic chelation is against the law. It does not prevent lead poisoning. It only hides lead poisoning. It does not protect you from lead. It is illegal for your employer to give you chelating drugs.

Chelating drugs are especially dangerous to your health if you take them while you are still exposed to lead. They can hide lead poisoning. Chelating drugs can make your body take in lead more easily. This can make you even more sick. Never take chelating drugs while you are working with lead.

Misuse of chelation treatment

The misuse of chelation treatment has been recorded repeatedly. Doctors have given workers chelating drugs even though the workers were still exposed to lead on the job. Taking chelating drugs while working a lead job is prophylactic chelation. It is very dangerous.

Never take any of these chelating drugs or get chelation treatment while you are still working with lead:

- Penicillamine
- Edetate calcium disodium ~DTA)
- Succimer (')MSA or Chemet)
- Dimercaprol

Your medical records

You have a right to have a copy of your medical records. Ask for a copy of your records each time you have a medical exam or blood test. Keep these records on file at home. Your employer must keep a copy of your medical records on file for as long as you are employed there. Once you leave the job, your employer must keep your medical records for 30 years if you were employed there for one year or more.

Under the OSHA "Medical Record Access" standard, you have a right to access your medical records kept by your employer or by outside contractors. You have the right to have your medical records sent to you or anyone you choose, such as your family doctor. You also have the right to have a doctor explain your medical records to you.

Your medical records may include:
-Medical and employment questionnaires or histories (including job
   description and occupational exposures)
-Results of medical examinations pre-employment, pre-assignment,
   periodic, or episodic)
-Results of laboratory tests (including X-rays and blood tests) Medical
   opinions, diagnoses, progress notes, and recommendations
-Descriptions of treatment and prescriptions
-Employee medical complaints

Ask for an exit medical exam

The current OSHA Lead Standard does not require your employer to pay for a medical exam when you leave the job. But, you do have the right to an exam-paid for by your employer-if you have any of the symptoms of lead poisoning before you leave the job. Remember to use that right-get a medical exam.

When you are no longer working around lead, your employer does not have to pay for your exams.

It is always a good idea to have a medical check up each year. When you go for your yearly check up, make sure you tell your doctor that you have been exposed to lead on the job. Tell the doctor all the information you have learned about how lead affects the body. Ask your doctor to examine you for any long-term effects of lead, each year.

Medical Removal
You must be removed from lead exposure on the job if:
1. Your blood lead level is ~ 50 ug/dl.
2. A doctor gives you a final medical determination. Some professional groups recommend medical removal at 30 ug/dl. OSHA recommends removal below 30 ug/dl if you want to have children.

Medical Removal Protection
If you are medically removed, your employer must provide you with another job where the lead level is below the Action Level or pay you your wages and benefits for up to 18 months until your blood lead level comes down or your job is done.

You have the right to see a second doctor.
The cost of this exam is paid for by your employer.

Medical treatment for lead poisoning is called "chelation."
Chelation can be painful. There are risks to your health.
Chelation should be done under the care of a health practitioner.
Get a second opinion before being chelated, if possible.
It is illegal for your employer to give you chelating drugs.

You have the right to have a copy of your medical records.

Key facts for Chapter 2, Part 2

When you work with lead you need special medical exams.
Your employer must provide these exams.

Initial medical surveillance
As soon as you start lead work, you need to get your blood tested.

Medical surveillance program
When you work with lead for 30+ days in a year, you need a medical surveillance program. There are three types of exams in this program:
1. Blood tests
2. Six-part medical exam
3. Medical exam and consultation

Blood tests find out how much lead is in your blood.

When you work with lead you need your blood tested at least:
- Every 2 months for the first six months.
  Then every 6 months as long as you work with lead at or above the Action Level.
- Every 2 months if your blood lead level is 40 ug/dl or above.
- Every month if your blood lead level is *50* ug/dl or above.

You need a six-part medical exam when your blood lead level reaches 40 ug/dl or above.

Medical exam and consultation
You have the right to a medical exam and consultation if you will **be** working with lead at or above the Action Level for more than 30 days a year and:
You feel sick with signs of lead poisoning. You're concerned about having a healthy baby. If your blood lead level is ~40 ug/dl. You're having trouble breathing with a respirator.

Chapter 3 – Identifying Lead Hazards

In this chapter you will learn about:
- **Lead dust**
- **Lead inspections**
- **When lead-based paint inspections are required**
- **How inspectors test for lead-based paint using:**
  - √ **Paint chip analysis**
  - √ **X-Ray Fluorescence analysis**
  - √ **Dust wipe tests**
  - √ **Wet chemical field tests**
  - √ **Soil sampling**
- **Risk assessments**

Lead dust

Lead dust is poisonous when you breathe or swallow it

Lead dust comes from lead-based paint. The dust is so small that you may not even see it. Lead dust is easy to breathe and swallow. Lead-based paint turns into lead dust when:

1. **It peels, chips, or flakes.**
   This happens when paint gets old, moisture-damaged, or damaged by weather changes.

2. **Surfaces covered with lead-based paint break or get disturbed.** This happens during abatement, renovation, or demolition. When you saw or drill a lead-painted surface, you create lead dust.

3. **Surfaces covered with lead-based paint rub against something.** This is called **friction.** Windows and doors have friction surfaces. When you open a window, painted edges get rubbed and create dust. When you walk on lead-painted floors, lead dust gets kicked up. The friction wears through the top layers of paint and exposes the older lead-based paint. When you sand or scrape lead-based paint, you create friction and lead dust.

4. **Surfaces covered with lead-based paint get hit with force.** This is called **impact.** Impact surfaces include floors, stairs, parts of walls, and doors. When you bang into a lead-painted wall with the back of a chair, lead dust gets released. When you close a door, there is an impact. If the door hits surfaces with lead-based paint' lead dust can be released.

Whenever you create dust from a lead-painted surface, lead gets into the air. When lead dust is in the air, you can breathe the particles into your lungs. When lead dust falls, it sticks to anything it lands on----floors and other surfaces, people, pets, and even food. If you get lead dust on your hands and put your fingers in your mouth, you will swallow lead particles.

Young children are very much at risk for lead poisoning. They play on the floor. They leave their toys around. They put their hands and toys in their mouths. If lead dust is on the floor and toys, children are likely to get lead in their mouths and swallow lead particles. Sometimes children eat paint chips. Sometimes they chew on lead-painted surfaces, like window sills. Even if the lead-based paint is in good condition, a child may still chew the paint and swallow lead particles.

Where is lead-based paint?

Any home built before 1978 may contain lead-based paint. Outside surfaces, kitchens, bathrooms, and windows are the areas most likely to have lead-based paint. However, lead-based paint can be found on any painted surface of a home. Sometimes the lead-based paint is buried under layers of non-lead-based paint.

You can't tell if paint has lead in it by looking at it. Painted surfaces must be tested for lead content. To be safe, find out if a surface has lead-based paint before working on it. If you do not test the paint for lead, assume that it is lead-based paint.

Inspections

Checking for lead-based paint is called an **inspection.** Inspections must be done by a trained lead inspector or risk assessor. The inspector tests the paint to see if it has lead in it or takes samples to be sent to a lab for testing. An inspector will do an inspection before a project begins. **Inspections identify where the lead-based paint is.**

States have different rules about how and when to test for lead-based paint. (Find out what your state laws say.) The Federal Department of Housing and Urban Development (HUD) developed guidelines for testing. The HUD guidelines apply to inspections of public housing and a number of non-public housing programs.

The 1992 Residential Lead-Based Paint Hazard Reduction Act (Title X) required that EPA develop regulations related to lead-based paint inspection in all housing built before 1978

HUD Guidelines (note refer to 2012 HUD guidelines)

Public housing units, HUD common areas, and exteriors of
HUD family projects must be inspected for lead-based paint if:

- It was built before 1978 (must be inspected by public
  housing authorities by 1994), and
- Children younger than 6 years old live or may live there

Title X

By October 1995, Title X requires that all known information about lead
hazards be provided at the time of sale or rental of any pre-1978 housing
unit. It also allows home buyers 10 days to arrange for a risk assessment or
inspection to identify lead hazards.

What surfaces need to be tested?

The HUD guidelines recommend testing all **types** of painted and varnished
surfaces. (Your state may **require** testing all painted surfaces or just some.)
Anything painted is a painted surface. Any painted or varnished surface may
contain lead. Painted or varnished surfaces are found both inside and outside the
home. They include:

•Ceilings	•Shelves	•Siding and trim
•Doors	•Staircase	•Gutters
•Floors	•Walls	•Roofs
•Molding	•Windows	•Sheds
•Radiators	•Porches	•And more

What a lead inspector does

Lead inspectors must have special training and certification. To start, the lead
inspector will get a sketch of the home. The inspector will number the rooms to
be tested and mark which way is north. The windows and doors can be
numbered clockwise from the entrance.

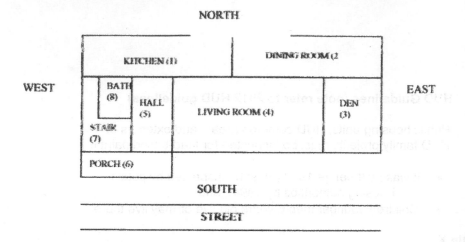

The inspector will take samples to test for lead. Each sample must be clearly labeled. The inspector will write down:

- What room the sample came from
- Which part of the room it came from
- The painted surface tested

For example, an inspector might take a dust sample from the window sill on the north wall of the kitchen. The surface area tested may be 3 inches by 36 inches.

The label might look like this

Sample#	1
Room#	1
Part of room	north wall
Surface	window sill
Area	3 x 36 inches
Condition	smooth

The inspector records this information on a record sheet called a "Sample Information" form. The inspector also writes down the testing method used and the test results on this form.

SAMPLE INFORMATION

Sample No.	Room	Part of Room	Surface	Area (l x w)	Condition	Test Method	Results
1	1	North Wall	Window Sill	3 x 36 inches	Smooth		

COMMENTS: Dust wipe samples

_____

_____

_____

Tests for lead in paint, dust, and soil

An inspector can use a number of ways to test for lead. Each test has advantages and disadvantages. The results are all measured differently. Let's look at each one:

1. Paint chip lab analysis

The inspector takes paint samples from painted surfaces. These samples are sent to a lab. The lab tests the paint samples for lead. The test shows how much lead is in the paint. The test is called paint chip lab analysis. The inspector must wear gloves when taking samples. Gloves must be changed after each sample.

Advantages

Paint chip analysis is very accurate when the inspector collects the sample correctly. The paint chip sample must include all the paint layers of the tested surface. (This is not always easy to do.)

Disadvantages

Paint chip analysis is expensive. It costs $25 to $75 per sample. It takes two days to two weeks to get the results, sometimes longer. To get a sample, you have to disturb the painted surface. Scraped patches in the paint get left behind. You will have to repair and repaint. This is an added expense. Your instructor will provide you with current estimates.

Results

Paint chip analysis measures the amount of lead in the paint by weight. The weight of lead in the sample is compared to the weight of the entire sample. The lead in the sample is reported as a percentage. If the sample is 0.5% lead or higher, HUD says that the surface tested should be considered a lead surface. Lead in paint chips can also be measured in milligrams per square centimeter (mg/cm^2).

2. X-Ray Fluorescence (XRF) analysis

The inspector can also use a machine called an X-Ray Fluorescence analyzer, or XRF. An XRF works a little bit like an X-ray machine at the doctor's office, but the process is different. Radioactive waves are used to find the lead in paint. But, instead of taking a picture, the XRF tells us how much lead is in the paint. This test is called XRF analysis. XRF machines must be used very carefully. Inspectors need special training to prevent radiation exposure.

Types of XRFs:

Direct Read XRF
A direct read XRF gives an immediate reading of how much lead is in the paint. The inspector will take several readings and average them together. The average gives a more accurate result. The direct read XRF is simpler and less expensive than the spectrum analyzer XRF.

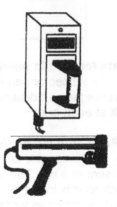

Spectrum Analyzer XRF
A spectrum analyzer XRF reads all the different metals in the paint—not just lead. It compares these readings. With the help of a small computer, it tells the inspector how much lead is in the paint. It is more complicated and more expensive than the direct read XRF.

Advantages
The XRF machine is small and can be used on site. It can tell right away whether or not lead is in the paint. It does not damage the painted surface like paint chip lab analysis does.

Disadvantages
XRFs are expensive. XRF inspectors must have radiation safety training. They also need special training on how to use the machine. After this training, they must get a permit to use an XRF. Permits, training, and replacement parts can be expensive-about $4,000 per year.

Many things can interfere with XRF readings. Brick, metal, and other building materials that the lead-based paint is on can effect the XRF readings. An XRF machine may not read paint accurately if it covers brick or metal. Temperature, humidity, radio waves, and vibration can cause false readings.

Some surfaces---like corners and narrow edges---cannot be measured by an XRF.

Results

XRF readings tell how much lead is in the tested surface area. Results are reported in milligrams (mg) per square centimeter (cm^2). A milligram is one-thousandth of a gram. A square centimeter is about the size of your thumbnail.

Usually more than one XRF reading is taken for each surface. If the average of those readings is equal to or greater than 1.0 mg/cm2, HUD recommends that the surface be considered lead. Check your state and local laws.

Back-up testing method

Often, an inspector will take a paint chip test sample from the same surface area to confirm the XRF readings. The paint chip lab results will be compared with the XRF results.

3. Dust wipe test

Dust tests measure lead dust on surfaces. High levels of surface lead dust are an immediate danger. Dust tests do not determine the presence of lead-based paint that is several layers down. They show whether there is lead in the dust.

The inspector collects dust from surfaces with commercial wipes. Inspectors must wear disposable gloves to protect them from lead dust. Inspectors should change their gloves after each sample to prevent sample contamination. The dust wipes are sent to a lab, where they are tested for lead dust.

How to collect dust samples:

1. Materials: commercial wipes, ruler, marking pen, plastic vials with caps or ziplock bags, disposable gloves, Sample Information form, and labels.

2. Put on the latex gloves.

3. Measure test area—a square foot for floors (the length and width of other surfaces)

4. Fill in the information on the label and Sample Information form.

5. Wipe over the entire area in an S-shape motion sideways. Fold the dirty side of the wipe into itself. Then wipe in the other direction in an S-shape motion using the clean side.

6. Put the folded wipe into the vial and put on the cap (or into the bag and seal). Attach the label.

7. Use the same method for all the dust samples you take. Be sure to change gloves before taking each sample.

8. Send samples to the lab.

Advantages

The dust wipe test is an easy test to do. The cost of processing is from about $15 to $30 per test. The results tell you whether lead is in the dust. It gives you a good indication if there is a lead dust hazard. Your instructor will provide you with local estimates.

Disadvantages

The dust wipe test cannot tell you exactly how much lead is in the paint. It cannot tell you which surfaces will need to be abated. It can tell you only if lead dust is present and gives you an idea of how much. Lead dust may be coming from sources other than lead-based paint.

Results

Results are measured in micrograms of lead per square foot (ug/ft^2). A microgram is one-millionth of a gram.

Dust wipe tests are taken at two times. First, they are used to test homes (especially if children live there) for immediate lead hazards. These dust tests are crucial in preventing lead poisoning. Extremely high lead dust levels indicate a lead hazard. It is common for a lead-painted window well to have lead dust levels above 10,000 ug/ft^2.

Homes often cannot be abated right away. While the family waits, they can do things to reduce the amount of lead dust. These actions are called "interim controls." When lead dust is reduced, the source of lead poisoning is reduced. (For more information on interim controls, see Chapter 6.) Dust wipe tests can show if interim controls are helping.

Second, dust wipe tests are used at the end of a lead abatement job for a clearance test or final inspection. The dust samples show whether the abatement and cleanup were done well enough. They tell you if the house is ready for the occupants to return.

HUD and many states require dust wipe testing of floors, window wells, and window sills. The dust tests must meet the clearance levels. If the dust levels are higher than this, workers must clean the work area again. (See "final clearance levels" in Chapter 10.)

After Abatement	
Surface	**Lead dust level**
Floors	Below 40 ug/ft²
Windows Sills	Below 250 ug/ft²
Window Wells	Below 400 ug/ft²

The Baltimore City Department of Health used wipe sampling to do A study of 20 houses that were lead abated. The average results are Below. During the abatement, work practices were carefully monitored. The use of heat guns and dry scraping were not allowed.

		STUDY RESUTS	
Surface	**Before abatement**	**After chemical Stripping**	**After replacement encapsulation, and enclosure**
Floors	1,300 ug/ft²	59ug/ft²	44ug/ft²
Window Sills	7,634 ug/ft²	125 ug/ft²	17 ug/ft²
Window Wells	59,202 ug/ft²	252 ug/ft²	49 ug/ft²

3. **Wet chemical field tests**

Some inspectors use wet chemical field tests (spot tests) to find out if paint contains lead. The sodium sulfide test and the sodium rhodizonate test are two examples. **The reliability of these tests has not been proven, so their use is not recommended by HUD.**

The chemical test solutions are clear liquids. To do the test, the inspector scrapes the painted surface down to the wall surface or substrate. All the layers of paint must be exposed. Then the inspector puts a drop of test solution on the painted surface.

Results
    If lead is in the paint, sodium sulfide turns grey, brown, or even black. Sodium rhodizonate turns pink or even red when lead is present.

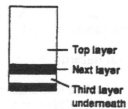

Top layer
Next layer
Third layer
underneath

Advantages
    This is a quick, easy test to do. It's done on site. It's inexpensive.

Disadvantages

1. Sodium sulfide works well only with white paint. Colored paints are hard to read.
2. The changes in color can be missed
3. Other metals can cause the same color change that lead does.
4. These tests do not tell how much lead is in the paint.
5. These tests only test exposed layers of paint. These tests will not tell you if coats of paint that are not exposed have lead in them.
6. Sometimes these tests say lead is present when it is not.
7. Dirt or plaster can hide a color change

5. Soil sampling

Soil can have high levels of lead. You usually find the highest levels of lead in soil close to the surface. Lead in soil can be a major hazard. Children play outside in the soil. They can get lead dust on their hands, clothes, and toys. Children can get lead poisoned by playing in soil with lead.

Composite soil sampling and analysis tells how much lead is in the soil. The inspector doing the test needs special training. The inspector will collect 3 – 10 sub samples and the top ½" only by an aseptic (clean) scoop or coring tool. The soil on all sides of the building should be tested out to the drip line.

The test results compare the amount of lead to the amount of soil in the sample. Results are reported in parts per million, or ppm. High levels of lead are usually found close to a house with lead-based paint. High levels of lead are often found in the soil close to the street. Lead in the soil close to the street comes from leaded gasoline. (Trigger level 400 ppm since 1994)

Risk assessment

An inspection tells you where the lead-based paint is in a home. A risk assessment tells you if the lead-based paint could be a health hazard to the people who live in the home.

A risk assessment looks at:

*   Lead-based paint hazards
*   How these hazards can be controlled
*   The people who live in the home

The person who does a risk assessment is called a risk assessor. A risk assessor has to get special training.

Lead hazards

The risk assessor first looks at the places where lead-based paint is in the home. This is the information that the inspector collected. Then the risk assessor figures out which lead-painted surfaces create lead hazards. Risk assessors are required to get special training and certification.

Chapter 3 – Identifying Lead Hazards

Any exposure to lead from contaminated dust, soil or paint that makes you ill is a lead-based paint hazard. Lead is a hazard when you breathe or swallow it. Dust from lead-based paint is a major hazard. Risk assessors look for sources of lead dust in the home, such as:

Deteriorating lead-based paint - Painted surfaces deteriorate for a number of reasons. The primary reason is moisture. Rain, leaks, condensation and spills can cause paint to break down. Sun, heat, cold and wind can wear down paint on exterior surfaces. Paint will also deteriorate if it is not put on properly. Putting paint on glossy or greasy surfaces or on rotting or termite-damaged wood is not proper application. Sometimes the new layer of paint is incompatible with the old paint layer. This can cause deterioration.

Friction surfaces - Paint dust also forms any place where a pained surface rubs against another surface. When two surfaces rub against each other, the movement causes **friction**. Friction causes paint to flake, chip and form dust. Lead-painted windows are the places where friction most

Lead close to the house

Lead close to the street

often causes lead dust. Whenever a window goes up or down it causes friction.

Impact surfaces – Paint can be weakened by impact or forceful contact. This happens when a door closes. A door has many impact points where paint can flake and chip.

Lead dust buildup – Lead dust is made of tiny lead particles. Lead particles are heavy and they stick to surfaces. They land close to the surface they came from. When a lead-painted wall is flaking and peeling, the lead dust particles fall close to the wall. Lead dust tends to build up in spaces close to friction surfaces, such as window wells.

Lead dust can also build up in areas that are not cleaned properly. Lead dust gathers in cracks. It builds up behind cabinets, between floor boards, and behind baseboards. The dust may come out of the cracks over time due to air movement, impact, pressure, or even a child picking at the floor.

People who live in houses with lead-based paint

Besides looking at possible lead-based paint hazards, the risk assessor looks at the people who live in the home. These are the people who could get lead poisoning. If there is a lot of lead dust, the risk increases that someone will get lead poisoning.

Children and pregnant women are at the highest risk for lead poisoning. A home with deteriorating lead-based paint where a young child and a pregnant woman live would be a very high-risk home.

Key facts for Chapter 3

A lead-based paint hazard is any exposure to lead from contaminated dust, soil, or paint that makes you sick.

Lead dust is a hazard when you breathe or swallow it.

Any painted surface can have lead-based paint.
HUD guidelines recommend testing all painted surfaces.
Test paint or assume it has lead.

Inspections show which paint has lead.
Lead inspectors must have special training and certification.
All samples must be clearly labeled.

Testing for lead in paint
Paint chip samples must include all paint layers.
Paint chip analysis is used on its own and to back up XRF tests. XRFs are used on site.
There are different types of XRFs: direct read XRFs, spectrum analyzers, and XLs.
Dust wipe tests tell you where there is lead dust.
Dust wipe tests are done after every abatement job as the final clearance test for the job. The test results show if the abatement is complete.

Risk assessments look at whether lead-based paint in a home is a health hazard to the people who live there.
Lead-based paint dust is a health hazard.
Sources of lead-based paint dust include:

- Deteriorating lead-based paint
- Friction
- Impact
- Places where lead dust builds up

Children and pregnant women are at highest risk for lead poisoning.

Chapter 4 – Worker & Community Rights

PART 1: KNOW YOUR RIGHTS

In this part of Chapter 4 you will learn about:

- **Your "Right-To-Know**
- **How to use your rights to solve problems on the job**
- **Community and building occupants rights**
- **What the community and occupants need to know about the lead abatement job.**
- **Your Rights as a lead abatement worker under the OSHA Lead Standard**

Your rights on the job

You have a right to a safe and healthy work site.

The Occupational Safety and Health Administration (OSHA) writes regulations to protect worker health and safety. According to OSHA, your employer must make your work site as safe as possible.

Your employer must protect you from known health and safety hazards. Lead is a known health hazard. You can be exposed to lead during all phases of lead-based paint abatement work. Your employer has to make working with lead as safe as possible. Your employer will do this in the following way:

1. **Identify the hazard source**
2. **Control the hazard source**
3. **Change the workplace and work practice**
4. **Provide personal protective equipment**

1. Identify the hazard sources

The first step to a safe and healthy work site is to identify all the possible hazards. This step is sometimes called "site characterization." Your employer must identify the worksite hazards before the job begins. He or she must continue to identify the hazards for as long as the job exists. To do this, your employer uses the inspection and risk assessment results. He or she will also test the air to see how much lead is being released and to monitor your exposure. Your employer will give you the exposure results and may have daily safety meetings to let you know about the hazards of your job.

2. Control the hazard source

The second step to a safe and healthy work site is to control the source of the hazard. Your employer can do this by replacing hazardous chemicals with safer ones. For example, many paint strippers have the dangerous chemical methylene chloride in them.

Your employer can use a safer stripper without methylene chloride in it. **Abatement can help control the major source of lead hazards.**

Your work will help to control the lead hazards in homes and in public and commercial buildings. You will help to prevent lead poisoning. After the lead-based paint is abated, a safer paint will replace it.

3. Change the workplace and work practices

OSHA requires your employer to control hazards by making changes to the workplace and using safe work practices. These changes will reduce the amount of lead that gets released into the air.

Changes to make the lead work environment safer are called engineering and work practice controls. These controls help protect you against lead poisoning. Engineering and work practice controls protect areas next to the work area and the environment from lead contamination. Some examples of engineering and work practice controls are:

Contained work area. Any time you disturb lead-based paint, you may be exposed. This exposure is a health hazard. The work area must be contained. Barriers must be made to keep lead dust inside the work area. The work area must be separate from all the other areas.

Clean changing area. Lead dust gets everywhere. Anything and anyone in the work site gets contaminated with lead. You need to change out of your street clothes and into disposable protective suits and foot coverings before you go into the work area. The OSHA Lead Standard says your employer must provide a clean changing area that is separate from the work area whenever you work above the Permissible Exposure Limit (PEL) or do any of the lead-related tasks listed in the standard. The change area must have separate storage for your clean street clothes. Your street clothes cannot come in contact with your work clothes or equipment.

Washing and toilet facilities. You will need to wash your hands and face every time you leave the work area. Your employer must provide a place where you call wash your hands and face. Your employer must also provide on-site toilet facilities.

**Washing
facilities**

Showers. Your employer must provide showers and towels where feasible when you work above the Permissible Exposure Limit.

An OSHA inspector can determine if a shower is feasible. You should shower and put on your clean clothes and shoes before going home at the end of the day.

Break area. Your employer needs to provide a clean break area that is separate from the work area. Never eat, drink, smoke, or put on makeup while in the work area. Your employer must also provide drinking water. Always wash your hands and face before you go into the break area.

The OSHA Lead Standard requires separation of the work area, wash area, and clean area. These areas are set up so that you can get clean. Getting clean is sometimes called decontamination.

Safe work practice. When you disturb lead-based paint you can create lead dust. All methods of lead abatement disturb lead-based paint. All methods of lead abatement create lead dust. Lead dust is a health hazard. The job can be safer if you:

- Use abatement methods that make as little lead dust as possible.
- Wet mist painted surfaces before you work on them.
- Use special tools with HEPA vacuum attachments. Wet debris before you bag it or wrap it in poly.
- Wet mop or wet sweep small debris - never dry sweep.
- Clean up as you work and at the end of every day.
- Use a special vacuum with a HEPA filter to clean up.

4. Provide personal protective equipment

Personal protective equipment - like gloves, goggles, and respirators - are not a substitute for making the job safer. Your employer must first try to control the hazard at the source and change the workplace and work practices to make them safer. Exposure to lead is dangerous. In addition to making the job safer, you will need to use personal protective equipment.

By law, your employer must give personal protective equipment to you:

- When you do any of the lead-related tasks listed in the OSHA Lead Standard
- If you are working above the PEL.
- Any time you work with lead and you request a respirator.

The equipment must be in good working order.

No matter what the exposure level is, anytime you work with lead on any job you can request a respirator if you want the extra protection. By law, your employer must give it to you.

Right-to-Know laws

As a worker, you have the right to know if you are working with dangerous

materials. This right is covered under the OSHA Hazard Communication Standard. Many states have their own Right-to-Know laws. Before the Right-to-Know laws existed, workers like you were exposed to dangerous materials every day and they didn't even know that the materials were dangerous to them and their families. Hundreds of thousands of workers have died from workplace exposures. Today, you have the right to know if you are working with a dangerous material. You must be trained in how to work with it safely.

OSHA Says your employer must provide:

- List of all hazardous chemicals that you could be exposed to;
- Label system and labels on all hazardous substances and containers;
- Training about each hazardous substance you come in contact with on your job;

* Material Safety Data Sheets (MSDSs) for all hazardous substances on site;
* Written hazard communication program.

Understanding what a dangerous material is and how to work with it takes time and effort. Your time and effort can keep you, your co-workers, your family, and even the community healthy. Your understanding and safe work practices can prevent illness and disease.

Training. Your employer must provide training in order for you to know what hazards you work with. The training must be given in the language of the worker. The training must include information about:

* Health effects of workplace hazards;
* How to identify hazards;
* How to protect yourself and work safely.

Material Safety Data Sheets (MSDSs). Material Safety Data Sheets are the key to identifying hazardous substances. Manufacturers must provide MSDSs for all hazardous products. Your employer uses the MSDSs to list and label hazardous products on site. Your employer also uses the MSDSs to provide training for you to understand the hazards of the product.

Your employer must have a MSDS for each hazardous material you may work with. These MSDS's must be at your job site.

On a large construction site, where there is more than one contractor, each contractor must supply the hazard communication information to the general contractor. The general contractor is responsible for the whole construction project.

Material Safety Data Sheets must include:

* Product identity and ingredients
* Physical and chemical characteristics
* Fire, explosion, and reactivity hazards
* Health hazards, risk of cancer
* Symptoms, routes of exposure
* Legal exposure limits
* Precautions for safe handling and use
* Protective control measures
* Personal protective equipment requirements
* Emergency and first aid measures
* Spill and leak procedures

MSDSs are the keys to knowing the hazards you work with.

OSHA 300 log of workplace injuries

You have a right to know about on-the-job injuries and illnesses. OSHA requires your employer to keep a record of all the injuries and illnesses that occur at your workplace. This record is called the OSHA 300 log. You have a right to see this information. It can help you identify the hazards of your job. Not all injuries or illnesses are listed in the 300 log. Workers go to private doctors and insurance companies pay. Some workers are afraid to report injuries or illness.

Right to file a complaint

Under the Occupational Safety and Health Act, you have a right to file a complaint with OSHA whenever your rights are violated. You must file your complaint to OSHA within 30 days of the incident. You may request that OSHA keep your identity secret from your employer. The OSHA regional offices are listed in the Resources Section in the back of this manual.

OSHA says your employer may not fire you for fighting for your health and safety. Your employer may not discipline you or discriminate against you. This is called "11-C protection."

Some people have been fired for fighting for their rights. If you win an 11-C case, you can get your job back, get back pay, and your employer can be fined. But 1 1-C cases often take a long time to settle. Even if you lose your case, you may still be able to get unemployment.

It's important to know your health and safety rights and fight for them. It's also important to do your job. It is illegal to fire someone because they are fighting for their rights. It is legal to fire someone because they didn't do their job. If you are fighting for a safer workplace, don't forget to do your job, too.

Is it worth it to fight for your rights? Only you can decide this. If changes are to be made in the workplace, it is important for you and your co-workers to assert your rights. It's best not to do it alone, but through your union or with other workers. Contact a local Committee on Occupational Safety and Health for advice.

Using your rights to solve problems on the job

What if you see something go wrong on the job? What if there is no poly laid on the outside where you have to take the window out and your employer tells you to forget it? What if you ask for a respirator and your employer tells you he's never heard of one?

What if there are no wash facilities on the work site? What if your employer tells you to wash up at the nearest bar, where he has made arrangements for you to clean up?

Many things can go wrong on a lead abatement job. If something goes wrong, you will have to decide if you are going to do anything about it. What can you do to solve these kinds of problems at work?

Chapter 4 – Worker & Community Rights

1. Talk to other workers.

If your union or company has a health and safety committee, talk to the members of the committee first. Talk to other workers. You will get better results if your employer sees that it is a problem for everyone, not just "a personal problem."

2. Collect information and records.

When did the problem start? Did anyone try to do anything about it? Talk to the industrial hygienist on the job, if there is one. Get copies of any air sampling results. Get information from the people who trained you. Call your local Committee on Occupational Safety and Health (COSH). Contact the organizations listed in the back of this manual (See the Resources Section in the back of the manual).

3. Find out what part of the OSHA Standard applies.

Your instructor will provide you with the parts of the OSHA standard that apply to that chapter.

4. Talk to your supervisor.

You may want to go to the president of the company right away, but it's not usually the best way to start. You are more likely to get results if you start with your co-workers and your supervisor. Present any solutions you have found. Document in writing what you do. Keep a record of whom you talked to and about what. Have a co-worker go with you to talk with the supervisor.

5. Go to a higher up.

If you are not satisfied with the supervisor's answer, then talk to a manager. Then talk to that manager's manager, if you must. If you go all the way to the top and you still don't think the work is being done right, then you might have to go outside the company for help.

6. Go outside for help.

You can contact OSHA or EPA. If the concern is worker protection, call OSHA. If the concern is about the environment - such as building contamination, waste disposal, or chemical releases to the outdoors - call EPA. Be persistent.

Before you ask OSHA or EPA to inspect the job, you should know what they can and can't do. They will try to come on the job. But sometimes jobs don't last long and EPA and OSHA inspectors can't always get to your work site while the job is going on.

If your company has broken the rules, EPA and OSHA can fine the company or they can shut the job down. If the problem with the job isn't covered by a regulation, then OSHA or EPA cannot fine the company.

For example, OSHA does not have rules about heat. Heat stress is a big problem on lead abatement jobs. Calling OSHA may not help in this case.

Calling OSHA and EPA is not a "quick fix." You may get good results, but it might take a while. It is worth it. If you call the government, it should be one part of an overall strategy.

Community and occupant rights

People who live in the community have a right to a safe and healthy community. The community and occupants need to know about the lead hazards. Some states require signs to be posted at least three days before abatement work begins. The building occupants should receive written information about the seriousness of the lead hazard. The people who occupy the building have special needs. Title *X* requires that EPA develop a lead hazard information pamphlet to be given to prospective home buyers and renters.

Occupants need to know:
- The dangers of lead dust
- How to clean and pack their possessions
- That they cannot re-enter the home until the area has passed final clearance What work will be done
- How lead is abated safely
- What happens to the lead waste
- How to clean and maintain their home after abatement
- Where to get blood tests for lead, especially for children
- What type of training workers have
- What other hazards exist in their home

The community needs to know workers are trained and working safely. Contractors must be certified to do lead abatement work by the state or local government or by the EPA.

Occupants and community members have a right to know if an abatement is stopped because it is not being done safely. They need to know how to protect themselves from the lead hazard.

Community members and occupants need to know about lead hazards. Everyone wants to live in a safe and healthy community. In 1986, that right was introduced into law by the Superfund Amendments and Reauthorization Act (SARA). Title III of SARA is referred to as the Community Right-to-Know Law. This law says that industry must give the community a list of all hazardous substances that may be released into the area. It also says that a list of all hazardous materials stored in hazardous waste sites must be available to community members.

SARA Title III only covers releases of material from industry. Today there is no Federal law that says a construction company must inform the community about hazards which may be created. When construction occurs with asbestos or lead, signs must be posted to keep the community out of the area. In many areas of the country, the local department of the environment must be notified by the construction company. Many state laws now provide added protection to workers and community residents.

If you live next door to an abatement job, you may not know how much lead dust is in the air or how dangerous the job may be. There is no law which requires the construction company to tell you if it is doing abatement work in your neighborhood. If there is bridge work or water tower work being done close to your house, you may not know it. There is no law that requires the construction company doing the work to let you know about the lead hazards created. Community members need to work together with local authorities to assure lead-safe and healthy communities.

As a lead abatement worker, you can make a difference. You can protect yourself and the community from lead poisoning when you work safely with lead.

Key facts for Chapter 4

You have a right to a safe and healthy work site.
The OSHA Standard protects you from being fired for fighting for your health and safety on the job.

Your employer must make working with lead as safe as possible
The best way to make working with lead safer is to:
1. Identify the hazard sources.
2. Control the source of the hazard.
3. Change the workplace and work practices to keep lead dust and fume levels down.
4. Give workers personal protective equipment.

The OSHA Lead Standard says your employer must provide you with:
1. A clean area to change your clothes.
2. Clean protective clothing to wear in the work place.
3. Washing and toilet facilities and a shower (where feasible).
4. A clean break area separated from the work area.

Use safe work practices to keep lead dust levels down.

The community and building occupants need to be informed about lead hazards.
Community members need to know how to protect themselves from lead poisoning. They have legal rights to know about industrial releases into their community. But there is no law that says they must be informed about hazardous releases-like lead dust-from construction sites.

Protect yourself and the community from lead poisoning by working safely.

HOW TO READ A MSDS

In this part of Chapter 4 you will learn about:

Reading Material Safety Data Sheets
Requesting an MSDS or environmental monitoring data from your employer
How to read a Material Safety Data Sheet

Each MSDS may look different. They are often difficult to read. All MSDSs must contain the same basic information on hazardous ingredients, health effects, legal and recommended exposure limits, physical properties, and control methods.

Section I - Material Identification
The product's name and the name, address, and emergency telephone number of the manufacturer must be provided.

Section II - Hazardous Ingredients/Identity
Which chemicals are covered?
The Federal OSHA Hazard Communication Standard requires that all hazardous chemicals be listed. Some state laws contain a list of thousands of chemicals that must be included. A few states require that all chemical ingredients be listed, even those that are not hazardous. All of the chemicals that you work with should be included unless the manufacturer or employer can prove that these chemicals are not covered by the law.

What are the names of the chemicals?
Trade name - The brand name the manufacturer gives the product (such as
"Safety Clean"). It does not tell you what chemicals are in the product. It
does not tell you whether the product is a mixture of chemicals or a single
chemical. The same chemical may be used in a variety of products with
different trade names. The trade name usually appears on the label and in
Section I of the MSDS.

Generic name - Name that describes a family or group of chemicals.
For example, there are several different "isocyanates," and thousands of
different "chlorinated hydrocarbons." Sometimes an MSDS will try to get
away with just listing the generic names. However, the law says that
chemical names must also be listed.

Chapter 4 – Worker & Community Rights

Chemical or Specific name-Name that describes the specific chemical. An example is *methyl chloroform,* one of the thousands of "chlorinated hydrocarbons," or *toluene diisocyanate, a* member of the "isocyanate" family. The chemical name is the easiest name to use when doing research on the health effects of chemicals and how to protect yourself.

CAS Number-Number given by the Chemical Abstract Service to each chemical. While different chemicals may have the same common name or the same DOT proper shipping name, they will each have their own CAS number that can be used to look up information. The Chemical Abstract Service publishes a book that contains a list of all CAS Numbers and the chemicals they represent.

The MSDS must list the chemical name of all hazardous ingredients that make up more than 1% of the mixture (or 0.1% for cancer-causing substances). Listing only the trade name, only the CAS number, or only the generic name is not acceptable.

Trade secrets-Manufacturers can sometimes hold back information from the MSDS if an ingredient is a trade secret. Under the Right-to-Know laws, manufacturers must provide trade secret identities to health care professionals and/or workers if they need to know the information or in a medical emergency. Consult your state law for more details. Remember, even if certain ingredients are trade secrets, the MSDS must still contain all other required information.

Exposure units-The MSDS must list these limits for hazardous ingredients:
- OSHA Permissible Exposure Limit (PEL)
- Threshold Limit Values (TLV) recommended by the American Conference of Governmental Industrial Hygienists (ACGIH)

The MSDS may also list workplace exposure limits recommended by the National Institute for Occupational Safety and Health (NIOSH). These are important because ACGIH and NIOSH often recommend exposure limits that are more up-to-date and protective than OSHA's PELs.

Section III - Physical/Chemical Characteristics
Physical and chemical characteristics include the chemical's appearance and odor, along with physical properties that indicate how easily a chemical will evaporate and release potentially harmful vapors into the air.

Boiling point-The temperature at which a substance evaporates and becomes a vapor. The lower the boiling point, the quicker the substance evaporates, and the easier it is to inhale. Chemicals with boiling points below 100 C (or 212 F) require special caution.

Vapor pressure-A high vapor pressure indicates that a liquid substance will evaporate easily. Chemicals which evaporate quickly are called "volatile." Volatile means that air concentrations of the substance can build up quickly, even though the substance is in liquid form. Liquids with high vapor pressures may be especially hazardous if you are working with them in a confined space or an enclosed area.

Vapor density-If vapor density is less than one, the evaporated substance will tend to rise in air. If the vapor density is greater than one, it will fall in air and concentrate in the bottom of tanks or confined spaces.

Appearance and odor - Qualities that may help identify a substance that spills or leaks in your work area. However, many chemicals are hazardous at low levels before they can be smelled. Never breathe hazardous chemicals on purpose.

Specific gravity-If specific gravity is greater than one, the substance will sink in water. If it is less than one, the substance will float on top of water.

Evaporation rate-The rate at which a substance evaporates as compared to a *reference standard.* The reference standard used with be indicated on the MSDS. If the substance has an evaporation rate greater than one, it evaporates faster than the reference standard. Examples of a reference standard are *ether,* which evaporates quickly, and *butyl acetate,* which evaporates slowly.

Section IV- Fire and Explosion Hazard Data
This section should provide information on the fire hazards of a product and special precautions necessary to extinguish a fire.

Flash point-The lowest temperature at which a liquid gives off enough vapor to form a mixture with air that can be ignited by a spark. Liquids with flash points below 100 F are considered flammable, and liquids with flash points between 100 and 200 F are considered to be combustible. Flammable and combustible liquids require special handling and storage precautions.

Extinguishing media-This information specifies what kind of extinguisher to use in the case of a fire. There are 4 classifications of fires:
- Class A for paper and wood
- Class B for more flammable materials such as liquids or greases
- Class C for electrical fires
- Class D for fires involving metals or metal alloys

Firefighting procedures and unusual fire and explosion hazards-Special instructions and information. For example, some chemicals (such as corrosives) must not be extinguished with water in case of fire.

Section V- Reactivity Data

When stored improperly, some chemicals can react with other chemicals and release dangerous by-products. "Reactivity" is the property that describes the reaction of a chemical when it is mixed together with another chemical, or when stored or handled improperly.

Section VI - Health Hazard Data

This section describes the health effects of the product, including signs and symptoms of exposure and medical conditions made worse by exposure. Unfortunately, a lot of MSDSs in circulation do not contain complete and accurate health hazard information. The section must include information on:

- Acute (short-term) effects of exposure
- Chronic (long-term) effects of exposure (often left out of MSDSs)
- Routes of entry (inhalation, skin contact, swallowing)
- Target organs (liver, kidneys, or central nervous system)
- Signs or symptoms of exposure
- Medical conditions generally aggravated by exposure

This section tells you what to do if someone gets exposed. It often specifies eye wash and safety showers in case of eye or skin contact. Employers must provide eye washes and showers if they are needed. It is important to read this section to be prepared. Whatever a worker needs if he or she is exposed should be immediately ready for use.

Section VII- Precautions for Safe Handling and Use
(Spill or Leak Procedures)

This section contains information on proper equipment to use and what precautions to follow if a spill or leak occurs. It should also describe safe waste disposal methods and precautions to be taken in handling and storing.

Section VIII- Control Measures

The MSDS must list control measures that can reduce or eliminate the hazard, including ventilation and other engineering controls, safe work practices, and personal protective equipment.

Chapter 4 – Worker & Community Rights

1.　　Requesting a Material Safety Data Sheet

Date

Employer Name
Address of Employer
City, State, Zip Code

Dear

With this letter, I am formally requesting a copy of the Material Safety Data Sheet (MSDS) and any other records, tests, or analyses you have on file regarding (trade name, chemical name, or common name of substance in question). I use this substance during the routine course of my work for (company name, address, city and state, zip code).

I am making this request pursuant to Section 1910.1200 of Title 29 of the Code of Federal Regulations. Your prompt attention to this matter is greatly appreciated.

Sincerely,

Name (title - optional)
Your Address
City, State, Zip Code

2.　　Requesting Environmental Monitoring Data

Date

Employer Name
Address of Employer
City, State, Zip Code

Dear

With this letter I am formally requesting a copy of all the environmental monitoring reports you have on file regarding (name of chemical) or any monitoring done in (the area(s) where you work).

I (use this chemical/work in this area) during the routine course of my work.

I am making this request pursuant to Section 1910.20 of Title 29 of the Code of Federal Regulations. Your prompt attention to this matter is greatly appreciated.

Sincerely,

Name (title - optional)
Your Address
City, State, Zip Code

Material Safety Data Sheet Checklist

This is not a test. This is an exercise to help you get better at reading MSDSs. Your instructor will review the answers with you at the end of the exercise.

Every Item below must be provided on each MSDS.
1. Is the product or chemical identity used on the label?
2. What is the name, address and phone number for hazard and emergency information?
3. On what date was this MSDS prepared?
4. What are the chemical and common names of the hazardous ingredients?
5. What is the OSHA Permissible Exposure Limit (PEL)? What is the ACGIH Threshold Limit Value (TLV)? Are there any other applicable limits?
6. Are the physical and chemical characteristics, such as vapor pressure and flash point listed?
7. What are the hazards of this product? (Include physical hazards, such as potential for fire, explosion, and reactivity.)
8. How does it get into the body? (breathing, swallowing, through the skin)
9. What can happen to you if you are exposed to this material?
10. Does this material cause cancer?
    Note: If a chemical does not cause cancer, or if there is no information about it causing cancer, then information about item 10 does not have to be listed unless a blank is included on the form.
11. What do you do if you or a co-worker is exposed? What are the emergency and first aid procedures?
12. How do you handle this material safely?
    Do you need a shower or wash area? How do you clean up a spill?
13. How can you protect your health when you use this material?
    What personal protective equipment do you need?
    Do you need ventilation?
    What work methods should you use with this material?

Key facts for Chapter 4, Part 2

Use safe work practices to keep lead dust levels down

You have the Right-to-Know about the dangerous materials you work with.

The Hazard Communication Standard says your employer must provide:

- A written Right-to-Know program
- MSDSs for all hazardous materials on site
- Training about each hazard
- A list of all the hazardous substances
- Labels on all hazardous substances

Material Safety Data Sheets

MSDSs are the key to knowing about the hazards with which you work.

MSDSs must tell you how the chemical can affect you and how to protect yourself and others.

A properly completed MSDS does not have any blanks. MSDSs must be at your job site.

Your employer should get the most recent and accurate MSDSs of any chemicals with which you are working.

NOTE: Refer to appendix EPA's Renovation, Repair, and Painting Program final rule (40 CFR Part 745) – April 22, 2008

Material Safety Data Sheet	**U.S. Department of Labor**
May be used to comply with OSHA's Hazard Communication Standard, 29 CFR 1910 1200. Standard must be consulted for specific requirements.	Occupational Safety and Health Administration (Non-Mandatory Form) Form Approved OMB No. 1218-0072
IDENTITY *(as Used on Label and List)*	*Note: Blank spaces are not permitted. If any item is not applicable or no information is available, the space must be marked to indicate that.*

Section I

Manufacturer's name	Emergency Telephone Number
Address *(Number, Street, City, State and ZIP Code)*	Telephone Number for Information
	Date Prepared
	Signature of Preparer *(optional)*

Section II—Hazardous Ingredients/Identity Information

Hazardous Components (Specific Chemical Identity, Common Name(s))	OSHA PEL	ACGIH TLV	Other Limits Recommended	% (optional)

Section III—Physical/Chemical Characteristics

Boiling Point		Specific Gravity ($H_2O = 1$)	
Vapor Pressure (mm Hg)		Melting Point	
Vapor Density (AIR = 1)		Evaporation Rate (Butyl Acetate = 1)	
Solubility in Water			
Appearance and Odor			

Section IV—Fire and Explosion Hazard Data

Flash Point (Method Used)	Flammable Limits	LEL	UEL
Extinguishing Media			
Special Fire Fighting Procedures			
Unusual Fire and Explosion Hazards			

(Reproduce locally)

OSHA 174 Sept. 1985

Section V—Reactivity Data

Stability	Unstable		Conditions to Avoid
	Stable		

Incompatibility *(Materials to Avoid)*

Hazardous Decomposition or Byproducts

Hazardous Polymerization	May Occur		Conditions to Avoid
	Will Not Occur		

Section VI—Health Hazard Data

Route(s) of Entry	Inhalation?	Skin?	Ingestion?

Health Hazards *(Acute and Chronic)*

Carcinogenicity	NTP?	IARC Monographs?	OSHA Regulated?

Signs and Symptoms of Exposure

Medical Conditions
Generally Aggravated by Exposure

Emergency and First Aid Procedures

Section VII—Precautions for Safe Handling and Use

Steps to Be Taken in Case Material Is Released or Spilled

Waste Disposal Method

Precautions to Be Taken in Handling and Storing

Other Precautions

Section VII—Control Measures

Respiratory Protection *(Specify Type)*

Ventilation	Local Exhaust		Special
	Mechanical *(General)*		Other

Protective Gloves	Eye Protection

Other Protective Clothing or Equipment

Work/Hygienic Practices

PART 1: RESPIRATOR TYPES

In this part of Chapter 5 you will learn:

•   **What respirators are**

•   **Why you should wear a respirator when you work with lead**

•   **How respirators work**

•   **Why respirators are not perfect**

•   **How respirators should fit**

•   **Who can wear a respirator**

•   **Which respirators are allowed on lead jobs**

•   **How to figure out if you have the right respirator for the job**

The last line of defense

Your employer has to change the workplace to make it safe. Your employer also has to train you in safe work practices for doing lead abatement. Lead is very hazardous. Making changes in the workplace and using safe work practices are sometimes not enough. You must wear protective clothing and respirators to protect yourself from lead.

Respirators are your last line of defense against lead.

You need to keep lead out of your lungs when you work with it. When you do abatement work, you need to control lead and keep it from getting into the air. But no matter what you do, some lead will still get in the air. This is why you have to wear a respirator.

What is a respirator?

YES!

A respirator is a mask that protects your lungs from hazards. It filters the air in the work room or supplies clean air from outside the work room.

Some respirators have filters that filter out lead particles from the air. Other respirators pump fresh air through a hose.

Paper dust masks are not adequate respirators. They will not protect you from lead. **Paper dust masks are not allowed on lead jobs.**

NO.

Respirators protect you

Respirators are absolutely necessary to protect your lungs from lead particles. Some workers don't like wearing respirators. Respirators are sometimes uncomfortable, hot, and heavy. They can block your sight and they make it harder to breathe. You need to wear these uncomfortable pieces of equipment to protect yourself from lead poisoning.

The OSHA Standard says that before you can wear a respirator, you must get training and a fit test. The OSHA Lead Standard also says that you should get a doctor's permission to wear a respirator.

A respirator is only as good as its fit

If you wear a respirator that doesn't fit you, air and lead will leak in around the sides of the mask. Instead of being caught in the filters, the lead will go into your lungs. This is why the law says you must have a fit test. A fit test tells you if the respirator is sealed around your face. A respirator that does not fit looks the same as one that does. There is no way to tell if a respirator protects you, just by looking at it.

Not everyone can wear a respirator

Get a check up

UN EXAMEN MÉDICO GENERAL

Some people have a hard time finding a respirator to fit their face. If you have a beard, you cannot wear a tight-fitting respirator. If your face is unshaven where the respirator seals the respirator will not protect you. Even a large mustache can break the seal of your respirator. You must shave if you have a beard or a mustache that interferes with the fit of a respirator.

Some people need special respirators. You may need a special respirator if you have:

. Broken nose
. Large scars
. A very narrow face
. A broad face

. Glasses
. Dentures
. Missing teeth
. A medical condition

If you need a special respirator, your employer must provide one for you.

Respirators make it hard to breathe. You need to have a medical checkup to be sure that your lungs and heart are strong enough to take the strain of working with a respirator. You need a doctor's permission before you wear a respirator on the job. Your doctor may require you to wear a special respirator if you have problems with your lungs.

If you feel very anxious, a little faint, and shaky when you first try a respirator on, you may not be able to wear a respirator. You may want to try the respirator on a second time to be sure. You may have claustrophobia, a fear of confined spaces.

When Do You Wear A Respirator?

You must wear a respirator whenever you work with lead.

Lead in the air is measured in micrograms (ug) per cubic meter (m^3) of air. A cubic meter is roughly about the size of a street mailbox. You breathe about one cubic meter of air every hour when you are working.

The OSHA Lead Standard says that you have to wear a respirator when lead in the air reaches 50 micrograms of lead per cubic meter of air in an 8-hour day. This is the average amount of lead particles over an 8-hour day. This is the OSHA Permissible Exposure Limit PEL. (If you work a 10~hour shift, your PEL is 40 ug/$m^{3)}$. Your employer must do air sampling to find out how much lead is in the air on your job.

The HUD Guidelines of September 1990 stated that: **"Respirators must be worn by all workers (who work on HUD projects and are) potentially exposed to lead."** This means that all workers on a HUD lead project must wear respirators. Any worker on an abatement site at any time before final cleanup is potentially exposed to lead.

The OSHA Lead Standard says that anytime you work with lead - regardless of your exposure - your employer must provide a respirator for you if you request one.

Tasks That Require You To Wear A Respirator

Sometimes you may be working with lead when your employer does not know how much lead is in the air. Air sampling takes time. The OSHA Lead Standard protects workers even before air sampling results are available. By law, your employer must assume there is a certain amount of lead in the air when you do certain tasks until air sampling is done. The OSHA Lead Standard divides these tasks into three classes. Each class requires the use of specific respirators. The chart on the next page lists these **"lead-related tasks"** 29 CFR 1926.62---Lead in Construction; 29 CFR 1910.134

Lead-related tasks

The OSHA Lead Standard requires you to wear certain respirators when you do certain tasks on **lead-painted surfaces**. The type of respirator you wear depends on the task you are doing and how much lead dust gets in the air.

Class 1 Tasks (up to 500 ug/m^3)

- Manual demolition of structures
- Manual scraping or sanding
- Using a heat gun
- Power tool cleaning with dust collection systems
- Spray painting with lead-based paint

Class 2 Tasks (up to 2,500 ug/m3)

- Using lead-based mortar
- Burning lead
- Rivet busting
- Cleaning up with dry abrasives
- Moving and tearing down enclosures used for abrasive blasting
- Power tool cleaning without dust collection systems

Class 3 Tasks (over 2,500 ug/m3)

- Abrasive blasting
- Welding
- Cutting
- Torch burning

Exposure assessment

The OSHA Lead Standard requires your employer to find out what your lead exposure will be. This is called exposure assessment. Exposure assessment can be air sampling, past exposure data from the same or similar jobs, or objective data from other sources such as research studies.

Your employer should check the air on the job for lead. He or she can check the air in the work area and in the air around the workers. This is called "air sampling". Air samples of the work area are called "area air samples". Air samples of the air around the mouth and nose of the worker are called "personal air samples".

AIR SAMPLING PUMP

Chapter 5 - Personal Protective Equipment

Personal air samples must be taken from a worker in each job type. For example, he or she might sample one scraper, one sander and one cleaner. Personal sampling pumps must be worn regularly. The pump fits on your waist. It must be calibrated before each use. The cassette attached to the pump must be placed high on your shoulder by your mouth, outside of the respirator.

Air sampling tells your employer which job types make a lot of lead dust. If the air samples show a high concentration of lead (that is, above 30 ug/m3), OSHA requires your employer to reduce the lead levels. Your employer must tell you what will be done to bring them down.

If your employer does exposure monitoring and air sampling, he or she must give you the air sampling results in writing within 5 working days after he or she receives the results.

How much lead can you be exposed to?

According to the OSHA Lead Standard, there are legal limits for how much lead you can be exposed to. The highest level of airborne lead you can be exposed to is 50 micrograms per cubic meter for an 8-hour day. This is called the Permissible Exposure Limit, or PEL. **You must wear a respirator when lead in the air reaches 50 ug/m^3**. Respirators should be worn even at lower levels of lead dust.

OSHA has another legal limit for airborne lead exposure called the Action Level. The Action Level for lead is 30 ug/m^3. If you are exposed to lead above the Action Level, your employer must measure the amount of lead in the air at least every 6 months.

These limits are average exposures over an 8-hour period. At the PEL, there is an average of 50 ug of lead in every cubic meter of air. At any one specific time there could be more than 50 ug of lead in the air, or there could be less. The same goes for the Action Level.

How much is 50 ug/m^3?

The PEL for lead - 50 ug/m^3 - is a very small amount.

A **microgram** is a measure of weight. 1 million micrograms make up a gram. A penny weighs about 2 grams. If you cut a penny into 2 million pieces, a microgram would weigh as much as one of those pieces.

A **cubic meter** is a measure of volume. It is equal to about the size of a street corner U.S. Post Office mailbox. The abbreviation for cubic meter is **m^3**. Imagine 50 of those tiny pieces of penny in the space that a mailbox takes up. That's how small 50 ug/m^3 is.

You breathe in at least 1 cubic meter of air per hour at work. If lead levels in the air are at the PEL, you will be exposed to about **400ug of lead over 8 hours**. ($8m^3$ x 50ug/m^3=400ug.)

400ug/m^3 is your maximum daily dose. If you work a 10-hour shift, your PEL becomes 40 ug/m^3. (10 m^3 x 40 ug/m^3 =400 ug.)

No respirator is perfect

The more lead in the air; the better the respirator you need.

Every kind of respirator has its good and bad points. Every respirator leaks. Some respirators protect you more than others. How much lead can a respirator handle? Some respirators are better than others at keeping lead out of your lungs.

There are many kinds of respirators used on lead abatement jobs. Which respirator you wear depends on the amount of lead in the air. Your employer must do air sampling. Then he or she decides what kind of respirator workers need, based on how much lead is in the air.

Each respirator on the following pages has a **Protection Factor (PF)**. A respirator's Protection Factor is a measure of how well it should protect you from lead. Protection Factors go from 10 to 2,000. You won't get the amount of protection assigned to a respirator unless it fits and is used properly. **The higher the Protection Factor, the more a respirator protects you**.

Types of respirators

Respirators fall into two big groups:

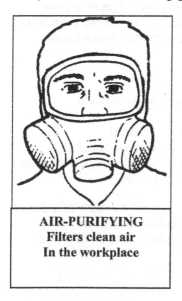

AIR-PURIFYING
Filters clean air
In the workplace

SUPPLIED-AIR
Clean air is supplied
To you through a hose

HALF-MASK, AIR-PURIFYING RESPIRATOR

Protection Factor = 10
Maximum Use Level= 500 ug/m3

A **half-mask, air-purifying respirator** is the simplest respirator you may use on a lead job. It is the **least** protective respirator the law allows. The bottom of the face piece (the wide part) goes under your chin. The top of the face piece (the narrow part) goes over your nose.

This **air-purifying** respirator filters the air in the room. Two filters catch the lead out of the air. The filters are called HEPA filters (High Efficiency Particulate Air). They are often purple or pink in color. The respirator will not protect you against lead unless you use HEPA filters.

This respirator works by **negative-pressure**. When you breathe in, your lungs and heart work to pull air through the filters. This makes a suction, or negative pressure, inside the mask. Breathing through a negative pressure respirator can take a lot of effort. The face piece has to fit perfectly on your nose, cheeks, and chin. It has to form an airtight seal. If your respirator does not fit perfectly, air and lead will leak in around the edges of the mask. **Remember, a respirator is only as good as its fit!**

If there is not enough oxygen in the work area, do not use an air-purifying respirator. If you create vapors when you work, or use chemical solvents, you will need a different type of filter-maybe even a different respirator.

FULL-FACE, AIR-PURIFYING RESPIRATOR

Protection Factor = 50
Maximum Use Level = 2500 ug/m³

A full-face, air-purifying respirator is legal for five times as much lead as a half-mask. It fits the same way as a half-mask, except the top of the face piece goes all the way around your face and across your forehead.

This is an **air-purifying** respirator. You must not use it if there is not enough oxygen to breathe. It is also a negative-pressure respirator. When you breathe in, it makes a suction, or negative pressure inside the face piece. The face piece has to fit perfectly on your forehead, the sides of your face, and your chin. If it does not form an airtight seal, air and lead will leak in around the edges of the mask. The lead will not get caught by the filters.

You cannot wear your regular glasses with a full-face respirator. The side bars of the glasses break the seal of the mask. The mask will not fit tightly on your face. If you wear glasses, your employer has to pay for special glasses and a frame that holds your lenses in place inside the full-face respirator.

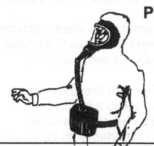

POWERED AIR-PURIFYING RESPIRATOR

Protection Factor = 50
Maximum Use Level = 2500 ug/m^3

A tight-fitting powered air-purifying respirator (or PAPR) is legal for 5 times as much lead as a half-mask respirator. It looks like a negative pressure respirator with an air pump. It has filters or cartridges. The air pump and the filters can be on a belt or on the face piece. The pump pulls the air through the filters. It blows the air through a hose into the mask. **If you work above the PEL, and you ask for a PAPR, your employer must give it to you.**

This respirator only filters the air that is already in the room. It is an air-purifying respirator. Because it has an air pump and a battery, this respirator is a powered air-purifying respirator PAPR).

The air coming through the hose pushes air and lead away from the sides of the mask. This is a **positive-pressure** respirator. The air pump makes a positive pressure inside the mask. One good thing about a positive-pressure respirator is that if it leaks, it leaks out. Lead is not supposed to leak in.

Because a PAPR is powered with a pump, your lungs do not have to work so hard to pull the air through the filters. The air pump does some of the work. But if the batteries are low, a PAPR is no better than a negative-pressure, full-face respirator. It becomes a negative-pressure respirator and air and lead can leak in around the sides of the mask.

A PAPR may also leak if the filters are clogged with dust or if you breathe too hard. The PAPR blows air at the same rate - no matter how hard you breathe. If you breathe in too hard, it makes a suction, or negative pressure, inside the face piece. The face piece has to fit perfectly on your forehead, the sides of your face, and your chin. If it does not form an air tight seal, air and lead will leak in around the edges of the face piece. This is called "over breathing" the respirator.

There are also PAPR's that are **loose-fitting**. Loose-fitting PAPR's are very similar to tight-fitting PAPR's, except that they have large, loose hoods. There is no tight fit. If the battery fails with a loose-fitting hood, you have very little protection. Loose-fitting respirators have lower protection factors than tight-fitting respirators.

Never use an air-purifying respirator if there is not enough oxygen in the work area.

Filters for air-purifying respirators
Air-purifying respirators clean the air that is already in the work area through filters. **Air-purifying respirators always have filters.** Sometimes filters are also called "cartridges."

You have to have the right filters for the job. The type of filter you use depends on the type of hazard you need to filter. There are many kinds of filters. **A chemical filter** will capture some vapors. A **mechanical filter** will capture dusts.

Filters are sometimes color-coded according to the hazard for which they are used. There is no standard to regulate color-coding. It is important to read the information on the filter itself--not just look at the color---to see if you have the right filter for the hazard.

The type of filter used for lead is called a **HEPA filter**. "HEPA" stands for **"High Efficiency Particulate Air."** HEPA filters are usually purple, magenta (hot pink), or orange. Sometimes you will need to use **Combination filters**. A type of combination filter is a HEPA cartridge combined with a chemical cartridge in one. You might use combination filters for chemical stripping.

You need to change your filters whenever it becomes hard to breathe. You must also change your filters when they get wet.

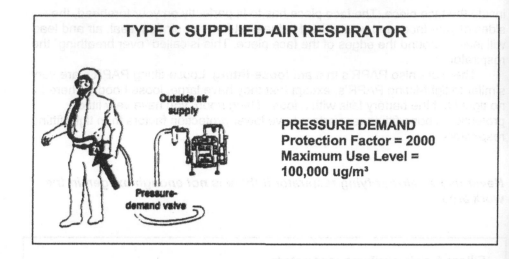

TYPE C SUPPLIED-AIR RESPIRATOR

Outside air
supply

PRESSURE DEMAND
Protection Factor = 2000
Maximum Use Level =
100,000 ug/m³

Pressure-
demand valve

A **Type C respirator** is very different from the other three respirators. It is a **supplied-air** respirator. Fresh air comes in through a hose from a source outside the room. Type C respirators are **positive-pressure** respirators. The air coming through the hose pushes lead particles away from the mask.

Type C **pressure-demand** respirators have a small valve which controls airflow. The valve makes sure the respirator gives you more air when you breathe harder. With a pressure-demand respirator, you always have positive pressure. Type C **continuous-flow** respirators do not have the airflow control valve. They pump air at a constant rate no matter how hard you breathe. They can become negative pressure. You cannot use Type C continuous-flow respirators for Class 3 tasks - they will not protect you enough. They have a Protection Factor of *50*. They are no more protective than a PAPR. **Pressure-demand is more protective than continuous-flow.**

There are problems with Type C respirators. You can trip on the hose or get it caught on equipment in the work area. If the hose gets damaged, your air supply may get cut off. So, you always need to carry an extra filter or a cylinder of breathable air.

Type C respirators are not used for residential lead paint abatement. **They are used for abatement of lead-painted bridges or other industrial steel structural.** The amount of lead dust during these projects is extremely high.

TYPE CE SUPPLIED-AIR RESPIRATOR

PRESSURE DEMAND
Protection Factor = 2000
Maximum Use Level=100,000 ug/m³

A type CE respirator is a **supplied-air** respirator **with a hood or helmet** attached to the mask. Your employer should give you a Type CE respirator if you are doing blasting work.

There are two different kinds of Type CE respirators available. The first type has a **flexible hood** made of a heavy-duty material called Hypalon™. Hypalon™ is nylon with a rubber coating. It is tough enough to protect you against flying grit or shot. The hood covers your head and shoulders. Some cover your body down to the waist. The respirator mask (either a half-mask or full-face mask) is built into the hood. A muff, or collar, fits around your neck.

The second kind of Type CE respirator has a **helmet**. The helmet will also protect you against grit and shot. It is rigid like a hard hat. A face shield covers your face and a flap covers your neck and shoulders.

Type CE respirators are **supplied-air** respirators. They supply fresh air to the worker through a hose from an outside source. They can be operated in a **pressure-demand** mode or a **continuous-flow** mode. **You must have pressure-demand for Class 3 tasks**. To tell if your CE respirator is pressure-demand, look at the mask - it must be tight fitting - and the regulator - it must be a pressure-demand regulator, which is usually shaped like a disk. A CE respirator is pressure-demand only if it has **both** a tight fitting mask and a pressure-demand regulator.

Rules for using supplied-air respirators

- Get training on how to use the respirator
- Use Grade D breathing air.
- Make sure someone monitors the air purification system.
- Make sure your helmet is tightly secured.
- Watch out for your airline hose. Make sure it is properly secured. Make sure it is away from any water or waste. Be careful not trip on it.

Other respirators

Respirators that are legal for lead abatement work may look different from those pictured in this chapter.

A half-mask respirator may be either air-purifying or supplied air. If it is supplied air, it may be operated in a continuous-flow or in a pressure-demand mode.

A PAPR or supplied-air respirator may have a loose-fitting hood or helmet instead of a full-face mask.

A self-contained breathing apparatus (SCBA) is a fire-fighter's respirator. When you wear a SCBA, you carry a tank of air with you on your back. A SCBA can be operated in a pressure-demand or positive-pressure mode. You should wear a SCBA if you are working in an area with explosive gases or with lots of lead dust.

Review of Protection Factors

The higher the Protection Factor, the more a respirator protects you. A respirator will not protect you unless it fits and has the right filters and parts.

Half-mask air-purifying respirators have a PF of 10 (For every 10 micrograms in the air, 1 leaks into the mask.)

Continuous flow Type CE respirators have a PF of 25 (For every 25 micrograms in the air, 1 leaks into the mask.)

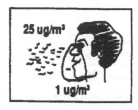

A full-face air-purifying respirator, a tight-fitting PAPR, and a continuous-flow supplied-air respirator all have a PF of 50 (For every 50 micrograms in the air, 1 leaks into the mask.)

A pressure-demand supplied-air respirator, including a Type CE respirator, has a Protection Factor of 2,000 (For every 2,000 micrograms in the air, 1 Microgram leaks in).

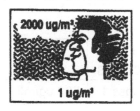

How do you know it's the right respirator?

When you see your air sampling results, how can you tell which respirator will protect you enough? You need to know the respirator's limit or Maximum Use Level (MUL). The MUL is the maximum amount of lead that a particular respirator can protect you from.

To figure out the MUL for a respirator, multiply the PEL *(50* ug/m^3) by the respirator's Protection Factor.

$$MUL = PEL \times PF$$

The PEL is the highest amount of lead the law says you can breathe. This means that OSHA says you can breathe 50 micrograms of lead for every cubic meter of air you breathe. The PEL is what you are permitted to breathe, not necessarily what is safe to breathe.

The Protection Factor (PF) tells you how much lead leaks into your mask as compared to the amount of lead outside your mask.

When you wear a respirator at its MUL, you breathe in lead at the PEL. This means that the law says you can breathe into your body 50 micrograms of lead for every cubic meter of air that you breathe. You need to keep the level of lead inside your respirator below the PEL (50 ug/m^3). You should change to a respirator with a higher PF if you get sampling results close to the MUL.

Respirators legal for lead work

Name	Class	PF	MUL
Half-mask, air-purifying	1	10	500 ug/m3
Loose-fitting PAPR Type CE, continuous flow	2	25	1,250 ug/m3
Full-face, air purifying Tight-fitting PAPR	2	50	2,500 ug/m3
½ mask, supplied-air pressure-demand	3	1,000	50,000 ug/m3
Full-face, supplied-air, pressure-demand, Type CE, pressure-demand	3	2,000	100,000 ug/m3
SCBA pressure-demand	3	≥ 2,000	100,000+ug/m3

TASK CLASS	MUC	RESPIRATOR TYPES
Class 1	500 ug/m3	Half-mask, air-purifying with HEPA filters
Class 2	1,250 ug/m3	*Loose-fitting hood or helmet PAPR with HEPA Filters *Hood or helmet with supplied air continuous flow *Type CE continuous flow
Class 2	2,500 ug/m3	*Full-face, air-purifying with HEPA filter *Tight-fitting PAPR with HEPA filters *Full-face, supplied air, pressure demand *Half-mask or full-face, supplied air, continuous flow
Class 3	50,000 ug/m3	*Half-face, supplied air, pressure demand
Class 3	100,000 ug/m3	*Full-face, supplied air, pressure demand *Type CE pressure demand
Class 3	100,000 ug/m3	*Full-face, SCBA, pressure demand

How to use air sampling results

Air samples can be used to determine which respirator to use. For example, the graph below gives air sampling results from different HUD-demonstration lead abatement projects. Your employer will do similar exposure assessments. He or she may get different results. Using the results, your employer will choose the appropriate respiratory protection.

Look at the HUD demonstration project air sampling results. The graph compares the lead dust levels created by different work methods. The results are the highest levels measured, not the average. Look at the category "Cleaning." The air sampling results -590 ug/m^3 are high because carpet removal is included under this category. Carpet removal creates large amounts of lead dust. What kind of respirator would you use for this type of job? The Maximum Use Level (MUL) for a half-mask, air-purifying respirator is only 500 ug/m^3.

You would need a more protective respirator, such as a full-face, air-purifying respirator or a PAPR.

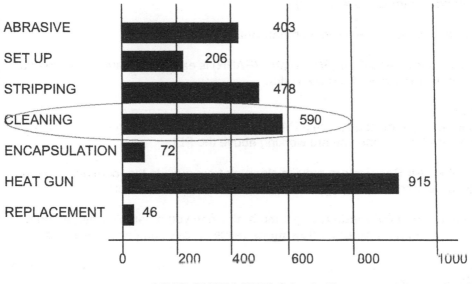

LEAD DUST LEVELS (ug/m3)

Air sampling results from HUD-demonstration lead abatement projects. Figures shown are the highest levels measured, not the average.

Key facts for Chapter 5, Part 1

You should wear a respirator whenever you work with lead.
Whenever you work with lead, you can request a respirator and your employer
must provide one for you.
When lead in the air is above 50 ug/m^3, you must wear a respirator.
You must wear a respirator when doing Class 1, 2, or 3 tasks.
Not everyone can wear a respirator.
You need a doctor's exam before wearing a respirator on the job.

Respirators don't protect you unless they fit properly.

Do not use paper dust masks for lead abatement work.
They are not allowed.
They will not protect you.

Positive pressure (motor pushes air into the mask and pushes particles away
from the edges of the mask) is better than **negative pressure** (your lungs and
heart work hard to move the air).

Full-face is more protective than **half-mask**.

A **Powered Air-Purifying Respirator** (PAPR) is easier and safer to use than a
non-powered air-purifying respirator.

PAPR's
Your employer must give you a PAPR instead of a negative pressure respirator,
if you ask for one and you are working above the PEL.

Supplied-Air Respirators provide clean air from outside the room and are more
protective than air-purifying respirators (filters the air in the room).

Pressure-demand mode (you get more air when you breathe harder) is more
protective **than continuous-flow mode** (air is always pumped at the same rate).

**You must use a pressure-demand, supplied-air respirator whenever you do
a Class 3 task.**

Choosing a respirator
Your employer chooses your respirator by looking at the air samples and/or the
Class tasks that you will do.

PART 2: RESPIRATOR CARE

In this part of Chapter 5 you will learn:

- **What your employer has to do before giving you a respirator**
- **How to make sure your respirator fits**
- **How to take care of your respirator**
- **How to clean, inspect, maintain and store your respirator**

What your employer has to do

Before your employer hands you a respirator, he or she has to do a lot of things. The employer has to find out if you can wear a respirator. Who will pick the respirators? Who will maintain them? These things have to be written down in a respirator program.

When OSHA inspects a job for health and safety reasons, OSHA looks to see if an employer is following OSHA regulations. More than 30% of the problems OSHA inspectors find are related to a company's respirator program.

The Respirator Bill of Rights

OSHA says your employer has to have a very strong respirator program. You can think of this as the "Respirator Bill of Rights."

1. **Your employer must assign someone to be in charge of the respirator program.**
   Find out who this person is. He or she can help you if you have a problem with your respirator.

2. **Your employer must have written procedures for choosing and using respirators.**
   Get a copy of these procedures from the person in charge of the program.

3. **Your employer must check the respirator program regularly.**
   Is it as good in reality as it is on paper?

4. **Your employer has to offer medical exams to everyone who wears a respirator.**
   You need a doctor to examine you to make sure you can wear a respirator. The OSHA Standard requires that if you have difficulty breathing in a respirator, your employer must provide you with a medical exam and consultation. This is required, if you are working at the Action Level or doing any lead-related task.

5. **Training**

Before you put on a respirator, you have to
be trained. You need training on each
respirator you use. You have to learn about
all the parts of your respirator. You have to
learn how your respirator works. You need
to know what a respirator can do for you.
You need to know what a respirator can't

do for you. You have to be trained in how to clean, inspect, and store your
respirator.

NOTE: *Refer to Appendix A - EPA's Renovation, Repair and Painting
Program Final Rule (40 CFR Part 745)* April 22, 2008

6. **Your employer must use approved respirators.**
Respirators and filters have to be approved by two agencies: the
Mine Safety and Health Administration (MSHA) and the National
Institute for Occupational Safety and Health (NIOSH).

7. **Your employer must choose a respirator for the hazard.**
A gas filter won't protect you from dust. A dust filter won't protect you from
a gas. A filter respirator won't protect you if there isn't enough oxygen in the
air. Your employer has to sample the air for lead and other hazards. He or
she will choose your respirator by interpreting the air sample results.

8. **Your employer must be sure your respirator fits you.**
Fit testing is a formal procedure which must include instructions on:
   - how to put the respirator on;
   - how to check the fit or seal of the respirator;
   - how to select a respirator that fits and feels comfortable. Your
     employer must provide several sizes and brands for you to choose
     from.

You must wear the respirator for at least 10 minutes before you are tested. The
test includes specific actions which you will do. A fit test is either a **qualitative fit
test** or a **quantitative fit test.**

Qualitative fit test
A qualitative fit test measures the quality of the seal
to your face. You stand in a bag or booth as the
tester pumps banana oil, saccharine, or irritating
smoke around the edges of the respirator. If the
material leaks into the mask, you will smell it or
taste it. This means the mask does not fit well
enough to keep lead out of your lungs. When using

irritant smoke, the booth must be ventilated. If the booth is not ventilated do not use it.

Quantitative fit test

The tester puts a computer probe inside your respirator. If a booth is used, the tester may spray a mist of salt or mineral oil into the booth. If the mist leaks into the mask, it does not fit well enough to keep lead particles out of your lungs. The computer measures how must mist leaks in. Today quantitative fit tests can be done without a booth or mist. Three fit tests must be done. The results must be at least 10 times the Protection Factor of the mask.

You must have a fit test on every respirator that is given to you for protection. A respirator is only as good as its fit. **You must** *have a fit test annually* if you have a respirator. When you first get a respirator, and annually after that, the fit must be tested. **You must also have a fit test if the shape of your face changes.** This could happen if you gain of lose more than 20 pounds, break your nose, lose teeth or get new dentures, get pregnant or have surgery on your face.

9.   **Your employer must check respirators and fix them**.
     If there is anything wrong with your respirator, your employer has to fix it before you can wear it. Your employer has to check the respirators to make sure they are in perfect shape. Your employer has to have trained people fix your respirator.

10. **Your employer must give you a safe place to store your respirator.**
     Your employer has to give you a clean, dry place to keep your respirator.

What you have to do

After your employer gives you the respirator, you have to use it safely. Do you have the right one? Did you get a fit test on your respirator? Does the respirator work? Is it clean?

You are the one who cares the most about whether your respirator works. If it is not in perfect shape, you could breathe lead. Learn how to use your respirator and take care of it.

1.   **Make sure you have the right respirator and filters.**
     Does your respirator fit you? Get a fit test for your respirator. Do you have an approved respirator? Look for the MSHA/NIOSH seals on your respirator box and on the filters. Do you have the right filters for the job? Read the label on the filter.

     Is your respirator good enough? You need to have the right respirator for the job. Look at the air sample results.

Figure out which respirator you need. **Respirators may not protect you as well as they are supposed to. If you can, get a respirator that's more protective (like a PAPR).**

Even if you have an approved respirator, it might not protect you enough from the amount of lead in the air. Respirator Protection Factors come from tests in labs. The respirator maker tests an average-size person. The tests are done in a clean, cool lab. Only new respirators are used. But you don't work in a lab. You may not have an average face. You sweat when you work. The respirator may slide on your face. Maybe your respirator isn't as perfect as when it was new. There are many reasons why a respirator may not work as well for you as it did in the lab.

2. Know how to use your respirator.

If you don't know how to use or maintain your respirator, it will not protect you. Get to know your respirator. Get training on the respirator you use. Inspect your respirator. Are all the parts where they belong? Always inspect your respirator before you put it on.

3. Inspect your respirator before each use.

A respirator can't help you unless it's in perfect shape. You need to inspect your respirator before you put it on. Make sure all the parts are there. Make sure all the parts are in good shape. Make sure all the parts are in the right place.

If you find anything wrong with your respirator, do not wear it until it is fixed. No one should fix your respirator unless he or she knows how to fix it.

Whenever you get a new respirator, look at the manufacturer's handbook. There should be a section or a page in the handbook that shows all the parts of your respirator. Make sure that your respirator has all its parts. (See the next two pages for more information on inspecting respirators.)

Respirator parts have to come from the same manufacturer that made the respirator. In other words, you may not use MSA™ brand filters on a Cesco™ brand respirator. You may not use 3M™ brand valves on an AO™ brand respirator.

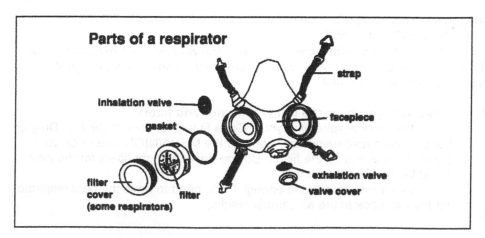

Parts of a respirator

How to inspect your respirator

Facepiece
The facepiece is made of rubber, silicone, and other materials. Check to see if it is ripped or worn. Is it warped or bent? Is it dirty?

Inhalation valves
Inhalation valves are two small rubber flaps behind the filters on the inside of the facepiece. This is where you breathe in. Make sure both of them are there. Are they ripped or bent? Are they dirty?

Exhalation valve
The exhalation valve is a small rubber flap about the size of a quarter. It is found underneath the valve cover on your chin. This is where you breathe out. Take off the cover---is the valve there? Is it ripped or bent? Is it dirty?

Gasket
Gaskets are rubber rings that make a tight seal between the filter and the facepiece. Not every respirator has gaskets. Are they there? Are they ripped or torn?

Filters
Filters filter contaminants out of the air. They are also called "cartridges." Make sure you have the right one for the job. When you work with lead, you need HEPA filters. When you use solvents or caustic paste, you will need other filters, too. Change filters regularly, especially when it becomes harder to breathe.

Straps
Elastic straps hold the respirator on your head. One strap goes over the crown of your head (it may be attached to two plastic straps, which go straight up and straight back on your head). The other strap connects behind your neck. Are the straps still elastic? Are they torn? Do the buckles and snaps work?

PAPRs

If you have a PAPR, you will need to check other parts.

Hose
If the PAPR's fan is on your belt, a hose carries air to your face. Check to see if it is bent or cut.

Fan
Check to see how much air the fan is blowing. Use a tube called a flow meter. If the flow meter reads at least a 4, the battery is charged.

Cord
If the fan is on your facepiece, a cord supplies it with electricity from the battery.

Battery
Every PAPR has a battery to run the fan. Check to see if it is fully charged. Make sure that it has been properly charged.

Supplied-air respirators

If you have a supplied-air respirator, you need to check other parts.

Air regulator
This valve controls how much air comes into the mask. It is either continuous-flow or pressure-demand.

Escape air bottle
Many Type C respirators have a small bottle of air. If air stops coming through the hose, you can breathe air out of the escape bottle. Test to see if the bottle is full before putting it on.

Escape cartridge
Many Type C respirators have a HEPA filter which is used if air stops coming through the hose.

4. **Know how to put on a respirator.**
   When you put on a respirator, put the mask on your face first.
   Smile and frown and move your face around. Be sure the edges of the mask
   fit your face. Fasten the bottom strap (the one that goes around the back of
   your neck). Tighten the bottom strap. The straps need to hold the respirator
   on your face. Do not make them too tight. The mask will dig into your skin. It
   will not be comfortable.

   Pull the top strap over your head. Tighten the top strap. Pull both sides at
   the same time. Then do the two fit checks (below).

   Fit check your respirator every time you put it on.

5. **Do fit checks every time you put a respirator on.**
   You also have to check the fit yourself every time you put on a respirator.
   The fit checks you do yourself are called a negative-pressure fit check and a
   positive-pressure fit check. You must do both of these fit checks every time
   you put on the respirator. Do the two fit checks every time **before** you go
   into an area where there's lead in the air. You can only do these fit checks
   on a tight-fitting respirator. (A tight-fitting respirator makes an airtight seal
   around your face.)

How to do a negative-pressure fit check

1. Cover the two filters or the air hose
   with your hands and suck in gently.
2. Hold for a count of ten.
3. **If the seal is good**, you will feel the
   area of the seal tightening to your face.
   If someone is watching you, he or she
   should see the respirator suck in a little
   at your nose. You will not hear a leak,
   or feel any air flow on your cheek.

4. **If there is a leak**, air will flow in through the leak instead of
   pulling the mask against your face. You will feel air move against your
   cheeks. It may feel like a feather brushing across your face. The air will
   move toward your mouth. You may hear the air flow.

How to do a positive-pressure fit check

Cover the Exhalation valve cover with one hand and puff out gently. Don't blow too hard, or you can blow out your intake valves and break a good seal.

If you have a good seal, you should feel the force of your breath balloon the respirator out a tiny bit. It is like the feeling you get when you first blow up a balloon. You have to blow harder to get over the resistance of the balloon. As the mask moves out, you will feel the seal of the respirator tighten on your face.

If there is a leak, air will flow out of the leak, instead of making the mask balloon out. You will feel air flow out against your cheeks. You will not feel the seal tightening to your face.

---

6.   **Keep your respirator clean.**
     Though respirators are never comfortable, they can become very uncomfortable if you do not clean and disinfect them regularly. It is very easy to clean your respirator, and you must clean it every time you use it.

     Take off the filters and wash the respirator in warm water with a mild soap. You may want to use a mild disinfectant. Wash the inside and outside of the face piece with a soft bristle brush or a clean rag. Rinse the respirator in clean water, and let it dry in the air. If you have a PAPR, do not drop the battery or motor in the water. Wipe these off with a damp cloth.

7.   **Store your respirator in a safe place.**
     Don't hang your respirator by its straps to dry. This can stretch out the straps. It is easy to damage a respirator. Keep your respirator in a clean, dry place. Your employer must provide you with a safe place to store your respirator. Check your employer's written Respirator Program for the company's procedure.

Key facts for Chapter 5, Part 2

A respirator will not protect you unless it fits
You must have a fit test before you can wear a negative-pressure respirator at work.

Fit testing

You must have a fit test every 12 months.
There are two fit tests:
1. **Qualitative fit-testing**. This test doesn't use machines. It uses your sense of smell.
2. **Quantitative fit-testing**. This test uses a machine that measures how much air leaks around the edges of your respirator.

Before you put on your respirator

Inspect your respirator before you put it on.
Do your own fit checks **every time** you wear your respirator.
There are two fit checks:
1. **Negative pressure fit check.** Cover the filters and breathe in.
2. **Positive pressure fit check.** Cover the exhaust valve on your chin and blow out.

Clean your respirator

Clean your respirator every time you wear it. Use soap and water.
Store your respirator in a clean, safe place.

Filter cartridges

Change the filters when it gets hard to breathe.
Use the right filter for the hazard---HEPA filters for lead. If you use solvents or caustic paste, you will need other filters as well as HEPA filters.

Respirator exercise

This is not a test. It is an exercise. Use it to see for yourself how well you understand the material in the chapter.

1. What is the difference between a negative-pressure respirator and a positive-pressure respirator?

2. Which one protects you more? Why?

3. If you are working on an abatement project and air samples show 70 ug/m^3, which respirator do you have to wear?

4. What is the difference between a qualitative fit test and a quantitative fit test?

5. Some people have a harder time getting a good fit on a respirator. Who are they? Why do they have a hard time?

6. Name three limitations of respirators-- that is, reasons why they protect you less than they are supposed to.

7. Are there times when you can't wear a negative-pressure respirator because it won't protect you enough?

8. Name two parts of the "Respirator Bill of Rights."

PART 3: OTHER SAFETY EQUIPMENT

In this part of Chapter 5 you will learn about:
- Disposable suits
- Gloves
- Hard hats
- Boots
- Goggles and safety glasses
- Other safety equipment
- How to prevent taking lead home

Protective clothing

A respirator is one of the most important pieces of equipment for protecting you from lead. Whenever you work with lead you must also wear protective clothing. Everyone in the work room should wear a suit at all times.

Everyone in the work area should wear a protective suit.

You will probably wear a disposable suit. The suit includes coveralls, booties, and a hood. Some suits are made in one piece, some are made with two or three pieces. Suits come in several sizes.

Usually you will wear disposable suits made of a white, paper-like material like Tyvek or KleenGuard.

If you are working with chemical strippers, you may need to wear protective suits that are poly laminated. Poly-laminated suits are usually made of a yellow, plastic, paper-like material.

YOU MUST WEAR
PROTECTIVE CLOTHING

How to use protective clothing

By law, your employer must give you clean protective clothing every day. Your employer must do this unless air sampling results show that airborne lead concentrations are above 200 ug/m³. If your exposure to lead is above 200 ug/m³, your employer must give you clean protective clothing at least once a week. Disposable suits must be replaced whenever they tear or rip beyond repair.

Before you enter the work area:

1. Take off your street clothes. Store them in a clean spot in the change area.
2. Put on your assigned respirator and protective gear.
3. Make sure the disposable suit and booties fit properly. You can shorten a one-piece suit by putting duct tape around the waist, wrists, and ankles.

Every time you leave the work area:

1. HEPA-vacuum lead dust from your protective clothing.
2. Take off and leave your booties in the work area.
3. Take off the rest of your gear in the dirty part of the change area.
4. Wash your hands, face and respirator.
5. Take off your respirator and wash your hands and face again.

At the end of the day:

1. Throw away disposable coveralls and booties. (see below)
2. If you wore shoes over your booties, throw them away with the waste or put them in a bag for your employer to store.
3. Clean your protective gear and respirator. Store it in a clean area.
4. Wash hands and face again.
5. Shower and wash your hair. If a shower is not available at work, shower as soon as you get home.

Non-disposable protective clothing
Your employer may give you non-disposable work clothes. They need to be washed. **Do not take your work clothes home or launder them yourself. By law, your employer must have your protective clothing cleaned.** You must put your work clothes in a special container located in the dirty part of the change area. This container must be closed and labeled.

Disposable protective clothing
Disposable suits do not get cleaned. You will throw away your disposable suits and booties in a special container located in the dirty part of the change area. The container must be closed and labeled. Disposable suits need to be changed whenever they rip and tear beyond repair. That usually means every day.

Making sure you have the right gear
Ask to see the Material Safety Data Sheets (MSDS's) for all caustics, strippers, solvents, and chemicals that you use on the job. Your employer is required by law to provide you with these MSDS's. Look under the section of the MSDS's that is labeled "Special Protection Information." It is usually around Section 8 of most MSDS's. This section is supposed to tell you what type of gloves, suits, and other protection you need.

Eye protection
Wear eye protection whenever you do abatement work. Wear goggles or a face shield whenever you use caustics or solvents. Make sure you know where the portable eye wash is located.

Gloves
When you do lead work, you should wear gloves. Read your MSDS's to see what type of gloves you need, if you are working with chemicals like caustics and solvents.

Footwear
Tyvek™ booties are very slippery, especially on the poly that is put down on the floor of a lead abatement work site. You can use duct tape on the bottom of tyvek booties for traction. Or you might wear canvas or rubber shoes outside the booties. **Don't wear booties on ladders or scaffolding.**

You may wear boots or steel-toed safety shoes. These keep you from slipping or being hurt by falling objects or electrical shocks. You should wear rubber safety boots if you work around live wires.

If you wear any kind of footwear outside the booties, you must take them off and leave them in the dirty work area before you leave the work room. You can't take these shoes off the job if they can't be cleaned. (Leather and fabric shoes **can't** be cleaned; rubber shoes without seams **can.**) **If you can't clean them, you have to throw them out or tie them up in a sealed plastic bag.** Rubber shoes can be tied up in a sealed bag and taken from one lead job to another. Never wear your work shoes home or in your car. They are contaminated with lead. If you wear them home, you will take lead home with you.

Hard hats

Hard hats are made to protect you if something falls straight down on your head. But they will not protect you if something hits you from the side. You should wear a hard hat if there are any overhead hazards, if you are doing demolition work, or if you are working around live electrical wires.

Ear plugs

You will need hearing protection when using a needle gun and other air compressor equipment.

Safety equipment training

Your employer should train you how to use safety equipment.

Sometimes, lead abatement work has many of the same dangers as ordinary demolition work. You will need to use all kinds of safety equipment. **OSHA has rules about protective equipment** like hard hats, goggles, and boots. Many of the rules for respirators also apply to other equipment. For example, goggles will not protect you unless they are in perfect shape. They have to be cleaned, stored, and maintained. Your employer must train you about the OSHA laws for safety equipment.

Do not take lead home

It is very important to wear a protective suit while working with lead, not your street clothes. Leave your work clothes at work. This includes the shoes you wear at work. Your work clothes and shoes are contaminated with lead. **If you take them home with you, the lead will come off in your home.** This is called "take-home lead." Your family could be poisoned by the lead you carry home.

Protect yourself and your family

Follow the correct procedures for using protective clothing on the job. Especially shower at the end of the day.

If you are working above the PEL, your employer must provide a shower. A wash facility must always be provided. Lead dust can get in your hair and on your skin. **If you don't wash up, you could poison yourself and your family. They may breathe or swallow the lead you take home.**

> Pete is not wearing a respirator or protected clothing while working on a lead abatement project.

Pete leaves work and drives home in this truck without showering and changing clothes.

Pete passes lead dust to his family. Now all three may get lead poisoned.

Pete wears protecting clothing and wears a respirator and showers after work.

No lead dust gets in Pete's truck.

Pete does not bring lead dust home.

Pete wears protecting clothing and wears a respirator and showers after work.

Pete does not bring lead dust home.

No lead dust gets in Pete's truck.

Chapter 6 - Controlling Lead-Based Paint Hazards

PART 1

In this part of Chapter 6, you will learn about:

- Title X
- Six situations where lead is a hazard
- Who will reduce lead hazards
- Lead paint abatement
- Interim controls
- Special cleaning
- How to use interim controls for a home
- Operations and maintenance programs

Reducing lead-based paint hazards

Children most often get lead poisoned because they swallow lead dust. The Congress of the United States found that:

- More than 3 million children are affected by low level lead exposure.
- The most common cause of lead poisoning in children is swallowing lead in household dust.
- There are more than 3 million tons of lead in lead-based paint in the total number of houses built before 1980.

In October 1992, Congress passed a law called the Housing and Community Development Act. This Act includes Title X of the Residential Lead Based Paint Hazard Reduction Act of 1992 (Public Law 102-550). The purpose of this act is to reduce lead-based paint hazards.

What is a lead-based paint hazard?

Title X defines a lead-based paint hazard as any condition that causes enough exposure to lead, to cause ill health. A lead-based paint hazard is possible wherever lead dust can be created. When lead dust is created, you can breathe or swallow it. It is a hazard to your health. **Title X lists six situations where lead is a hazard.**

1. **Lead dust from lead-based paint which is damaged.**
   All building materials get damaged and deteriorate. All building materials with lead-based paint can create lead dust.

2. **Lead dust from lead-based paint on any friction surface.**
   A friction surface is any surface that rubs against another surface.
   Windows and floors are friction surfaces.

3. **Lead dust from lead-based paint on any impact surface.**
   An impact surface is any surface that has forceful contact over and over
   again. Doors have impact surfaces.

4. **Lead-painted surfaces that a child can chew on.**
   The child chews on the surface and swallows the lead particles. These
   surfaces are called accessible surfaces.

5. **Lead-contaminated dust** anywhere in the home that is above the
   acceptable standards that are set by EPA.

6. **Lead-contaminated soil** that is bare soil with lead above the acceptable
   standard that are set by EPA.

Where is lead-based paint found?

Lead-based paint can be found in buildings built before 1978. That
includes our homes, schools, community centers, libraries, hospitals, and other
public and commercial buildings built before 1978. Lead-based paint is almost
always found on bridges and stell structures becasue it prevents corrosion.
Anytime there is bridge repair, lead dust is likely to be created. Anytime an
older house is renovated, there is a potential lead hazard. Anytime demolition
is done on an older building, there is a potential lead hazard.

Who will reduce the lead hazards?

Reducing the lead-based paint hazards in the United States is a huge job.
It will take many years and a lot of resources. Many different people will work to
help reduce the lead hazards.

- **Certified small contractors** will abate homes using certified workers.
- **Certified large contractors** with trained certified workers will abate large
  building complexes, facilities, and steel structures.
- **Community organizations and tenant associations** will have members
  trained to reduce lead hazards in the homes, playgrounds, and community
  facilities.
- **Public employees** of schools, housing, and state and municipal agencies
  will be trained to provide lead-safe facility maintenance and custodial care.

How will lead hazards be reduced?

Title X gives a detailed plan to reduce lead hazards. Here are some of the important parts of Title X's plan:

- EPA, OSHA, and HUD will work together to develop standards, regulations, and funding to reduce lead hazards.
- Federal government will educate the public about lead hazards.
- If a property seller or landlord knows about lead hazards on the property, he or she must inform potential buyers or renters about them.
- Home buyers have the right to get a lead inspection of that home before the purchase contract is legal.

Title X's 2-step plan for reducing lead hazards

1. Evaluate the lead hazards

Evaluating lead hazards will help answer very important questions.

- Which homes need to be taken care of first?
- Who in the home might get poisoned?
- What actions will reduce lead hazards?

The information gathered in the inspections and risk assessments (Chapter 3) will help answer these questions.

2. Reduce the lead hazards

Once the lead hazards are identified they need to be reduced. Reducing lead hazards means to get rid of the lead that is dangerous to a person's health. Title X states two ways of reducing lead hazards. They are called **abatement** and **interim controls.**

Abatement

Lead abatement is a set of actions that remove or control the lead hazard. Some of these actions are permanent, as long as the protective material stays intact. These actions are sometimes called abatement strategies. Title X includes the following as abatement activities:

- Replacement
- Removal
- Enclosure and encapsulation
- Cleanup of lead dust
- Removal or covering of lead contaminated soil
- Site preparation and cleanup
- Waste disposal
- Final inspections and clearance testing

Interim controls

Interim controls are actions that reduce the lead hazard temporarily. They are a temporary solution. They can be very helpful. They keep the lead dust levels down and can prevent lead poisoning. Areas where interim controls are being used need to be regularly inspected to make sure the controls are still working. HUD is developing a schedule of inspection for each interim control activity. Interim controls listed in Title X include the following:

1. **Education programs**
2. **Special cleaning**
3. **Repairs, repainting, and maintenance**

Education programs

Anyone who uses interim controls should have special training. You create lead dust when you use interim controls. You will move lead dust around. This creates a hazard. You need to know how to work safely with lead. This course is an example of such training.

Other education programs would be lead hazard awareness training for building occupants and workers who won't be doing lead work. Both groups need to be aware of lead hazards. They need to know where the lead-based paint surfaces are and what is being done to make the building lead safe.

Special cleaning methods

Special cleaning methods must always be used when you work with lead-painted surfaces. Special cleaning can be used by itself to control lead dust. Special cleaning must be used with all other interim controls and all abatement methods. Research shows that there are two cleaning methods that work well to reduce lead dust:

1. **HEPA-vacuuming**
2. **Washing with a lead cleaner**

These cleaning methods work best when they are used together, one right after the other. You will learn more about special cleaning methods later in this chapter.

Repairs, repainting, and maintenance

The purpose of interim controls is to reduce the lead hazard, until the hazard can be abated. Repairing lead-painted surfaces and repainting them with a non-lead paint is one way to reduce lead dust until those surfaces can be abated. You must monitor and maintain any surface you repair or repaint. Many actions are included in the repair maintenance of lead-painted surfaces.

A small repair job at home

A heavy mirror was held on the wall of your bathroom. The weight of the mirror caused the hook and nail to pull out of the wall. The mirror fell onto the sink. Fortunately, it did not break. The wall now has a hole where the nail used to be. The hole is as wide as a penny and an inch deep. The paint around the hole is chipped.

The small and simple repair could include:

- **Wet washing the paint dust and chips**
- **Wet scraping the chipped paint**
- **Repairing the hole with caulk or putty**
- **Repainting the surface**
- **Wrapping and disposal of debris**

An interim control plan for a house

Here is a set of actions that can be used as interim controls for a home. Combined, these actions can reduce lead exposure. Make sure interim controls are allowed by state and city laws before using them.

Before you begin, make sure you contain the area. Set up signs and barrier tape to keep non-workers out of the area. Wear protective clothing and a respirator until you are ready to repaint.

1. **Do a special cleaning.**
   Vacuum the whole house with a HEPA-vacuum. Then use a lead cleaner to wash the whole house. Pay special attention to the window wells.

2. **Do small repairs to the windows to reduce lead dust.**
   Cut a piece of sheet metal or plastic the same size as the window well. Back caulk the piece and nail it in place. This repair will enclose the well and create a cleanable surface. It will reduce the lead dust the window creates, and make the window easier to clean later on.

3. **Wet scrape edges and loose paint.**
   Wet scrape the leading edge of the window stools (inside window sills). Wet scrape any other loose, peeling paint.

4. **Wash the whole house with a lead cleaner again.**
   Then HEPA vacuum the whole house again.

5. **Have an inspector do clearance dust wipe tests.**

6. **Repaint the wet-scraped surfaces with a non-lead paint.**

   These actions will reduce the amount of lead dust in the home and make it a safer environment for both children and adults. The home will still need to be monitored for lead hazards on a regular basis.

In-place management

In-place management is necessary whenever you use interim controls. Keeping a lead-based paint surface in good condition prevents damage and dust. Controlling lead dust and paint chips during routine cleanup and maintenance activity also helps reduce lead hazards.

In schools, hospitals, and other public and commercial buildings, custodians and maintenance personnel clean and repair the building. Any facility that has lead-painted surfaces should have an in-place management program.

A good in-place management program can help prevent lead poisoning. It can help make and keep a building lead safe. A good program should include the following:

- An education program for workers and building occupants to make them aware of lead-based paint hazards, where the lead-painted surfaces are located, and what actions are being taken to make the building lead-safe;
- Safe work practices training for the custodians and maintenance workers;
- A written program for each building that identifies all sources of lead exposure;
- A lead program manager who is in charge of all activities related to lead, and who communicates with workers, outside contractors, and occupants regularly;
- On-going monitoring and checking of the condition of lead-painted surfaces; and

- Records of all inspections, work activities, maintenance, ongoing monitoring, worker medical exams, exposure monitoring, waste disposal and other activities.

Everyone in the building is involved in preventing lead hazards when an in-place management program is working.

Holistic approach to lead-hazard control

The goal of planning and doing lead-hazard control is to create a safe environment at an affordable price.

Lead work should always be part of a maintenance approach. Maintenance work should always be done as part of lead in-place management or abatement work. Lead paint work should never be done without looking at long-term maintenance issues. Consider the following issues:

- It makes no sense to replace windows if the replacement doesn't benefit energy conservation. Energy-efficient replacement windows will increase the value and efficiency of the building.

- Moisture problems lead to lead paint failure and can encourage termite damage and structural problems. Repair all sources of moisture before or during abatement.

- Carpets can store lead dust as well as bacteria and mold that cause respiratory disease. Bacteria, mold and lead dust are almost impossible to clean out of carpets. Whenever possible, carpets should be removed and replaced.

Key facts for Chapter 6, Part 1

Lead-based paint hazards
Lead-based paint is the major cause of childhood lead poisoning.
Lead dust can be found any place where lead-based paint is flaking or damaged.
Lead-based paint can be found in many buildings built before 1978.

Title X ("Residential Lead-Based Paint Hazard Reduction Act") U.S.
Congress passed Title X in 1992 to reduce the hazard of lead-based paint.
Title X has a two step plan for reducing lead hazards: evaluating and controlling lead hazards.

Abatement means controlling the hazard.
Title X states that abatement means "removing lead-based paint hazards permanently." Anyone doing lead abatement must be trained.

Interim controls reduce lead-based paint hazards temporarily. Interim controls keep lead dust levels down and can prevent poisoning.
Careful cleaning is important in abatement and interim controls. A good in-place management program can help prevent lead poisoning.
Monitor any area that you repair, to make sure it stays in good condition.
Make sure the interim controls you use are legal in your area. Anyone using interim controls must be trained.

Community members, building occupants, and workers need to know about lead hazards in the building.
They need to know what is being done to make a building lead-safe.

PART 2: SPECIAL CLEANING METHODS

In this part of Chapter 6, you will learn about:
- **The parts of a HEPA vacuum**
- **How to use a HEPA vacuum**
- **What is a lead cleaner**
- **How to use the 4-step system**

Special cleaning methods

Special cleaning methods must be used when you work with lead-painted surfaces. Special cleaning can be used by itself to control lead dust. Special cleaning **must** be used with all other interim controls and all abatement methods.
Research shows that HEPA-vacuuming and washing with a lead cleaner are the methods that work well to reduce lead dust. They work best when they are used together, one right after the other:

1. **HEPA-vacuum all surfaces**
2. **Wash all surfaces with a lead cleaner.**
3. **HEPA-vacuum all surfaces again.**

HEPA-vacuum

Always use a HEPA-vacuum on a lead job. A HEPA-vacuum is an industrial strength vacuum cleaner with a HEPA filter. HEPA stands for "High Efficiency Particulate Air." HEPA filters can catch lead dust. A regular shop vacuum will not filter out the lead dust. A shop vacuum just blows the lead back out into the room.

True story:
What can happen if you don't use a HEPA vacuum?
   Mr. B. and his wife stripped all the lead-based paint from their home in New York. The family lived in two rooms of the house, while work was done on the rest of the home.
   Mr. B. wanted to protect his infant daughter, Mary, from lead. He vacuumed the entire house every day. He used a regular vacuum. The regular vacuum blew the lead dust back into the area where his family was living, every time he vacuumed. As a result, Mary's blood lead level went up to 37 ug/dl. She had to receive chelation therapy. Two years later, her blood lead level returned to normal.

   Blakelee, S. "Lead-Calcium Time Bomb." American Health. November 1990

How a HEPA vacuum works
   Most HEPA-vacuums have three filters: a HEPA filter, a secondary filter, and a pre-filter.
1.   Debris gets sucked in through the hose into the vacuum bag.
2.   The air and dust get filtered through the pre-filter, the secondary filter, and the HEPA filter.
3.   The HEPA filter captures the lead dust before the air is released into the work area again.

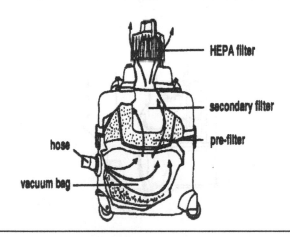

How to use a HEPA-vacuum

1. **Lightly mist the area with water to keep dust levels down.**
    Some HEPA vacuums can combine a wet wash with the vacuum. Read the manufacturer's instructions on how to use it.

2. **Move slowly.**
    Remember, lead dust sticks to surfaces. Vacuum slowly so the HEPA-vacuum can pick up all the lead dust.

3. **HEPA-vacuum all surfaces**
    Start at the end farthest from the main entrance/exit. As you vacuum, move towards the main exit and finish there.

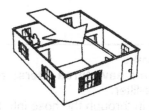

Begin at the top of each room and work down. For example, start with the top shelves, the top of the woodwork, and so on, and work down to the floor. Do every inch of the window, especially the window wells.

4. Use special attachments.

Use the rubber cone where the floor meets the baseboard and along all the cracks in the floor boards. Use the brush tool for walls and woodwork. Use the wheeled floor nozzle for bare floors and the carpet beater for rugs.

5. Maintain the HEPA-vacuum.

Every now and then, you should check the HEPA-vacuum for:

• Damaged wires
• Worn gaskets and switches
• Torn vacuum bag (if used)
• Damaged and clogged filters

Whenever you repair the HEPA vacuum, wear protective clothing and your respirator. Repair and replace parts for HEPA vacuums in a contained work area. Replace parts as needed. Check the pre-filter often for dust and debris. Change the pre-filter when appropriate. This keeps the HEPA-vacuum working properly. Use parts and filters that are the same make as the originals. Never use shop vacuum parts on a HEPA-vacuum.

Wear protective clothing and your respirator. When checking the HEPA-vacuum, clean it off using a second HEPA-vacuum. Remember to clean up the area when you are done.

Lead cleaner

Trisodium phosphate (TSP) is a special ingredient in some detergents that bonds with lead dust. Lead dust sticks to the TSP. Washing with the lead cleaner TSP helps get lead dust particles out of the cracks and crevices. Remember to rinse surfaces well after washing them with TSP or any other lead cleaner.

Lead cleaners, like TSP, should not be used on certain surfaces, such as finished furniture. Use a tack cloth (a soft, lintless cloth such as a handkerchief) on such surfaces.

Phosphates like TSP are harmful to the environment. A number of other lead cleaners may be used instead of TSP. Some states and local governments do not allow the use of TSP. Other states require you to use TSP as a lead cleaner. Be sure to check your state and local laws.

1. **Use detergent that contains 5% TSP or an equivalent lead cleaner.**
   You can buy this detergent in most hardware or janitor supply stores. (Dishwasher detergent may contain 5% phosphate. If so, this is okay to use-- but it is more expensive.)

2. **Wear gloves and eye protection.**
   Lead cleaners are skin and eye irritants. Always wear gloves and protective eye gear when you use a lead cleaner. A portable eye wash should also be on site.

3. **Mix the lead cleaner with water.**
   Follow directions on the package to make the solution. Do not use it stronger than the instructions say.

4. **Wash the area in the same order you HEPA-vacuumed it.**
   Wipe from the far end of the area to the entrance and, from the top of each room to the floor. Wash and rinse each room one at a time.

5. **Use the "4-step system"**
   When you wipe down surfaces with the lead cleaner, you will need three containers: one to hold the wash, one to *squeeze* the rag or mophead into, and one with clean rinse water.

   There are four steps in washing with lead cleaner. (See below.) Go through these steps for each room in the work area. Wash and rinse each room one at a time. **Rinse carefully and thoroughly**. Lead cleaner leaves behind a film. If you do not rinse it off once it dries, the cleaner can damage surfaces. It can also prevent new paint from bonding to the surface.

Step 1: Spray or pour the lead cleaner solution.
Use a plastic jug or a garden sprayer to hold the solution. Pour out the lead cleaner onto the rag or mophead. This will help avoid contaminating the cleaning solution.

Step 2: Wash surfaces with lead cleaner.
Use rags for woodwork and a string mop for floors. Sometimes a sponge mop is used for walls. Sometimes cloth rags are used for all surfaces.

Step 3: Squeeze out the dirty rag or mophead.
Squeeze out the dirty rag or mophead into an empty container.

Replace the wash rag or mophead whenever it gets loaded with dust and debris.

Repeat Steps 1 through 3 until you finish washing one room.

Step 4: Rinse the surfaces.

Fill a container with clean water. Use a clean rag or mophead and rinse all the surfaces you washed.

Squeeze the rinse rag or mophead into an empty container. Replace it when you need to.
Repeat Step 4 until you finish rinsing the room you washed. Replace rinse water as often as necessary to keep it clean. Repeat all four steps for each room in the work area. Check your state and local laws for instruction on how to dispose of the cleanup waste water, rags, mopheads, and debris.

Remember to repeat the HEPA vacuum process.

Key facts for Chapter 6, Part 2

Special cleaning requires HEPA-vacuuming and washing with a lead cleaner.
1.   HEPA-vacuum all surfaces in the work area.
2.   Wash all surfaces with lead cleaner.
3.   HEPA-vacuum all surfaces again.

Use a HEPA-vacuum on lead jobs.
HEPA-vacuum all surfaces from top to bottom.
Wear protective clothing and a respirator whenever you use, repair, or clean the HEPA-vacuum.

Special cleaning methods must be used when abating lead.
Special cleaning removes lead dust.
Special cleaning is one of the most important jobs in abatement.

Use a lead cleaner on all surfaces (where appropriate)
Use trisodium phosphate (TSP) or another lead cleaner to wash surfaces.
Check what your state and local laws require. Lead cleaner can burn your skin and eyes, so wear gloves and eye protection when you use it, and have an eye wash nearby. Use 3 containers: (1) lead cleaner; (2) empty (3) rinse water.

Use 4-step system:
(1)   Pour or spray the lead cleaner from a jug or garden sprayer onto the rag or mophead.
(2)   Wash all the surfaces in a room with lead cleaner. Move from top to bottom, starting from the point farthest from the exit.
(3)   Squeeze out the dirty rag or mop head into empty bucket.
(4)   Rinse all surfaces very carefully. Use clean water, rags, and mop heads. Wash and rinse each room - one at a time.

Check your state and local laws for instructions on how to dispose of the cleanup waste water, rags, mop heads, and debris.

Special cleaning methods can be used as an interim control.

Chapter 7 - Lead Abatement Setup

In this chapter you will learn about:

- How to keep lead out of the air
- Wearing a respirator and disposable suit
- What a lead job looks like
- How to clean the work room
- How to set up the work room
- How to set up a decontamination area
- How to use the decontamination area

Working with lead

All lead-paint abatement methods create lead dust.

- Lead dust is poisonous if breathed or swallowed.
- Lead dust is made up of very small particles of lead.
- Lead dust is often too small to see.
- Lead dust is heavy.
- It usually falls within 6 feet from its source.
- Lead dust settles on whatever surface it lands on.
- You can get lead dust on your hands if you touch any surface that has lead dust.

Burning lead creates lead fumes.

- Lead fumes are very dangerous.
- Lead fumes contain many tiny lead particles.
- Lead fumes stay in the air a long time.
- Lead fumes are very easy to breathe.
- Lead fumes easily go through a dust mask.

Rules for lead work
The following steps will keep lead from spreading outside of the work area. It will also make final cleanup of the work area much easier.

1. Keep dust levels down
2. Contain the work area
3. Follow good hygiene practices
4. Use personal protective gear and clothing
5. Clean up

---

1. Keep dust levels down

The purpose of lead abatement is to reduce a hazard. But, while you do the abatement you will stir up and even create new lead dust. **It is very important to keep lead dust levels down**. According to the law, your employer must use methods and tools which create the least amount of lead dust. This program must be in writing, and is called a compliance program. As a worker, you can control lead dust levels by:

- Avoiding methods that create a lot of dust and waste.
- Using a HEPA vacuum.
- Using wet methods.
- Cleaning up as you work.
- Never dry sweeping.

2. Seal off the work area

The OSHA Lead Standard says that the work area must be separated from the non-work area. HUD says the work area must be sealed off. The work area can be contained with sheets of 6-mil polyethylene, called "poly."

Containing the work area:
- Protects non-leaded surfaces from lead dust.
- Keeps lead dust from spreading outside the work area.
- Keeps everyone but workers away from the lead.
- Makes clean up easier.

It is important to look for rips in the poly every day before you begin work. Repair any rips with duct tape as soon as you see them.

3. Use personal protective gear and clothing

Wear a respirator, disposable coveralls, booties, and gloves while on the job site. Sometimes you will have to wear protective eye gear, too. Take off your disposable coveralls and booties whenever you leave the work area. Throw them away in the container labeled "LEAD CONTAMINATED WASTE" at the end of each workday. **Do not take lead dust home on work clothes.**

4. Wash up, shower, change

Wash your hands and face each time you leave the work area. Lead dust will get on you while you work. Washing up each time you leave the work area prevents you from getting lead dust in your mouth. Washing prevents you from poisoning yourself. Never eat, drink, smoke or put on makeup in the work area.

Don't take lead dust home! When your exposure to lead is above *50* ug/m^3, your employer is required to provide showers whenever feasible. Take a shower at the end of the work day. Do not wear contaminated work clothes or shoes home.

5. Cleanup

Cleanup is very important. It prevents future exposures to lead. It protects you while you work. It keeps harmful lead dust levels down. It prevents you from spreading lead dust outside the work area. Good cleanup is required for the abatement job to pass the final inspection.

Setup

A good setup is very important on an abatement job. There are many different parts of the setup job. You have to turn off and seal off the ventilation system. You have to clean and protect the room. You may have to bring in extension cords. A good setup makes the rest of your job much easier. It also prevents many safety problems. The exact type of setup you do will depend on your job.

It is important to think about how to set up without creating a bigger lead dust hazard. Identify the contaminated areas. Identify where the shower or wash area will be set up, and **how you will move in and out of the contaminated area.**

Setup check list

_____ Put up warning signs.
_____ Identify work site safety hazards.
_____ Clean and remove anything you can move. Clean, cover, and seal the things you cannot move.
_____ Shut off and seal off ventilation system.
_____ Provide airflow for workers.
_____ Do necessary repair work.
_____ Shut off and lock out electricity.
_____ Set up the decontamination area and wash area.
_____ Clean, cover, and seal everything left in the work area.
_____ Mop and seal the floor.
_____ Bring in equipment and tools.
_____ Seal off the work site.
_____ Separate "dirty work" area from the rest of the work area.
_____ Set up locked storage space for waste.
_____ Secure the work site.

1. Put up warning signs

Only the people working on the lead abatement job should enter the work area. People who live in homes where work is done will need to pack up their belongings, and stay somewhere else until the abatement job passes final inspection. Even on jobs where interim controls are being used, occupants should be out of the house during work.

The building owner needs to warn everyone in advance that lead work will be done. Warning signs need to be put up at the exits and entrances of the area to be abated. Many states and local governments say you must post warning signs. Make sure you check your state and local laws.

```
┌─────────────────────┐
│     CAUTION         │
│                     │
│       LEAD          │
│      HAZARD         │
│       KEEP          │
│        OUT          │
└─────────────────────┘
```

Some states say the contractor performing the abatement must put up warning signs on the doors leading to the work area. They must say:

```
┌─────────────────────────────┐
│        WARNING              │
│    LEAD WORK AREA           │
│        POISON               │
│  NO SMOKING, EATING         │
│      OR DRINKING            │
└─────────────────────────────┘
```

These signs prevent anyone from wandering into the work area. The signs tell everyone there is a lead hazard. The OSHA Lead Standard says these signs must be posted if you a re working above the PEL. Warning signs should be written in the language of the occupants and the workers.

2. Identify work site hazards

It is important to identify work site hazards before starting the job. You and your co-workers need to map all the safety hazards on the job site. You will look for problems like:

- Exposed electrical wires and switches
- Water damage
- Water leaks
- Collapsed or damaged ceilings, walls, floors, stairs
- Any other structural damage

You will need to put up warning signs that say "DANGER", until you repair the problems.

3. Clean off and take out anything you can move

Clean and move anything you can out of the room. Large appliances such as refrigerators, washers and dryers may be left. But gas stoves and refrigerators must be disconnected. You will move:

- Chairs
- Books
- Machines
- Computers
- Tables
- Cooking Pans

- Office supplies
- Desks
- Lamps
- Paintings
- Bookcases
- And so on

Clean everything off with rags and a lead cleaner like TSP. Immediately, rinse off the lead cleaner with clear water. Do not use TSP on finished furniture. Use tack cloth instead. Put the used rags in 6-mil poly bags and label the bags "LEAD CONTAMINATED". Dispose of them with other waste. The washer water must be stored in non-corrosive containers. It may be hazardous waste. In some states it is illegal to pour wash water down the drain.

All cloth must be removed and cleaned. Cloth includes clothes, curtains, carpets, and upholstered furniture. Removing carpet kicks up a lot of dust. Workers must wear protective gear, especially respirators.

Rugs and fabric on furniture must be cleaned. It is very difficult to clean cloth and carpets. If they cannot be cleaned, they should be removed. Warn the owner about the things you cannot clean.

Do _not_ throw anything away without the owner's permission.

If the owner agrees to throw contaminated items away, wrap them in two layers of 6-mil poly. Seal them up with duct tape. Label the items "LEAD-CONTAMINATED WASTE", Dispose of them with other abatement waste. (See Chapter 10 on Cleanup and Disposal.)

4. Shut off the ventilation system and seal it

The ventilation air system carries air through the building. **It can carry lead through the building.** Lead goes where air goes. The ventilation system, for the work area, must be shut off at the electrical box.

Lock the box and label it with a tag that says:

The ventilation system is often called the **HVAC system.** HVAC stands for Heating, Ventilating, and Air Conditioning. Cover and seal the air vents with poly and duct tape.

Since the heat is turned off, in cold weather it is necessary to bring in alternative heat sources. Also, be sure to protect water pipes and fixtures from freezing. If necessary, drain the pipes and wrap the water entrance from the street with electrical tape.

5. Provide ventilation (airflow) for workers

There are times when extra ventilation is necessary. Your employer might use a negative air machine to both ventilate the work area and clean the air. A negative air machine is like an exhaust fan with a HEPA filter. When you use a negative air machine, there must be an opening for fresh air to come in. This is called "make up air." The OSHA Lead Standard says you must have extra ventilation if you are working above the PEL.

6. Do necessary repair work

Some of the structural problems you identified at the crew's pre-job meeting have to be fixed. Collapsed stairways, ceilings, and floors can make the work area too dangerous to start the job. You will have to fix these problems before you can start the abatement work.

Check for moisture damage. If you find any moisture damage, determine the source of the moisture or water damage. Fix the source problem, or inform the owner of the need to have it fixed. Roof leaks, poor flashing, bad plumbing and other water leaks must be repaired. Uncorrected water leaks will cause the abatement to fail. Walls must be allowed to dry out. Moisture in a wall can cause abatement to fail.

Any damaged plaster will need repair if it is going to be abated. Otherwise, the method will fail. Remember to contain the area before you do this repair work.

You also need to make sure the water system is working. You will need on-site running water to wash up. You will need water for some abatement methods and for cleanup procedures. If the water service is shut off, you will have to bring water to the site.

7. Shut off electricity and lockout the electrical system

Lead abatement jobs use water. This is an electrical hazard. Water can leak into an electrical outlet and kill you. For small residential jobs, you can cut off the electricity at the fuse or breaker box for the rooms that you are working on.

For large jobs, the electrical system should be shut off at the electrical box. Lock the box and label it with a tag that says

"DANGER - DO NOT OPERATE."

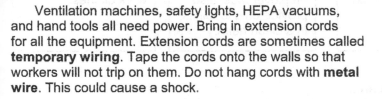

Turning off wall switches is not enough. Someone who does not know about lead abatement work could electrocute you by mistake.

Machines also have to be shut off. A machine with moving parts could hurt someone. It has to be turned off and locked so people can work safely around it.

Ventilation machines, safety lights, HEPA vacuums, and hand tools all need power. Bring in extension cords for all the equipment. Extension cords are sometimes called **temporary wiring**. Tape the cords onto the walls so that workers will not trip on them. Do not hang cords with **metal wire**. This could cause a shock.

Cords should be hooked up to sensitive switches. These are called **Ground Fault Circuit Interrupters (GFCIs)**.

8. Set up the decontamination area (decon)

You go into and out of the work room through a special area. It is called the **"decontamination unit" or "decon."** This is where you **decontaminate** or **get clean.**

Your employer needs to set up a decon. **Set up the decon in a clean area.** The kind of decon you use depends on the size of the job. Some contractors build their own decons. Some use hard plastic decons. Others use decon trailers that go outside the building.

For a large-scale job, the decon may be separate rooms. These rooms should be lined with two layers of poly (hung with duct tape) and have poly flaps between them. The decon should be sealed to the work room. For small-scale work, like single unit abatement or interim control work, you may not be able to use a full decon. Your employer is still required to provide an area to decontaminate, a wash area, and a clean changing area that are separate from the work area.

The decon has three rooms. They have to be in this order (starting from the work room):

DIRTY AREA - WASH AREA - CLEAN AREA

1. Dirty area	2. Wash area	3. Clean area
The dirty area must have a container to put your dirty protective clothing and used respirator filters in. This container has to have a lid that closes. The container should be labeled.	The wash area must have an eye wash station, running warm water, clean towels, and soap. When possible, there should be a shower. Your employer must also provide on-site toilets, in a clean nearby area.	The clean area must have a clean place to store your street clothes and respirator. Your street clothes should never be in contact with your dirty work clothes.

Entering the work area

Before you begin to work, you should change into your protective work clothes and shoe covers in the **clean area**. Store your street clothes in the clean area. Inspect, put on, and fit check your respirator. Put your hood over your respirator straps and secure with duct tape. Walk through the wash area into the equipment or dirty room. Take whatever equipment you need and go into the work area.

Exiting the work area

Every time you leave the work area, **you must exit through the decon**. Before stepping into the decon, HEPA-vacuum the protective suit that you are wearing. Remove your booties and leave them in the work area. Then enter the **dirty area** of the decon. Take off your protective clothing by rolling the inside out. At the end of the day, you need to put your contaminated protective clothing in the labeled laundry container. Your employer must give you clean protective clothing.

Move into the wash **area. Wash your face with your respirator on.**
Remove your respirator and wash your hands and face.

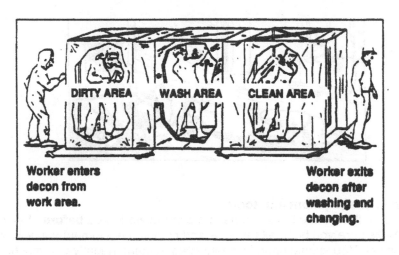

Clean your respirator. When you leave at the end of the day, you need to shower and wash your hair, as well as wash your hands and face. Don't take lead out of the work area on your body.

Move into the **clean area** with your clean respirator. Put on your clean clothes and shoes. Never wear contaminated work clothes home, or bring them home to wash. They are contaminated with lead. If you take your work clothes home, you could expose yourself and your family to lead.

9. Clean, cover, and seal everything left in the room

HEPA-vacuum and wipe off with a damp rag anything that you cannot remove (like a refrigerator, oven, piano, etc.). Wet clean all surfaces. Wait until the surfaces dry. Then cover and seal them with 6-mll poly and duct tape. This seal may not be broken until the final inspection. Remember to duct tape the poly to the floor.

10. Put up critical barriers

Duct tape poly on air vents, heat ducts, windows, and any other openings. This helps prevent lead dust from escaping the work area.

11. Seal the floors

Wet-mop the floor, particularly where the floor meets each wall. Let it dry. Cover the floor with 6-mil poly, taping it around the outside edges with duct tape. Cover the first sheet of poly with a second sheet of poly where demolition or removal will create high dust levels. Tack this layer down with a small piece of duct tape so the second layer can be taken up without pulling up the first layer.

It's important to look for tears in the poly every day before you begin working. **Repair any rips as soon as you notice them.**

12. **Bring in equipment and tools**
    Be sure that all the tools you need are in the work area **before** abatement begins. Make sure you bring all the tools and cleaning equipment you will need for abatement. You should bring in cleaning equipment, negative air machines (if required), scaffolding, and ladders before the decon area is built and before the area is sealed.

13. **Seal off the work area (from the rest of the building)**
    If you're only removing paint from **one room or one part of a building,** and another part of the building is occupied, **seal off the work area from the rest of the building.** The barrier must prevent people from passing through accidentally. Examples of this kind of barrier are a locked door or plywood nailed to a frame. The edges must be sealed on all sides with duct tape to make them dust tight. This seal may not be broken until the work is complete in this area, the area is cleaned, and the area passes final clearance.
    Workers should enter and exit from the work area through a door. If this is not possible (for example, the work area is more than three floors up), a full decon system must be used between the work area and the rest of the occupied building.

14. **Separate "dirty work" areas from rest of work area**
    Demolition, chemical stripping, and any other work that will generate a lot of lead dust or waste is called **"dirty work."** It is a good idea to separate "dirty work" areas from the rest of the work area. Doing so helps control the transfer of dust.
    - Put up two layers of 6-mil poly over the dirty area exit
    - Seal off ventilation registers
    - (If possible) do not remove debris through other areas.
    - Avoid tracking dust from the dirty area when you move to other parts of the work area.

15.   Set up a locked storage space for waste

Use a locked dumpster or an area that can be locked. The waste storage area must not be accessible to children or animals. Put up a warning sign that says: "**DANGER! LEAD WASTE**". If you use a dumpster, be sure the rental company knows you will be storing lead waste in it. Lay out a path of poly to the storage space. Do not track lead dust from the work area to the storage area.

16.   Secure the work site

Secure the building at the end of each work day. This prevents vandalism and loss of property. It also keeps people from entering the contaminated area. Take particular care to lock doors and windows.

Setup for outside work

Checklist for outside setup
_____ Post warning signs
_____ Rope off the area
_____ Put down the poly

Put 6-mil poly on the ground and seal it to the wall with duct tape. You need to extend 6 feet of poly from the wall for every 10 feet in height of the surface to be abated - up to a maximum of 20 feet. (Make sure you check with state and local laws.) A disposable tarp may be laid loosely over plants. Put weights around the edge of the tarp to keep it down.

Good setup will prevent soil from getting contaminated. When water is used to remove the lead, you need to collect **all** of the water. You can use 2 x 4s to build drains. Turn up the edge of the poly and attach the boards. Water must be contained and disposed of properly.

It is not advisable to do outside abatement work if average winds are more than 10 miles per hour. At the end of each day, wrap up the poly, seal it with duct tape, and store it with the other waste.

Lead tracking

When you walk on lead dust, it can stick to your shoes or boots. It then falls in another area. This is called **"lead tracking."** Set up a path of poly to prevent lead tracking. Areas of heavy traffic should be covered with a layer of plywood.

Tracking lead dust is a big problem on lead abatement jobs. Lead dust can be tracked on your shoes from the work area to outside. Sometimes lead dust from the outside soil is tracked into the work area. Lead dust from a porch or non-work area can get tracked into a clean area. When this happens, the whole area must be cleaned again.

Setup for interim controls

Anytime you disturb lead-painted surfaces you will create lead dust. Even small jobs require appropriate set up. When performing an interim control or a maintenance repair activity, it is possible to create lead dust.

Setup checklist for interim controls

_____ Post warning signs and mark off work area with barrier tape.
_____ Keep people out of the work area.
_____ Wear protective clothing and respirators.
_____ Clean and remove nearby objects. Send rugs out to be
cleaned, after labeling.
_____ Clean and seal what remains in the area.
_____ Seal air vents and other openings.
_____ Set up dirty area, wash area, and clean area.
_____ Lay layers of poly at least 6 feet in every direction
from the area where you will be working.
_____ Bring all work tools and equipment into the work area
_____ Seal off the work site from the rest of the building.

The following activities are not interim controls:
- Stripping
- Demolition
- Paint removal (scraping, sanding, etc.)
- Replacement
- Removal of wall to wall carpeting

You must use a full abatement setup when you do any of them.

Chapter 7 - Lead Abatement Setup

Key facts for Chapter 7

Good setup makes cleaning up at the end of the job easier.

When working with lead, you must:
Keep dust levels down.
Seal off the work area.
Repair tears in poly as you work.
Wear disposable suits and booties while in the work area.
Wash your hands and face each time you leave the work area.
Shower at the end of each shift.
Clean up as you work and at the end of each shift.
Secure the work site.

To set up you will use the following materials:
Disposable coveralls and booties
Poly and duct tape
HEPA vacuum
Lead cleaner, buckets, rags, and sponges

Before doing the abatement:
1. Clean and remove everything that you can from the work area (such as furniture, appliances, etc.).
2. Clean and cover anything that you cannot remove with poly.
3. Remove all carpeting.
4. Cover all floors with poly.
5. If you're only removing paint from one room or one part of a building, then seal off the work area from the rest of the building with poly.

When doing outside abatement, keep lead from getting into the soil.
Good setup can prevent lead contamination.

During interim controls, setup is important to contain any lead dust that gets created.

In this chapter you will learn about:

- **Replacement**
- **Enclosure**
- **Encapsulation**
- **Paint removal by**
    Wet scraping and planing
    Electric heat guns
    HEPA-sanders
    HEPA-needle guns
    Chemical strippers

Lead paint abatement

The Lead-Based Paint Hazard Reduction Act of 1992 states "abatement" refers to the methods used to permanently get rid of lead-paint hazards. Getting rid of lead-based paint hazards means making lead-based paint unavailable, so that it is no longer a hazard. There are four basic methods of lead abatement:

1. **Replacement**-Removing the building part with lead-based paint on it and replacing it with a new one.
2. **Enclosure**--Covering the lead-based paint with a solid barrier.
3. **Encapsulation**--Coating the lead-based painted surface so that it is not accessible.
4. **Paint removal**.

Enclosure and encapsulation are not permanent solutions, but these methods do reduce the lead hazards.

1. Replacement

Replacement means removing the lead-painted building part (like a window), and replacing it with a new one. This method is mostly recommended for windows, doors, and other woodwork that are painted with lead-based paint.

Advantages

Replacement is the easiest and quickest way to get rid of lead-based paint Replacement removes lead-based paint forever. It's a **permanent solution**. When combined with overall modernization, replacing windows can be used to upgrade the building itself. Replacement can lower heating bill and maintenance costs.

Disadvantages

Replacement is expensive. It takes a lot of work. Skilled carpenters are often needed to put in the new parts - especially windows and doors. Surfaces next to the part being removed may get damaged. The replacement part may not be as good as the original.

Replacement can involve demolition work. It can create a lot of dust. To keep lead levels down, wet mist and HEPA-vacuum the old building part before removing it. Replacement often requires manual demolition. Old building parts must be torn out and removed. Manual demolition is a Class 1 Task. You must wear a respirator and protective clothing. After removing the building part, wet - mist the part again, wrap it in poly, and seal it with duct tape. Store it until it can be disposed of properly. Wet down and clean up debris as you work. This helps keep lead dust levels down. You will learn more about cleanup and waste disposal in Chapter 10.

2. Enclosure

Enclosure means covering the lead-based paint with a solid, dust-tight barrier. The lead-based paint is enclosed behind the barrier. An enclosure keeps the lead-based paint away from the rest of the building. It keeps lead away from the building occupants.

The materials used to enclose the lead-painted surface must be durable. Common materials used to build enclosures include:

- Underlayment
- Aluminum
- Paneling
- Fiberboard

- Vinyl
- Plywood
- Drywall
- Tile
- Acrylic sheets

Wall paper and contact paper are <u>not</u> enclosure materials. They are not dust-tight.

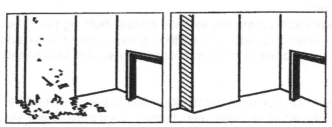

AN ENCLOSURE KEEPS LEAD PAINT AWAY FROM OCCUPANTS AND THE REST OF THE BUILDING

Before you enclose a surface, remove all peeling and chipping paint. Also fix any "source problems" such as water leaks or moisture sources. If so urce problems are not fixed, the encl osure that you build will get dam aged and fail. After fixing the source problem, HEPA-vacuum the area to be enclosed. This will collect any loose lead dust.

Label the surface "LEAD PAINT" before you enclose it. Use spray paint or something similar.

When you enclose a surface, make sure that the lead dust will not leak out of the edges or seams. Seal all seams with caulk. Back-caulk the perimeter of the enclosure material before you install it. Then, mechanically attach the enclosure material to the lead-painted surface. Use nails or screws. You need to use both adhesive and physical fasteners to create a dust-tight seal. A dust-tight seal prevents lead dust leaks.

The new surface must be in place permanently. The enclosure must be made so that no one, especially not a small child, can remove it. The enclosure material must be strong and durable. If there are building plans, the areas where enclosures cover lead-based paint need to be marked and identified in the plan. This will show workers, who work in the building in the future, that lead is located there.

Disadvantages

Enclosure may not be a permanent solution. The lead source still remains underneath the covering. Any renovation or repair work to enclosed surfaces will disturb the lead-based paint. It will release lead dust that has collected behind the enclosure barrier. Enclosed surfaces and joints of the enclosures must be monitored for damage and deterioration.

3.   Encapsulation

Encapsulation means coating the lead-painted surface with a thick, durable sealing material. Some systems include a mesh as well. The coating prevents lead dust from being released. Encapsulants are best used on building materials that are in good condition. You need an encapsulant with mesh for surfaces that are chipping or peeling.

Encapsulants must be strong enough so you can't easily break the surface or chip them. They must completely cover the lead surface and have a dust-tight seal. Encapsulants must be flexible and strong. You should not be able to damage the encapsulated surface with impact. Make sure that the encapsulant you use is not toxic, and that it is flame resistant. Read the MSDS. Wall paper, contact paper, and new paint **are not** encapsulants.

There are many different kinds of encapsulants on the market. The quality and reliability of encapsulants vary greatly. Right now there are no standards for approving encapsulants. More research is needed to test how they last. Check your state and local laws. In many areas of the country, encapsulants must be approved by state or local government on a case-by-case basis.

Preparing the surface

You must follow all of the manufacturer's instructions on how to prepare the surface. The wall or surface must be in good condition to use encapsulants. Encapsulation will not work if the wall is separating from the wood or lath. It will not work if the plaster is separating. It will not work if the surface is damaged or deteriorated.

The surface to be covered needs to be prepared before being covered. Moisture sources must be eliminated and the surface allowed to dry. Peeling paint should be wet scraped. The surface should be TSP cleaned and allowed to dry. (You can use a HEPA-vacuum to clean the surface instead of TSP.) If these steps are skipped, the encapsulant will fail.

Applying the encapsulant

You must follow all of the manufacturer's instructions on how to apply the encapsulant. Encapsulants are usually easy to apply. Often they can be applied like you apply paint. **If the encapsulant is improperly applied, it will fail.** It can separate from the paint. This will cause the paint to peel and create lead dust.

Do a test patch

Not all encapsulants can be used on all surfaces. Some encapsulants will not work on certain surfaces. For this reason, you must do a "test patch" of the encapsulant on the surface to be covered. Read and follow the manufacturer's instructions. If the test patch bubbles or cracks, then it has failed. If the test fails, do not use this encapsulant on this surface. Test other encapsulants or use another abatement method.

Use the right personal protective equipment

The type of personal protective equipment you need depends on the type of encapsulant you use. Suits and respirators should be worn when you do any repair work before applying the encapsulant. For some chemical encapsulants, you will need special filters, chemical-resistant gloves and suits. When using some encapsulants, you will need to use an organic vapor filter as well as a HEPA filter on your respirator.

Make sure the area has a good flow of air. You might need extra ventilation. Good ventilation is very important when using an encapsulant. Be sure to check the product MSDS for specific safety measures.

Disadvantages

Encapsulation may not be a permanent solution. The lead source still remains underneath the covering. Any renovation or repair work to encapsulated surfaces will disturb the lead-based paint. Encapsulants do not work on all surfaces. They need to be tested. "Patch testing" the encapsulant takes time.

Encapsulated surfaces need to be inspected regularly for damage and deterioration. Encapsulants can fail. Sometimes encapsulants separate from the surface. This is called encapsulant failure. If the encapsulant is not applied well, it will fail. If the surface is not prepared correctly, it will fail. Encapsulants should not be used on impact or friction surfaces.

Using some encapsulant products will create hazardous waste. Hazardous waste has to be properly disposed.

4.   Paint removal

Removal means taking off lead-based paint. **Removal methods create a lot of lead dust and waste.** To begin, wet-mist and HEPA-vacuum old building parts. Clean up debris as you work. Keep lead dust levels down. Paint can be removed by using one or more of the following methods:

a.   **Wet scraping down to the substrate**
b.   **Wet planing**
c.   **Electric heat guns**
d.   **Local exhaust hand tools**
e.   **Chemical stripping**
f.   **Vacuum and water blasting (exterior only)**

a.   Wet scraping

Wet scraping means misting loose paint before scraping it. Dry scraping paint creates a huge amount of dust. Never dry scrape lead-based paint. Mist the loose paint before you scrape it. Continue to wet it while you scrape. Doing this keeps lead dust levels down.

Wet scraping is often used to prepare a surface for painting. It does not mean removing all of the paint----only the loose paint. Wet scraping and painting can be used as an interim control.

> **WARNING:**   Never wet surfaces near electrical outlets even if the circuit is turned off. You could get an electric shock.

SCRAPER
A scraper is a blade-like tool used to remove paint. They come in different sizes. Scrapers should be kept sharp at all times. A mill file is good for keeping scrapers sharp.

Clean up the paint scrapings and dust as you work. Wet and bag the debris as you go. This keeps lead dust levels down. Manual scraping is a Class I Task. To be safe, wear a respirator and disposable suit, gloves, and goggles when you wet scrape. You will get a lot of paint scraps and lead dust on your disposable suit. HEPA-vacuum the outside of your suit as you exit the work area.

b.   Wet planing

Wet planing is much like wet scraping. It means misting the surface before you plane it. Wet-planing creates dust. Wear a respirator and protective clothing to be safe.

135

WOOD PLANE

A plane is a carpenter's tool for shaving a wood surface. You can use a plane to remove lead-based paint from impact surfaces like the edges of a door. You can use a plane on friction surfaces, like the edges of windows that rub together when you open or close the window.

c.   Electric heat guns

Using heat guns is not recommended. Electric heat guns work by forcing warmed air onto a painted surface. The heat softens the paint. The loosened paint is then scraped off with hand tools.

Use heat guns very carefully. Heat guns can cause serious burns on your skin. They can damage the building material from which you are removing paint. They can even cause a fire. Before using a heat gun, check the building material and the other side of the wall. Heat guns can ignite a fire on the other side of the surface material. **Have an ABC-fire extinguisher on hand.**

Extreme heat causes lead to give off toxic fumes. Extreme heat is 1,100° F or above. These fumes are dangerous. Fumes are created when a solid is heated. Lead fumes contain many tiny particles of lead. These tiny particles are very easy to breathe. The lead fumes quickly travel into your lungs and then to the blood. Lead fumes are dangerous. Heat can also cause the paint to release organic vapors. Organic vapors come from chemicals used to make paint. High heat can turn the chemicals into dangerous vapors.

You are dry scraping when you use a heat gun. This creates a lot of dust. Using a heat gun is a Class 1 Task. The OSHA Lead Standard says you can ask your employer for a Powered Air Purifying Respirator (PAPR). Your employer must provide you with a PAPR if you are working above the PEL and you ask for one. You should wear a PAPR when you use a heat gun to protect yourself against dust and fumes. The PAPR should have both a HEPA filter and an organic vapor cartridge. Some states say you must wear a PAPR when using a heat gun.

d.   Local exhaust hand tools

Local exhaust hand tools are power tools that you can hold in your hand. They have a hose that attaches to a vacuum. The vacuum has a HEPA (High Efficiency Particulate Air) filter. This system is called a local HEPA exhaust system. There are a number of local exhaust hand tools for lead abatement work. Using local exhaust hand tools is a Class I Task. You must wear a respirator and protective clothing.

Follow the manufacturer's instructions for proper use of local exhaust hand tools. Never remove or pull back the shroud or cover. The cover is needed for the

vacuum to work. Shrouded tools are difficult to use. Sometimes you cannot see what you are doing.
You must move the tool very slowly to keep the shroud in place. The tool must be used flat against the surface. If you work too fast, the shroud seal will break and lead dust will get into the air.

1. **HEPA sanders**
   Sanding generates huge amounts of dust. HEPA sanders are power sanders fitted with a HEPA vacuum to catch and filter lead dust as it is created. Always use a HEPA sander when you sand lead-based paint. Limit the use of HEPA sanding to flat surfaces for feathering or finishing only.

HEPA SANDER

2. **Needle gun with HEPA filter**
   A needle gun has many metal rods. The rods are contained inside a shroud (cover). The rods loosen and break the surface paint. The shroud catches most of the lead dust. The local exhaust pulls them into the HEPA filter.

NEEDLE GUN

Needle guns are best used on metal or masonry surfaces. They are useful on pipes, and structural steel. They will damage wood surfaces. **Wear hearing protection when you use a needle gun.**

3. **HEPA saws and drills**
   Other hand tools can be fitted with HEPA exhaust systems, like saws and drills. The HEPA system catches and filters most of the lead dust as it is created. The drill has a cover like the needle gun. **Wear hearing protection when you use a HEPA saw or drill**.

HEPA SAW

HEPA DRILL

e. **Chemical Stripping**
   The use of chemicals to strip off paint is called chemical stripping. Chemical stripping works with solvents or caustic paste. Chemical solvents dissolve the paint. Caustic paste melts paint into a goo that is scraped off with hand tools. Chemical stripping always involves manual scraping. Wear eye and hand protection, a respirator, and protective clothing to be safe from the chemicals and from lead. Chemical strippers may give off harmful chemical vapors. You may need to wear combination filters on your respirator.

After the paint is removed, carefully clean the surface. Then use a special rinse to neutralize the surface. The rinse balances the acid or base of the stripping chemicals. Check to make sure the neutralizer worked. The surface may need to be smoothed and re-glued before it is repainted.

Chemical strippers are dangerous!

Read your Material Safety Data Sheets.

Material Safety Data Sheets (MSDS's) give you safety instructions about using chemical products.

Any chemical which can remove paint will harm you if it touches your skin or gets in your eyes.
Caustic strippers will burn your skin. When you scrape a caustic, it can create a dust or mist that can get in your eyes, nose, mouth and throat. Solvent strippers can be very dangerous. Some solvents can damage your skin; others pass through your skin into your blood. Solvents can damage your brain, nervous system, blood, liver, kidney, and heart.

- Find out where the eye wash station is, so you know where to find it if you need it.
- Never do chemical stripping above your head.
- Keep chemicals off your skin and out of your eyes.
- Wear rubber, chemical-resistant gloves and suits. Wear gloves that extend up your arm towards your elbows and eye goggles.

Some stripping chemicals have toxic vapors which you should not breathe.

* **Do not use strippers that contain methylene chloride.** Methylene chloride is extremely toxic. It can cause cancer and other major health problems.

* Only use chemical strippers in well-ventilated areas.

* Use the right respirator filters. Make sure your respirator cartridges will protect you from the chemicals in the stripper. You may need a combination filter, when you are removing lead with a chemical stripper.

Some strippers can cause a fire.
The vapors they give off create a fire hazard.

• Do not use them around electric heaters, heat guns, or any l equipment.
• Have an ABC-fire extinguisher on hand.
• Have a plan in case of a fire.
• Mark and know where the emergency exits are.
• Post the emergency phone numbers.
• Know how to use the phone.
• Have a designated meeting place outside the work area.

Off-site stripping

You can send painted material off-site to be stripped. Wet down and clean up any debris generated when you remove the component. Mist the building part with water and remove it. Wrap it in poly. To be safe, wear a respirator and protective clothing when you do this.

Send the component to a professional stripping shop. At the shop, it will be dipped in a tank full of chemical stripping agents. The paint will dissolve right off the surface.

When the component is returned, be sure to wash it before you reinstall it. Make sure it is properly neutralized. You may also need to refinish and re-glue it. Remember to wear a respirator if you sand the surface-chemical stripping always leaves some lead behind.

Advantages

Chemical paint strippers are useful to preserve the detail on decorative doors, molding, and trims. They are used on old antique trims or molding that can not be replaced.

Sending the work somewhere else keeps hazardous chemical strippers out of your work area.

Disadvantages

Chemical strippers create hazardous waste. Strippers are often made of hazardous materials, and must be disposed of as hazardous waste. The liquid waste generated through rinsing and cleaning may also be hazardous waste. Hazardous waste has to be contained and disposed of in a special way. It must be handled correctly, or it can hurt workers and the environment. Sending the work off-site protects you and your work site. It does not protect the work site or workers where the stripping takes place. You will learn about hazardous waste in Chapter 10.

Chemical stripping leaves some lead behind. This leftover lead soaks into the pores and cracks of a surface, especially wood, where it hardens. Wear a respirator if you sand the surface. Clean the stripped surface carefully or the leftover lead will mix with the new non-lead paint. When the new paint chalks, chips, or peels, the lead will get in the dust all over again.

Caustic strippers can damage the building material.

Leftover stripper will cause the new paint coat to fail. It will damage the building material. This can happen if the surface was not cleaned right. Cleaning takes a lot of time. It is an important job. Another reason the new paint might fail is that the neutralizer did not work properly. It is very important to test the surface to see if the neutralizer has worked. If the surface is not neutral, you must clean and neutralize it again. Do this process over and over until the surface is neutral. This could take days.

Removing a building component for off-site stripping will create dust. An old building component may break when you try to remove it. To keep dust levels down, mist the component with water before you remove it. Wet down and clean up any debris generated. Wear respirators and protective clothing, and follow proper hygiene practices.

f.   Vacuum and water blasting (exterior methods)
Paint can be removed by vacuum blasting and water blasting. These methods are to be used for **exterior work only**. Vacuum blasting requires a HEPA vacuum. Both methods are very expensive. They create a lot of waste. They can damage the treated surface, especially wood. Neither method is used very often. **Vacuum blasting** can be used on a variety of surfaces, but it works best on flat surfaces. **Water blasting** creates waste water that is considered hazardous. It must be contained and disposed of properly.
After the lead-based paint is removed, the bare surface must be cleaned and smoothed. Then, the surface must be inspected. If it passes inspection, it can be repainted with non-lead paint, or covered with other materials.

Prohibited methods

There are some methods which HUD and some states do **not** allow on residential lead abatement jobs. These methods are not allowed, because they are hazardous or they just do not work.

- Torch or flame burning
- Open abrasive blasting
- Uncontained water blasting
- Machine sanding (unless equipped with a HEPA filter)
- On-site use of methylene chloride
- On-site use of flammable solvents
- Solutions of potassium or sodium hydroxide (caustic paste allowed with special precautions)
- Dry scraping (allowed in Massachusetts)
- Wall papering or repainting as an abatement method.

NO FLAME BURNING!

NO DRY SANDING!

Key facts for Chapter 8

Always wear a respirator and protective clothing when doing abatement work.

Clean up as you work.

There are four methods to abate lead-based paint:
1. Replacement
2. Enclosure
3. Encapsulation
4. Paint removal

Replacement is a permanent solution.
Replacement can increase the value of the building.
Replacement can be demolition. It can create a lot of dust.
Wet mist before removing the old part.
Clean up as you work.

An enclosure is a dust-tight solid barrier.
A dust-tight enclosure prevents lead dust from leaking out.
An enclosure may not be a permanent solution.
The surface must be HEPA-vacuumed before enclosure.
The enclosure must be strong and durable.

Encapsulation means coating the lead-painted surface with a thick material.
Encapsulation is best used on building parts in good condition.
Whenever you encapsulate, you must prepare the surface first.
Always do a "test patch."
Encapsulation may not be a permanent solution.
Encapsulants may fail.
Make sure the encapsulant you use is legal in your area.

Paint removal methods create a lot of lead dust.
Mist the paint before you scrape or plane it.

Heat guns may create dangerous lead fumes and toxic vapors.
Do not use a heat gun above 1,100°F
Heat guns can burn you and the building.

Only use local exhaust tools that have a HEPA vacuum attached to them to remove lead-based paint.
Mechanical hand tools create large amounts of dust.
Only use sanders, saws, needle guns, or drills with HEPA attachment.

Chemical stripping removes paint with solvents or caustic paste.

Chemical strippers are dangerous!
Chemical stripping often creates hazardous waste.
Wear chemical-resistant coveralls, gloves, and booties.
Always wear eye protection.
Do not use strippers that contain methylene chloride.
Some strippers can create a fire hazard.
Make sure you have an ABC fire extinguisher on site.

Vacuum and water blasting should only be used for outside work.

HUD and some states do not allow these lead abatement methods for residential work:
Torch or flame burning
Open abrasive blasting
Uncontained water blasting
Machine sanding without local exhaust
Using flammable solvents
Using strippers with methylene chloride
Dry scraping

Chapter 9 - Lead Abatement in the Home

In this chapter you will learn how to treat lead-based paint on:
- **Windows**
- **Doors**
- **Woodwork**
- **Walls**
- **Ceilings**
- **Floors**
- **Staircases**
- **Porches**
- **The outside of a home**

Doing the abatement

Abatement means getting rid of lead-based paint hazards. There are four different abatement methods. They are:
- Replacement
- Encapsulation
- Enclosure
- Paint removal

Whenever you do abatement, you must use the personal protection described in chapter 5. You must also follow the setup procedures defined in chapter 7. The following chart shows which methods are used for different parts of a home.

Method	Where can you best use it?
REPLACEMENT	• Windows, doors, moldings • Any easily removed component
ENCAPSULATION	• Walls, ceiling, trim
ENCLOSURE	• Floors, pipes, ceilings, exterior trim, etc.
PAINT REMOVAL Wet Scraping	• May be used as an interim control for loose paint • Should not be used as a removal method for large areas
Heat Gun	• Flat surfaces • Thick layers of paint (softens them)
Caustic Paste	• Decorative molding • Soft wood, brick, cement
Solvents	• Metal substrates • Clean residue left by other methods
Off-site Chemical Stripping	• Restoration work • Doors, mantels, metal railing and trim

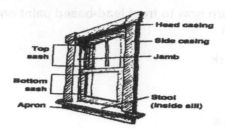

Windows

Lead-painted windows are often the highest source of lead dust.

The opening and closing of windows causes friction between painted surfaces. This **friction** creates dust. Windows are exposed to water, sun, wind and temperature changes. These all cause paint to deteriorate and create dust.

Put extra poly up when you work on windows. Attach the poly to the wall underneath the window, and extend the poly out at least 6 feet. Do this both inside and outside the window.

Window abatement
Replacing lead-painted windows is a good choice because:
- They cause lead dust
- Children like to play at windows
- Old windows are expensive to maintain
- New windows save energy
- New windows increase property value

If you must keep the old sashes, you can:
1. Remove the sashes and have them stripped off site. Clean, re-glue, refinish, and paint them before reinstalling.
2. Replace the stops and the parting bead.
3. Enclose or chemically strip the jamb.
4. Replace the casing and the apron.
5. Replace the stool (inside sill) or enclose it.
6. Enclose the outside of the window with wood or coil stock.
   WARNING: Enclosing wood with coil stock may cause exterior wood to rot.

Interim controls
If you are not going to abate lead-painted windows right away, you can still treat them so they create less lead dust. (Make sure these options are legal in your state and local area!)

The sashes

The goal is to eliminate friction against leaded surfaces.

- **Fix the top sash in place**
  Nail or screw in wood blocks under the top sash to hold it in place. (Make sure this is legal to do in your area.) This way you will only have to work the bottom sash.

- **Remove and dispose of inside stop.** Do the same with the **parting bead** if you are treating the top sash as well as the bottom.

- **Remove the bottom sash.** If the counter-weight ropes or chains are in place, do not let them drop into the weight compartment.

- **Remove the paint from edges** that rub against stop, stool, and parting bead. Wet planing is a good method.

- **Rehang the sash(es)** in a compression track. If there is no counter weight or spring system, install one.

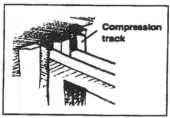

The well and the stool

When there is a storm window frame, a "well" is created between the storm window and the stool. This area is one of the highest dust areas.

- **HEPA vacuum the well.**

- **Create a cleanable surface.**
  Enclose well with vinyl or metal coil stock. Back caulk the material and nail it down. Caulk the edges from the top.

Open or drill out weep holes.
(Weep holes are drain holes in bottom of storm window.)

- **The stool** is at the base of the window, inside the house. Children often look out the window and may put their mouths on the stool. **Wet plane or enclose the edge facing the room.** You may also need to enclose or remove the paint from the top surface.

The casing, apron, jamb

- If the paint on the casing, apron and jamb is in good shape, you may be able to just wet scrape and repaint. Remember, paint is not an encapsulant. Repainting is only a temporary solution!

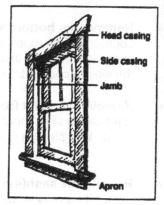

If the outside jamb is still exposed and the outside casing is damaged, wet scraping and painting may not be enough. Seal any exposed wood with boiled linseed oil (or equivalent) and paint.
  Enclosing the trim with coil stock will also work, but may cause exterior wood to rot.

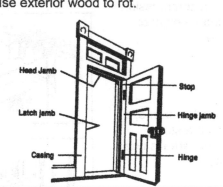

Doors

Lead-painted doors are a source of lead dust.

Opening and closing doors creates an impact. When you **impact** a surface again and again, you create dust. Outside doors are exposed to water, sun, wind, and temperature changes. These cause paint to **deteriorate** and create lead dust.

Door abatement

Replacement is often the easiest, most cost effective method. There are a number of ways to do this:
* Replace door and door stop.
* Install a pre-hung door and keep old jamb.
* Install a pre-hung door and new casing.

Taking out old casing can damage the surrounding wall. New casing should be wide enough to cover any damage. It should also cover the jamb edge, and the area where the old casing met the wall.

Remove the paint off-site

If you must preserve the door and casing, send them to be **stripped off-site**. Clean them when they come back. Re-glue, fill in any holes or cracks, and sand them. Reinstall and paint after inspection.

Remove the paint on-site

You can remove the le ad-based paint on-site with chemi cal stripping, wet scraping, or by using a heat gun. For metal doors, you might use a needle gun equipped with a HEPA filter. These methods require time and patience.

Interim Controls

If you are not going to a bate lead-painted door systems, you can still treat them so they create le ss lead dust. (Make sure these options are legal i n your state and local area!)

1. **Replace the stop---or wet plane it.**

2. **Wet plane the corner edges** of the door on its latch side where it contacts the stop.

3. **Re-set the hinge screws If necessary.**
   The door should not make any wood -to-wood contact, except a gainst the latch (knob) side stop. If it does, re-hang the door or plane the hinge side of the door, until there is about 1/8-inch space between the door and the jamb on all sides. The door should not scrape the threshold or make contact with the hinge side stop.

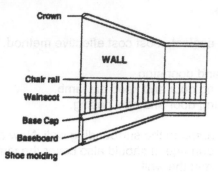

Woodwork (not including doors and windows)

Lead-painted woodwork can be a source of lead dust, especially impact points such as chair rails, baseboards, and jamb edges.

Woodwork abatement

1.   **Replacement**. All woodwork can be replaced. Remember to back caulk and nail down replacement parts when you install them.

2.   **Encapsulate** (if the paint is in good shape).

Interim controls

If you are not going to abate lead-painted woodwork, you can still treat it so it creates less lead dust. (Make sure these options are legal in your state and local area!)

1.   **Wet plane and enclose any edges** from surfaces where children may put their mouths.
2.   **Where paint is intact, paint over with a high grade paint.** Paint is not an encapsulant Repainting is only a temporary measure!
3.   **Cover impact points** (chair rails, baseboards, jamb edges, etc.) with a strip of solid lattice or corner protector.

Walls

Kitchen, bathroom, and basement walls were often painted with lead-based paint. Sometimes other walls in a home can have lead-based paint, too. Encapsulation and enclosure are the methods most often used to abate lead-painted walls.

Wall abatement

1.   **Encapsulating walls**
     The wall must be sound. Plaster or plaster board must be in good shape. There cannot be any major delamination (coming apart) of the existing paint layers. If not, the encapsulant could pull right off the wall. If the wall is sound, but has minor cracks or chips, a mesh system works well. It will

seal the cracks and chips. Old wallpaper should be removed, because it can cause the encapsulant to fail.

- **Prepare the wall.** Wet scrape any loose paint. Clean off any oil, dirt, and grease with a solvent or detergent.
- **Wear the right protective gear.** You may need to use chemical-resistant protective gear. Wear your respirator and goggles. Check the encapsulant MSDS. Make sure you have the right filters for your respirator. You may need a combination filter.
- **Mix the encapsulant** Follow the manufacturer's directions.
- **Do a "test patch."**
- **Ventilate the area.** Some products need extra ventilation.

2. **Enclosing walls**
    Before you enclose a wall, label the wall surface "lead paint." This will alert anyone who works on the wall later that they are disturbing lead-based paint.
    Both sound walls and damaged walls can be enclosed. Enclosure is recommended where the substrate (wall material) is damaged. Before you install an enclosure, you have to get rid of all moisture sources and let the walls dry out.

Fur out the wall

When plaster is damaged, you must install enclosure material to studs or furring strips. Furring strips are thin strips of wood you fasten to the studs. This way, even if the plaster fails, the enclosure will stand. Furring strips should be attached with adhesive **and** screws into the studs. Putting up furring strips is called "furring out the wall."

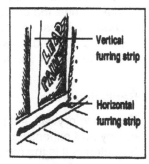

Vertical furring strip

Horizontal furring strip

- First lay out a horizontal furring strip along the base of the wall.
- Then put up vertical furring strips. Line them up with the studs.

Enclosure material

Screws

Mastic or adhesive

Fasten the enclosure material

Fasten the enclosure material to the studs. If you furred out the wall, fasten the enclosure material to the furring strips. Use both adhesive and screws. If the wall is plaster on masonry, and the plaster is sound, the enclosure material can be attached with a combination of mastic and masonry fasteners.

Create a dust-tight seal

Paint deteriorates more quickly behind an enclosure.

All edges of an enclosure-especially the bottom-must be sealed well. If you don't create a good seal, lead dust will leak out.

Seal the bottom edge

- Caulk the enclosure material at the bottom.
- Back-caulk and nail the baseboard in place.
- Back-caulk, bottom caulk, and nail the shoe molding in place.

Seal the seams and other edges

- Back-caulk all the seams that aren't taped and spackled. Use a high quality adhesive caulk.
- Use a "**J-channel**" where drywall meets a finished surface. A J-channel is a final strip you attach to the rough edge of drywall to make a finished edge. It's called a "J--channel" because of its shape. Caulk the outside edge so it seals with the finished surface. Screw the drywall in place.

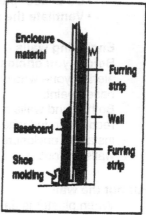

3. **Replacing walls**

Replacing drywall and plaster is extremely messy and expensive.

Sometimes it is the most practical solution-for example, when partition walls will be built or new electric, plumbing, or heating systems will be installed within a wall.

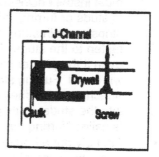

Taking out the old walls or wall substrate (plaster) is demolition work.
Follow all worker and environmental protection rules.
- Remove all furniture and personal items and seal off the area.
- Put down a second layer of poly on the floor for added protection.
- Keep area misted to lower dust levels.
- Clean up often and dispose of waste.
- Wear protective suits and respirators, and use extra ventilation.

Interim controls

If the lead-painted walls are not damaged, flaking, or peeling, you might just wet scrape and repaint them. Remember, paint is not an encapsulant. Repainting is not an abatement method; it is only a temporary solution.
When the new paint does chip and peel, the old paint may chip with it. Then it will create lead dust.

Ceilings

If a lead-painted ceiling is damaged, it must be enclosed. Ceilings can be enclosed with drywall or any other type of covering that seals the seams and edges. An enclosure must be dust-tight. It must be sealed along all edges, joints, and seams. **A drop ceiling is not an enclosure.**

Ceiling abatement

New drywall must be attached to the ceiling beams-called "joists' '-with drywall screws. You can find the joists by cutting through the old plaster ceiling with a drywall dagger. Never attach the new ceiling to the old ceiling itself. The new ceiling must be fastened to the joists. To find the joists, use a dry wall dagger and:

1. Cut to the joists on both sides.
2. Mark the center of each joist on the wall.
3. Draw a chalk line across the ceiling from center mark to center mark.
4. Screw the new drywall into the joists along these lines.
5. Tape and spackle all edges.
6. Where new dry wall meets a finished surface, use a J-channel.

Interim controls

If the ceiling is not damaged, flaking, or peeling, you might repaint it to take care of the lead hazard in the short run. Remember, paint is not an encapsulant. Repainting is not an abatement method it is only a temporary solution. When the old paint does chip and peel, it will create lead dust.

Floors

Lead-painted floors are a major source of lead dust. They are impact and friction surfaces. People walk on them. Children and pets play on them. Things get dropped on and dragged around on them. These activities create lead dust.
Floors should be abated last. Ceilings, walls, and windows need to be done first. This will reduce the amount of lead dust that gets on the new lead-free floor. The less dust that gets on the floor, the easier it will be to clean at the end of the job.

Floor abatement

1. **TSP-clean the floor to remove lead dust**.

2. **Install a subfloor before installing the finished floor** (unless you are installing a new tongue-and-groove floor). Use 1/2-inch or thicker plywood or tempered underlayment. Do **not** use masonite. Back caulk the edges, especially the borders. Nail it down. HEPA-vacuum the floor and all cracks. Fill large cracks with a filler that won't turn brittle or break.

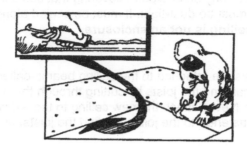

3. **Install the finished floor**. You can use vinyl, tile, or wood. (If you use urethane, use extra ventilation and follow instructions carefully.) You can also use carpeting, but wait until final cleanup is complete before installing. Carpeting alone is not an enclosure. Wall-to-wall carpeting is discouraged in homes with lead-based paint because it is not cleanable.

Carpet removal

Carpets collect more lead dust than bare floors.

Lead dust falls on and sticks to carpet fibers. Lead dust settles under the carpet. Taking out lead-contaminated carpets can be dangerous. You will be exposed to high levels of lead dust.

1. Seal the area from other parts of the house.
2. Wear a respirator and protective clothing.
3. Ventilate the area.
4. Dampen rug and any dust under it to keep the dust levels down.
5. Wrap up the carpet in 6-mil poly and seal it with duct tape.
6. HEPA-vacuum the area, and wash over it with a TSP solution.

Carpets contaminated with lead are very difficult to clean. You or your employer should advise the owner of the carpet to remove it. **Do not** remove the carpet without the owner's written permission. If the carpet is not removed, it must be HEPA-vacuumed, very slowly.

After the abatement
Lead-free floors will collect lead dust.

Floors should be abated at the end of the job---after windows, doors, walls, and ceilings. It is very difficult to clean floors of lead dust. Once you finish abating

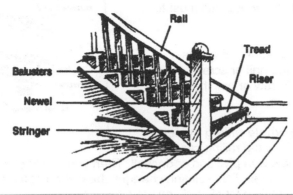

the floor, seal off the area until the final cleanup and an inspection can be done.

Staircases
Staircase abatement can be done in a number of ways. The entire staircase can be replaced----but this is extremely expensive and Is not recommended. Parts of the staircase can be replaced, while other parts can be enclosed or encapsulated.

Staircase abatement

1. **Stringers and newels.**
   Stringers and newels cannot be removed without taking out the whole staircase. This is very expensive. It is better to remove the lead paint on site or use an encapsulant that will take impact.

2. **Railings, newels, and balusters.**
   Railings, newels and balusters can be treated with some onoapoulanto. However, the rail is a high friction area. An encapsulant may not work on the rail. The outside corners of the newel post and the top edge of the railing may need to be enclosed, wet planed, or chemically stripped.

   In some cases, the balusters and rails can be removed and off-site stripped or replaced. The paint in between balusters must be removed on-site.

   As an **interim control** for square railing caps, you could wet-plane them across the top side.

3. **Enclose treads and risers.**
   A rubber tread with metal nosing works well. Rubber nosing may work, if it fits snugly on the nose of the stair and the stairs are not used very often.

- Enclosed risers with thin plywood (like luan plywood) or some other hard material. Whatever you use must fit snugly.

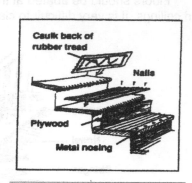

- Back caulk the edges of treads. Place them and nail or screw them down. Screw or nail the metal nosing on.

4. **Enclose the whole railing system.**
   You can enclose the railing cap, balusters, and newels with plywood or drywall. Then you would cap the new system with a wooden rail. This solution changes the design of the room a lot. It also takes a long time, is a lot of work, and is expensive.

After abating the staircase

Once the staircase is abated, cover it with 6-mil poly. Staple down some type of non-slip material on top of the poly for worker safety. You can use cardboard stapled to the treads.

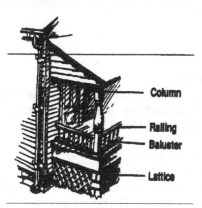

Porches

Wooden porches with lead-based paint are serious lead hazards because:
- Surfaces get worn down from weather changes.
- Children spend a lot of time there.
- Railings are at the right height for kids to put their mouths on.

Porch floors should be replaced or enclosed. Use treated planks, treated tongue-and-groove, or exterior or marine grade plywood. Make sure the floor slants down away from the house. The slant allows for proper water drainage.

Balusters may be on-site stripped or encapsulated. They are often in such bad shape that they need to be replaced.

Rails can be replaced, stripped, or wet planed.

Structural columns can be wet scraped, encapsulated, or stripped.

Lattice (crisscrossed strips of wood or metal) should be replaced.

Ceilings may be enclosed with exterior grade plywood. Remember to back-caulk the perimeter.

Outside brick and cement

Abatement

Enclosing outside surfaces with a dust-tight material, and a vinyl or aluminum siding, is often the method of choice. This method provides weatherization and increases the efficiency of the house. It also creates less waste than other abatement methods.

HUD allows vacuum blasting and water blasting for outdoor work. Chemical stripping can also be used. These methods are very costly and generate a lot of waste. Waste from water blasting and chemical stripping is considered hazardous, and must be disposed of properly. You will learn about waste disposal in the next chapter.

When working on outside structures, setup is very important. You need to protect the soil, bushes and plants, and the surrounding environment. Tape poly to the base of the structure. Extend the poly out at least 6 feet for every story. Place boards under the edge of the poly to create a curb. The curb directs the waste water into a low spot, where it can be pumped into a 55-gallon drum.

Clean and take down the entire outside setup at the end of each day. Lock up waste before leaving the work site.

Interim controls

Wet scraping is sometimes used to remove loose lead-based paint from outside brick and cement structures. This is a very labor intensive method. Masonry wet scraping should be done with maximum pressure to remove all paint that has separated from the substrate. Repaint with a high-grade masonry paint, or use an encapsulant recommended for masonry application.

Soil abatement

Soil with high lead levels is a major health hazard, especially to children. Government agencies used to recommend removing and replacing 6 to 24 inches of soil. But studies in three cities around the nation showed that removing this much soil is very expensive and may only reduce the blood lead levels of children living in these areas by small amounts. Often the best approach is to remove 2 to 3 inches and test the new lead levels. If the lead levels are still high, more soil may need to be removed. Most states require abated soil to be tested to see if it is a hazardous waste.

If the soil has low levels of lead, the best method is to contain the soil. Open dirt with lead in it is the most dangerous. You can contain the soil by planting grass. You can put mulch or sand on top of the soil. This reduces the lead hazard. Landscaping with sod to cover the soil can also be very effective.

Gardens in soil contaminated with lead can be a major health risk. Leafy vegetables and vegetables that grow in the ground (like carrots and potatoes) can absorb lead. People who eat large amounts of these vegetables can get lead poisoning.

Key facts for Chapter 9

The four abatement methods used in a home are:

1. Replacement
2. Enclosure
3. Encapsulation
4. Paint removal

Replacing lead-painted windows, doors and woodwork is a good way to reduce lead hazard.
Back-caulk and nail (or screw) in replacement parts when you install them.

Do not use encapsulants on structurally damaged walls or walls that are separating from the substrate.

Enclosure is often used for lead-painted floors and ceilings.
Create a dust-tight seal when you enclose a surface.
Back-caulk and nail (or screw) in enclosure materials.

When working on outside structures, setup is very important.

Interim controls are only temporary solutions.
They are actions you can take to reduce lead dust levels until you do an abatement.
Interim controls should not take the place of abatement.
Interim controls may not be allowed in your state or local area.
Check your state and local laws.

In this chapter you will learn:

- The importance of good cleanup
- What cleanup materials to use
- How to do daily cleanup
- How to do final cleanup
- What the clearance levels are
- What to do with waste

Cleanup of lead-paint dust

Cleanup is the most important step.

If you do not clean up, lead dust levels will increase! Careful cleaning prevents future exposures to lead. Careful cleaning protects the family who will move back into the homes you work on. Any lead dust that remains can poison them. Careful cleaning also protects you while you work.

Lead dust is difficult to remove
- Lead dust is very fine
- It may not be visible
- It sticks to surfaces
- It has to be rubbed off
- It collects and packs into cracks

Cleanup materials

- Protective suit and respirator
- Work gloves and eye protection
- Hand pumped water sprayer
- Water
- Labeled heavy-duty plastic bags (6-mil poly)
- Plastic shovels and/or dust pans
- HEPA-vacuum cleaner (with special attachments)
- Lead cleaner
- Buckets (at least 3 mop buckets, one with a wringer)
- Sponges and rags
- Clean step ladder
- String mops, sponge mops, and extra mop heads for both
- Special containers for hazardous waste (if needed)

Daily Cleanup

Cleaning the work site every day helps to keep lead dust levels down. It keeps the work area as clean as possible. The OSHA Lead Standard says all surfaces must be kept as free from lead dust as is practical. This keeps lead out of the air. Cleaning the work site prevents you from spreading lead dust around. It also helps make final cleanup-and passing the final inspection-much easier. You may be exposed to high levels of lead in cleanup. You must wear a respirator and protective clothing during cleanup. Daily cleanup takes place at the end of each work day.

1.   Wrap up and label large debris.
Wrap large debris (like doors, windows, etc.) in 6-mil poly. Seal the wrapped debris with duct tape. Put a label on it that says "LEAD CONTAMINATED." Store waste in a secure area until it can be tested and disposed of properly.

WRAP LARGE DEBRIS IN 6-MIL POLY

2.   Wet mop the floor. Bag and label small debris.
Water mist dust and small debris with water. Wet mop or wet sweep it all up. Do not dry sweep! This stirs up lead dust. Put the debris into 6-mil plastic bags and seal the bags. Bag, tape, and throw away the mop heads with the debris. Put labels on the bags that say "LEAD CONTAMINATED." Store waste in a secure area until it can be tested and disposed of properly.

WET MOP FLOORS   DON'T DRY SWEEP!

3.   HEPA-vacuum all surfaces in the work area.
The OSHA Lead Standard says that you should not allow lead dust to build up. It says wherever possible use the HEPA-vacuum. **Do <u>not</u> use a regular shop vacuum** - it can't filter lead dust. Start at the far end of the work area and move towards the exit through the decon.

4.   Check poly and repair any tears or rips.

Check for tears in the poly throughout the day. Repair any rips as you find them. At the end of each day, inspect the whole containment for holes, rips and tears in the poly. Make sure you check the poly covering the air vents and heat registers.

Final cleanup

The cleanup done at the end of the abatement job is called a **final cleanup**. Final cleanup must be done slowly and carefully. Final cleanup might even take longer than the abatement itself. **There are three stages of final cleanup.** Each stage is very important and must be done thoroughly.

Many abatement jobs fail the final inspection because the final cleanup was not done properly. If an abatement job fails, you will have to do cleanup over again. You will have to redo cleanup as many times as it takes for the job to pass. Redoing cleanup is expensive and takes a lot of work time. It is better to do it right the first time.

Wait one or more hours after you finish the abatement before you start final cleanup. (Check with your state and local laws.) This allows the lead dust that is in the air to settle. The time that it takes for the lead dust to settle depends on the type of work methods you used. Dust may settle onto surfaces within a few hours of encapsulation or enclosure. Smaller particles created with a needle gun or heat gun will take much longer to settle out of the air.

Stage 1: Special cleaning

1.   Wear protective gear.

Put on plastic gloves to protect your hands from the lead cleaner. Wear protective goggles or other eye gear to shield your eyes. You will also wear your respirator, disposable suit and booties or rubber boots.

2.   HEPA-vacuum all surfaces.

HEPA-vacuum all surfaces in the work area, including areas that had been covered with plastic.

Start at the far end and then work towards the decon. Begin with ceilings or the top of the walls and work down, cleaning the floors last.

Do every inch of the windows, especially the wells. Use the corner tool to clean where the floor meets the baseboard and all cracks in the floor boards. Use the brush tool for the walls. Move slowly and carefully to get all the dust.

3. **Collect waste in sealed plastic bags or wrap in poly.**
    Place any remaining disposable items in 6-mil plastic bags and tape the bags shut. If they are too large, wrap them in 6-mil poly; seal them with duct tape; and put labels on them that say "LEAD CONTAMINATED."

4. **Wet mop and bag dust**
    Use the spray bottle to wet down all dust and debris with a fine mist of water. This will help control the dust during cleanup. Wet mop the entire work area. Bag and seal the debris. Label the waste "LEAD CONTAMINATED."

5. **Take off first layer of poly.**
    If you used two layers of poly, now is the time to remove only the first layer. Wet mist the poly before removing it. This contaminated plastic must be removed carefully. Remove the upper plastic that covers cabinets and counters first. Then carefully remove the poly on the floor. Do not remove floor poly until all other poly is removed. Fold top layer of poly onto itself - from the edges into the center in order to trap any remaining dust inside. Seal up with duct tape and put into plastic bags for disposal.

    If you did not do any demolition or replacement, you may have only used one layer. If so, do **not** remove that layer and skip to step **#6**.

6. **Wash all surfaces with lead cleaner.**
    Wash all surfaces in the work area with a lead cleaner (such as TSP), including areas that had been covered with plastic. Some wallpaper should only be HEPA-vacuumed and not washed.

TSP is a special ingredient in some detergents that bonds with the lead in the dust. The lead in the dust sticks to the TSP. You want to use a detergent that contains 5% TSP. There are some phosphate-like substances that may be just as good as TSP and less harmful. (Check your state and local laws.)

Use the 4-Step System you learned about in previous chapter.

Start from the top and work down. Start with the ceiling and work down to the floors.

Mix up a new solution of lead cleaner often, so it stays clean.
Change the rinse water, rags, and mop heads at least once every *500* square feet. The number of times you must change both the TSP water and the rinse water will depend on how dirty the area is. After washing each room, go back over the surfaces with a clean water rinse.

Dispose of TSP waste according to state and local laws.

7. **Remove the bottom layer of poly. Clean the floor.**
    After all the work above the floor has been cleaned, carefully remove the bottom layer of poly from the floor. Fold the contaminated side of the poly into itself. This will contain the lead dust and moisture. Seal the bundle with duct tape, and place it in a 6-mil bag or wrap it in 6-mil poly. Label it "LEAD CONTAMINATED." HEPA-vacuum the floor. Use the lead cleaner to wash it. Rinse it with clean water.

8. **HEPA-vacuum all surfaces again.**
    After all surfaces have dried, HEPA-vacuum a second time. Vacuum until no dust or residue can be seen. Move slowly and carefully.

9. **Collect used cleaning items in sealed plastic bags.**
    Discard all items used for cleaning (towels, sponges, rags, mop heads) in 6-mil plastic bags. Seal the plastic bags and label them "LEAD CONTAMINATED."

Visual inspection

The work area should be visually inspected before you repaint abated surfaces. The inspector may come in and <u>look</u> at the surfaces chosen for abatement to see if they have been abated. The inspector will also look for signs of dust.

If all the abatement work is done and no dust can be seen, the job passes the visual inspection. If the job does not pass visual inspection, you will have to reclean the area until no dust can be seen.

In some states there is no requirement for visual inspection. It is still a good idea to make sure you don't see any signs of lead dust before repainting an abated surface.

Stage 2: Painting and sealing

All abated surfaces should be primed with the correct type of primer for the surface. Repaint all abated surfaces. A final coat of gloss or semi-gloss is recommended. Enclosures may not need to be painted. Wooden floors should be sealed with clear polyurethane based paint. Other floors, like tile or linoleum, should be sealed with wax. Concrete floors need to be sealed with a concrete sealer.

Stage 3: Repeat special cleaning

Allow at least 24 hours between stage 2 and stage 3 for the paint and sealers to dry or follow the manufacturer's specifications. Then HEPA-vacuum all surfaces. Wash all surfaces with a lead cleaner. Then HEPA-vacuum all surfaces again.

Final Inspection

Once the area has been cleaned and repainted, an inspector will take dust samples for the final inspection. These samples are called clearance dust samples. Review Chapter 3 for more information on collecting dust samples. The job must pass final inspection before occupants can move back into the building.

The inspector will take samples from each room in the work area. The inspector will take at least three samples for each room; one from the floor, one from a window sill, and one from a window well. The actual number of samples will depend on the abatement method you used and Federal standards. The inspector will take more samples for surfaces that were chemically stripped, than for enclosed surfaces. **The purpose of the final inspection is to make sure that dust levels are as low as they can be.**

Clearance dust levels

The lead dust levels from these samples must be acceptable for clearance. Clearance means that the area is lead safe. Remember, lead in dust is measured in micrograms (ug) of lead per square foot (ft^2) of area tested.

HUD clearance levels	
Surface	**Level of lead in dust**
Floors	Below 40 ug/ft²
Window sills	Below 250 ug/ft²
Window wells	Below 400 ug/ft²

If the dust samples meet these levels, then the job passes final inspection. If they are above these levels, you will have to redo cleanup. You will have to redo cleanup as many times as it takes for the job to pass the final inspection.

Why measure lead in house dust?

All abatement methods create lead dust. Dust tests show if dangerous levels of lead dust still exist in a home. Lead dust is a major source of lead exposure for young children. Children have been poisoned after abatement jobs, **because cleanup was not done well**. If lead dust gets left behind, the families who return to their homes can be poisoned. This is why cleanup is so important. This is why passing final inspection is so important.

**Protect the families whose home you work on.
Do cleanup right!!**

Waste from a lead abatement job

There are many waste materials from lead abatement jobs.

- Lead-based paint chips
- Lead-based paint dust
- Bulky items that were removed (windows, doors, etc.)
- Poly and duct tape
- Sludge from paint removers
- Solvents from paint stripping
- Liquid waste (from cleanup, neutralizing surfaces, water blasting)
- Used cleaning supplies
- Disposable work clothes and respirator filters

Your employer must find out the federal, state, and local rules on how to dispose of each type of waste likely to be created, before the project begins. The building owner will need to know that all of the waste was disposed of legally.

Handling waste on the job

According to federal law, if your job is creating more than 220 pounds of waste per month, your employer will need to take a small sample from each type of waste and have it tested. If your contractor is creating less than 220 pounds of waste per month, the waste still needs to be tested. Dispose of the waste according to state and local laws.

Separate each type of waste on a job. Your contractor will take a sample from each type of waste to see if it is hazardous. Hazardous waste is waste that can poison people and the environment if it is not handled carefully. **All waste should be kept within the contained area on the job until it is tested to determine if it is hazardous.**

Warning! Sometimes regulations call all waste "solid waste" until it is tested. Sometimes the regulations call all non-hazardous waste "solid waste," including non-hazardous liquid waste. **In this manual, "solid waste" means solid material and "liquid waste" means liquid material.**

Liquid waste

Liquid waste includes wash water from cleanup, the neutralizing solution used for paint strippers, and waste from water blasting. Store liquid waste in non-corrosive containers.

Contact the local sewage treatment center and the state Department of the Environment for directions on how to dispose of liquid waste properly. Never pour it down toilets, drains, or storm sewers.

Liquid waste from a lead abatement is often hazardous waste. If you are generating lots of liquid waste, store the waste in 55-gallon steel or plastic drums until it is tested.

Testing waste
In most states all waste from lead abatement jobs must be tested to see if it is hazardous waste. Hazardous waste is liquid or solid waste that could poison people if it is not disposed of correctly.

Your employer will test different types of waste to see if they are hazardous. This is done with a special test called a "Toxicity Characteristic Leachate Procedure" test. This test is often called a "TCLP" test. The TCLP test looks at how the waste material will break down. It checks to see if the waste material will leak or release a hazard.

Lead waste - including paint chips, sludge from chemical strippers, and water from water blasting - are some of the types of waste that must be tested.

Non-hazardous waste disposal

1. **Bag or wrap solid waste in 6-mil poly.**
   Seal with duct tape. Do this as part of cleanup every day and at the end of the job. Do not use a bag labeled asbestos when you are bagging lead. Label the bag "LEAD CONTAMINATED."

2. **Store waste in a secure space.**
    Store waste in an area closed off to
    people other than workers. Protect
    waste from children, animals, the
    weather, and anything else that can
    disturb it. Sometimes you can use a
    locked dumpster. Put signs that
    say "DANGER! CONTAINS LEAD
    WASTE" on the storage space.

3. **Take waste to a landfill in a covered vehicle.**
    Transport solid waste to a municipal or lined landfill. Always transport waste
    from a lead abatement job in a covered truck. This keeps lead dust from
    getting into the environment.

    WARNING: <u>Do not</u> take waste from a lead abatement job to an incinerator.
    Burning lead waste creates lead fumes that get into the air. Lead fumes are
    very easy to inhale, and are very dangerous to your health.

Hazardous waste disposal

When possible, avoid abatement methods which generate hazardous
waste, such as chemical stripping. If you use such methods, your employer must
plan how to contain, transport, and dispose of the hazardous waste before the
project begins. Hazardous waste is much more expensive to dispose of than
non-hazardous waste.

There are several laws for hazardous waste disposal. The law which
applies depends on how much hazardous waste a contractor makes.

Amount of hazardous waste	Laws that apply
220 pounds or less per month	State
More than 220 pounds per month	State and Federal

If you generate less than 220 pounds of hazardous waste per month, you
have to follow state laws. Some states require you to take even small amounts of
hazardous waste to a licensed hazardous waste facility. Your employer must find
out what your state requires.

If you generate more than 220 pounds of hazardous waste per month, you
have to follow Federal laws. The Federal law that covers hazardous waste is the
Resource Conservation and Recovery Act (1976). It is called **"RCRA"** for
short. (Some states have their own laws about hazardous waste. They must be
as strict or more strict than the RCRA.)

RCRA says that if your employer (or contractor) makes over 220 pounds of waste per month, he or she will have to get an EPA hazardous waste generator identification number. Your employer must also have you do the following:

1. **Store all hazardous waste in special containers.**
    Store hazardous waste in 55-gallon drums, tanks, or other containers that match the type of waste. The Department of Transportation or state waste management agency will give you the information you need to choose the right container. All containers must be marked "HAZARDOUS WASTE" in bright red and yellow colors. All containers must have a label that lists their contents.

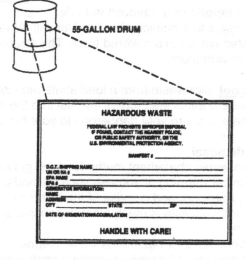

2. **Store hazardous waste in a secure area.**
    Store waste in an area closed off to people other than workers. Protect waste from anything else that can disturb it. Regularly inspect containers for leaks or corrosion. Hazardous waste can be stored at the company's facility for up to 90 days.

3. **Use a licensed transporter.**
    The person or company that transports hazardous waste must be approved by the **EPA**. Be careful when you move hazardous waste containers. Use hand trucks, dollies, pull carts, and ramps whenever you can. This will prevent containers from breaking and protect everyone from exposure to hazardous waste.

4. **The hazardous waste must be brought to a licensed disposal site.**
    The transporter must take the hazardous waste to a disposal facility that is licensed to accept this type of hazardous waste. The site must be approved by EPA. All hazardous waste must be disposed of within 72 hours of final cleanup.

5. **Use a Hazardous Waste Manifest.**
    An EPA form called a **"Hazardous Waste Manifest"** must be with every shipment. Your contractor, the transporter, and the receiver at the disposal site must all sign the manifest.

Other requirements

Some contractors have to follow even more requirements for hazardous waste. They include contractors who:

- Generate more than 2200 pounds of hazardous waste per month.
- Abate more than one housing unit at a time.
- Abate commercial, public, and industrial buildings.

EPA studies of paint abatement waste

EPA sponsored two studies of lead abatement waste. They used jobs from the HUD demonstration project in 1991.

After the first study, EPA found that certain types of waste generally were hazardous or not hazardous. For some kinds of waste, they did not have enough data to draw conclusions. So, they did a second study.

The results from the second study are in the following chart. These results only give you an idea of what might happen on your project. You can separate the waste into these two groups before the TCLP tests are done. The following results from the second study are not conclusive.

ABATEMENT WASTE

Hazardous	Usually not hazardous
• Paint chips • Paint dust (from HEPA vacuums and air filters) • Rags, sponges, mops, HEPA filters, other cleaning materials • Air monitoring cartridges • Scrapers • Unfiltered wash water • Solid waste with lead level higher than 5 ppm • Poly and tape from jobs where heat guns used	• Filtered wash water • Disposable work clothes and respirator filters (HEPA - vacuumed before disposal) • Solid waste, such as window frames, with lead level less than 5 ppm (measured at lab) • Poly and tape from encapsulation and enclosure jobs (HEPA-vacuumed before disposal)

RCRA requires that any contractor generating more than 220 pounds of waste per month sort and test waste from each project. Local and state regulations may require that even waste from small jobs be tested.

Key facts for Chapter 10

Cleanup is the most important part of the abatement job.
Cleanup must be done slowly and thoroughly.
It may take longer than doing the abatement.

Daily cleanup
1. Wrap large debris in poly.
2. Wet mop or wet sweep small debris and bag it.
3. Check the poly and repair any tears or rips.
4. HEPA-vacuum all surfaces.

Wait 24 hours after finishing abatement before you begin final clean up. (Check your state and local laws)
Final cleanup must be done slowly and thoroughly

Final cleanup - Stage I
Every step of final cleanup is important:
1. Wear protective clothing, including a respirator and goggles.
2. Wet mop the entire area and bag all dust
3. Take up the first layer of poly.
4. HEPA-vacuum all surfaces.
5. Wash all surfaces with a lead cleaner and then rinse. Follow state and local laws about disposal of lead cleaner
6. HEPA-vacuum all surfaces again.
7. Dispose of all cleaning items in sealed 6-mil plastic bags.

Some states require a visual inspection of the abatement job after the first stage of final cleanup.

Final cleanup - Stage 2
Paint and seal all the abated surfaces.

Final cleanup - Stage 3
HEPA-vacuum all surfaces. Wash all surfaces with a lead cleaner and rinse well.
HEPA-vacuum all surfaces again.

Final inspection
Every lead abatement job must pass a final inspection.
Dust wipe tests measure the amount of lead in the house.
If lead dust levels are too high, you must redo cleanup.

Waste from a lead abatement job

1. Store waste in a locked place until it can be disposed of.
2. Waste should not be removed from the contained area on the job site until your employer knows if it is hazardous or not.
3. Waste should be tested to determine if it is hazardous.
4. Hazardous waste can be stored up to 90 days at the company's facility. All other waste must be removed from the site within 72 hours after final cleanup.

Handling non-hazardous waste

Wrap or bag solid waste in 6-mil poly.
Label waste "Lead-Contaminated."
Transport solid waste to a lined dump in a covered truck.
Never burn lead waste.
Do not pour liquid waste down a drain.

Handling hazardous waste

Store hazardous waste in special, labeled containers.
Use a licensed transporter to take the hazardous waste away.
Hazardous waste must go to a licensed disposal site.
A Manifest must go with every shipment of hazardous waste.

Chapter 11 - Industrial Removal of Lead-Based Paint

In this chapter you will learn about:

* **Methods to remove lead-based paint from steel and concrete surfaces**
* **The dangers of blasting and burning lead-based paint**
* **How to protect yourself from lead dust and lead fumes**

Removing lead-based paint

Lead-based paint was not only used in houses. It was used on metal, steel, concrete, wood, and other surfaces. It was used in factories and power plants. It was painted on bridges, water towers, and pipelines. In fact, it was even painted on highways. When repair work must be done on these painted surfaces, lead-based paint may need to come off. The lead-based paint may also be removed before demolition of these structures.

Lead-based paint can be removed from steel or concrete by grinding, sanding, or using a needle gun on the painted surface. Grinding and sanding creates a lot of lead dust. They are considered Class 2 tasks. Lots of dust is released into the air. Collecting the lead-based paint dust can be difficult. Lead dust is easy to breathe and can get on your clothing.

Sometimes lead-based paint is blasted off of steel structures. Rather than scraping or removing a piece of structure intact, the paint is removed by blasting. Blasting is very dangerous. It can make large amounts of lead dust. It also makes the dust smaller. Instead of chips, small particles are made. Some of these can be seen but many are invisible. You can breathe the particles. The particles can also get on your hands, clothing and tools. Blasting is a Class 3 task.

Sometimes lead-based paint is burned off. When painted steel beams are cut using torches, the paint is burned off. This also happens when welding is done on metal with lead-based paint. Heating the paint to high temperatures puts lead into the air. This causes lead fumes. Lead fumes are easily breathed. Whenever you burn lead-based paint, you will be breathing lead fumes. Burning is the most dangerous removal method, and is prohibited in many states. Burning lead is prohibited in residential work by HUD. Burning lead is a Class 3 task.

Finally, you may remove lead-based paint from metal or concrete surfaces using a chemical stripper. This is the same method of chemical stripping used in residential removal of lead-based paint. The chemicals used are usually either solvents or caustics. Industrial chemical strippers are often stronger and more hazardous. Chemical stripping makes less dust than some methods. However, solvents and caustics may be dangerous to breathe and get on your skin. Using this method also makes lots of liquid waste which can be hazardous. The lead in the waste is dangerous. The chemicals may be dangerous. They have to be handled carefully. If you are using an air-purifying respirator, you must always use an organic vapor, as well as a HEPA cartridge in combination, whenever you are chemical stripping lead-based paint. Just like in home abatement jobs, you should avoid using chemical strippers with methylene chloride. If you must use a chemical stripper with methylene chloride, then you must wear a supplied air respirator.

Work safely!

Blasting, power tool removal, and burning lead-based paint can make large amounts of lead dust. You must use special work practices and respirators to protect yourself. This work can also harm the environment. The lead dust can get into water and soil. People in communities nearby can also be exposed if work is not done right. Let's look at the different types of lead-based paint removal on steel and concrete surfaces. There is a safe way and an unsafe way of working. If work like this is not done correctly, you may get sick. Workers who operate the tools or equipment are at risk. Other workers who are exposed include:

- Cleanup workers
- Helpers
- Workers loading or tending pots
- Supervisors or inspectors
- Workers performing tasks in containments

Industrial removal of lead-based paint can create high levels of dust. There have not been enough good studies done on what these levels usually are. However, the following table shows some of the lead levels found on different industrial jobs.

TYPE OF JOB	EXPOSURE LEVEL	SOURCE
Blasting/Bridge	1,070-10,400 ug/m³	Rekus, 1988
Blasting/Boiler	640-1,400 ug/m³	Adkinson, 1989
Blasting Bridge	3,690-29,400 ug/m³	NIOSH, 1991
Riveting/Bolting	1-189 ug/m³	NYCDOH, 1992
Burning/Power Plant	2,100-22,400 ug/m³	Rekus, 1988
Burning/Cutting Industrial Demo.	21,330 ug/m³	Holness et al. 1988
Disc Sanding Ship Overhaul	5.6-1,570 ug/m³	Booher, 1988
Rivet Busting Bridge Overhaul	18-3,653 ug/m³	NYCDOH, 1992
Power Tool Cleaning	80-790 ug/m³	Adkinson, 1989

Class 2 and Class 3 tasks are jobs that create lots of lead dust or fumes.
Class 2 tasks include:
- Removing lead-based paint with power tools not connected to a HEPA vacuum
- Cleaning up with dry abrasives
- Rivet busting lead-painted surfaces

Class 3 tasks include:
- Torch burning
- Welding and cutting lead-painted surfaces
- Abrasive blasting

Build a work area containment

Your company will have to build a containment for many industrial paint removal jobs. The removal work takes place inside the containment. Containing the work area helps with two things:

- Keep lead dust out of the air in the environment
- Collect the lead-based paint and other debris (including water) created during removal.

The containment is built to protect people who may live near your work site. It also protects the air, water, and soil in the area near your job. If ventilation is set up right, it can protect workers on the job, too.

Containment can be built with rigid or flexible materials.
Rigid containment's can be built with plywood and metal, or wood framing. Flexible containments are built using mesh screens, heavy-duty plastic sheeting, or tarpaulins (tarps). Mesh screen allows some air to go through. They also allow some dust to get out. They can be hung using wires and cables. Tarps do not allow air through, so dust cannot get out. They must be attached to the structure using rigid staging.

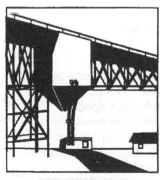

RIGID CONTAINMENT   FLEXIBLE CONTAINMENT

Sometimes flexible containments can be moved along the structure. This is done with a pulley and winch system.

When a containment is built on a tower or large bridge, the wind can be dangerous. An engineer should approve the design of the containment.

Containments are also built to collect debris. Blasting with non-recyclable materials produces a lot of debris. If you are doing water jetting, a lot of liquid sludge is made. Containments for these jobs must channel the debris or sludge and collect it in containers for waste disposal. Setting up, moving, and tearing down these containments can cause high lead exposure.

The inside of containment may be very dusty. Special work practices are required when you work in containment:

1. **Keep your respirator on! Don't take it off!**
   This means no eating or drinking, no smoking or chewing tobacco, and no putting on makeup while you are in the containment.

   Use a HEPA vacuum to clean dust and debris. OSHA requires you to use a HEPA vacuum whenever possible.

3. **Clean all surfaces - except bare steel - with a lead cleaner regularly** (at least once per shift). Do not wet clean bare steel surfaces. Bare steel will rust very quickly. This is called "flash rusting." Bare steel must by dry-cleaned.

4. **Do not use compressed air** to clean surfaces, unless you use the compressor in a containment that is hooked up to a ventilation and filtering system.

Set up and use ventilation
Ventilation may be set up on many jobs. Ventilation can keep dust out of the air. It can be used on jobs in three different ways:

1. **Local exhaust ventilation**
   Local exhaust ventilation collects dust almost as soon as it is released. An example of local exhaust ventilation is a power tool connected to a HEPA vacuum. The tool must have a special hood around the grinding wheel or sanding disk. The hood has a place for the vacuum hose to attach. When the vacuum is turned on, it pulls the dust through the hood into itself. Some tools have a flexible hood also known as a shroud. **Local exhaust ventilation keeps the dust away from you and out of the air.**

HEPA DRILL

NEEDLE GUN WITH HEPA FILTER

Rules for using tools with local exhaust ventilation
- Don't use the tool if the attached HEPA vacuum doesn't work.
- Hold the shroud tightly against the surface. Leaks will release dust into the air.
- Move the tool slowly. Keep the shroud flat to the surface.
- Always wear a respirator and protective clothing.
- Use the right tool for the job.

2.   General ventilation

Ventilation that is designed well will make the work area safer.

General ventilation is used with containments. The containment is built with air intakes at one end and portable air moving machines at the other. The ventilation machines have heavy-duty fans that can move as much as 20,000 cubic feet of air each minute.

The air may come through ducts built right into the containment. The fans push or pull the air through the containment. Ducts can be used to distribute the airflow. The air moving machines have HEPA filters which take out lead and other dust. Heavy debris still falls to the floor of the containment.

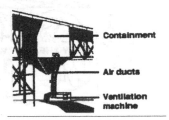

Containment

Air ducts

Ventilation machine

Rules for using general ventilation
- Organize the work process so ventilation pulls air and dust away from workers.
- Test the ventilation system to ensure that it works properly.
- HEPA-filter the air that is being blown out of the containment. Make sure a HEPA filter is used.

3.   Negative air ventilation
Some job specifications require negative air ventilation. This type of ventilation makes the air pressure inside the containment lower than the air pressure outside. Air with lead dust cannot leak out of the containment. Only air from outside can leak in.

The equipment is the same as for general ventilation. An air moving machine is set up at one end of the containment. The machine pulls air across the containment into the machine. The air then goes through filters and lead dust is trapped. **The difference is that with negative air ventilation more air is forced out than is let in.**

By forcing more air out than you allow in, a negative pressure is created. If there are leaks in the containment, air will go in, not come out.

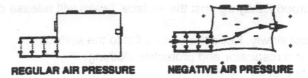

REGULAR AIR PRESSURE   **NEGATIVE AIR PRESSURE**

Set up and use a decontamination area

A decon entrance must be built. Both flexible and rigid containments will have a decon entrance. The decon consists of a dirty change area, a shower, and a clean area. The decon may be attached to the containment. It can also be located on the ground near the containment. You must use the decon to wash lead dust off your hands and face. You must also change out of work clothing and shower before going home. Do not take lead dust home to poison your family.

DIRTY AREA   WASH AREA   CLEAN AREA

Use Type CE respirators

When blasting, wear a pressure-demand Type CE respirator.

TYPE CE RESPIRATOR

Blasting to remove lead-based paint makes a lot of dust. It can send steel shot, grit, or other hard particles into the air at high rates of speed. A very protective respirator is needed. Protection for your head and face is needed as well. For most blasting work, you will use a Type CE pressure-demand respirator. This respirator is a supplied air respirator with a helmet or hood attached to the mask. There are different types available. Some CE respirators are pressure demand, and others are continuous flow. You need pressure demand when you do blasting work. Type CE respirators supply breathing air from an outside source to the user. A pressure-demand CE respirator will protect you in areas with high dust levels, and the helmet will protect against grit and shot. Your employer should give you a Type CE pressure-demand respirator if you are doing blasting work.

You will also need a pressure-demand CE respirator if you are welding, cutting, or torch burning surfaces covered with lead-based paint.

Rules for using Type CE respirators

- Get training on how to use Type CE respirators.
- Get medical approval to use the respirator.
- Use Grade D breathing air.
- If breathing air comes from compressed air tanks, be sure they are properly secured.
- If breathing air is supplied by a compressor, it must have an air purification system and CO alarm or monitors.
- Have someone monitor the air purification system.
- Make sure your helmet and air supply are tightly secured.
- Watch out for your air hose! Make sure it is secured. Keep it away from water and waste. Be careful not to trip on it.

Wear protective gear

You also must be provided with protective clothing to keep lead dust off of you. **Never take work clothing from a lead job home!** Your employer must give you clean work clothing and launder it for you. You also have to have a clean place on the job to change into work clothing at the beginning of each shift. Use the same place to change back into street clothing to go home. OSHA requires your employer to provide clean work clothing **weekly** if your exposure is above 50 ug/m^3 and **daily** if your exposure is above 200 ug/m^3.

Protect your hearing-wear earplugs or ear muffs underneath the hood of your respirator. Blasting, using needle guns, and other methods of paint removal create high levels of noise that could permanently damage your hearing and cause stress-related problems.

Methods of removal

1. **Power tools**

   Power tools are used on industrial lead-based paint removal jobs to remove small amounts of lead-based paint, rust, and mill scale. Power tools you may use include:

. Sanders	.Grinders
. Needle descalers	. Drills
.Oscillating saws	. Roto-peeners

Power tools work best when used for small jobs. They can be fitted with local exhaust ventilation. The tools have a shroud (or cover) on them. This cover is connected to a HEPA vacuum. When the HEPA-vacuum is turned on, the dust is sucked into the shroud and then into the vacuum. Power tools with local exhaust attachments put less dust in the air. Power tool cleaning with local exhaust ventilation is a Class 1 Task under the OSHA Lead Standard. Power tool cleaning without local exhaust ventilation is a Class 2 Task.

2. Burning, cutting, brazing

Avoid burning lead-based paint----it is very dangerous!

HYDRAULIC SHEARS

Do not burn, weld, or braze lead-based paint. These methods heat the paint and release high levels of lead fumes in the air. HUD and many states prohibit burning lead-based paint in residential work. Your employer should always try to use another way of getting the job done. For example, if you are doing demolition of structural steel or architectural metal, do not torch cut the metal. Cut the metal with a backhoe attached hydraulic shears or remove the paint first with power tools or chemical strippers, then torch cut it. When your are welding a piece of lead-painted metal, first remove the paint with power tools or chemical strippers; then weld.

3. Chemical stripping

Chemical stripping is the use of chemicals to loosen paint on metal or concrete surfaces. The chemicals used can be very dangerous. Think about it if it can loosen paint it has to be strong. The chemicals used fall into two categories: solvents and caustics.

Solvents are liquid chemicals that dissolve dirt, oil, paint and other substances easily. Oil-based paints can be cleaned with gasoline, which is sometimes used as a solvent. Other solvents include toluene, trichloroethylene, and methylene chloride. These chemicals evaporate easily. This makes them easy to breathe. Solvents can also be absorbed into your skin. Solvents can damage your nervous system, cause liver and kidney disease, and may cause cancer.

Caustics are strong chemicals that can loosen paint and other products. They can also burn your skin and mucous membranes. If you get these chemicals in your eyes, sinuses or lungs, they can burn and cause damage. Examples of caustics are sodium hydroxide, lye, potassium carbonate, and potassium hydroxide. These chemicals may also cause long term health problems like permanent lung disease.

Avoid using chemical strippers with methylene chloride, toluene, trichloroethylene, or any other solvents that are dangerous to your health.

When stripping metal or concrete surfaces with chemicals, make sure that you wear protective clothing, such as gloves, a polyethylene suit, and a respirator. Your eyes need protection, too, so make sure that you have on a full-face respirator **or** wear eye goggles or a face shield.

Wear a face shield or goggles when you use chemical strippers.

Chemical strippers are applied to the paint using a trowel or spray system. Usually it has to sit on the paint for hours, sometimes overnight, before you can scrape the paint off.

When you scrape the paint and chemical off, the debris (paint and chemical) is usually hazardous waste. Your employer must test it using the TCLP test. This waste can be very dangerous to the environment. Don't let it go down the sewer system, into water, or onto soil. When doing chemical stripping jobs, put down canvas and poly sheet plastic to catch the paint and chemical waste. The plastic and canvas system must have edges. This is so that the sludge cannot spill out. All the waste sludge is collected and put into drums for disposal.

Canvas with sheet plastic
Drums for Waste disposal

4.   Blasting

Blasting creates a lot of lead dust

Always build a containment for the work area whenever you are blasting.

Blasting has been done for many years to remove paint on steel structures. But blasting is prohibited in residential work by HUD and many states. There are many kinds of blasting. All blasting uses compressed air to make very high pressures. The high pressure is used to propel an abrasive material against the paint. Some of the common kinds of blasting are:

Sand blasting---a powerful machine blows sand out of a nozzle. The machine uses compressed air to blow the sand out. It is blown out at high pressures. The sand blows the paint off of the metal or concrete. Paint, sand, and debris get thrown into the air. Sand blasting exposes you to silica. It is very dangerous.

Other non-recyclable blasting----other abrasive materials that are used to blast are corn cob pieces, coal slag ("Black Beauty"), and carbon dioxide pellets. Like sand, the corn cob is used once and thrown away. The carbon dioxide evaporates into the air. These kinds of blasting make a lot of dust and debris which have to be disposed of.

Recyclable blasting---Some blasting machines use abrasive materials that can be collected and used again. Steel grit or shot, aluminum oxide, and plastic pellets are some of these. Compressed air is used to blow out the material at a very high pressure. These machines recycle the grit or pellets, and the material can be used again. This makes less debris to clean up, but lots of lead-based paint dust is blown into the air.

Water blasting----This kind of machine mixes water with an abrasive material. The water or mixture is blown out of the machine at very high pressures. The paint is blown off of the surface. This kind of blasting makes less dust than dry blasting, but creates lots of water waste with lead-based paint in it.

Water jetting---This machine sprays water at very high pressures, usually over 20,000 psi (pounds per square inch). The force of this water alone can remove paint and rust. The force of the water can also cut flesh. Workers operating this equipment, and working inside the work area, must be protected.

Vacuum blasting----This machine has a shroud, or cover, which seals against the surface being cleaned. The abrasive is contained in the shroud, and sucked along with the lead-based paint debris into a vacuum.

All of these kinds of paint removal can cause lead poisoning. Sand blasting also can cause a lung disease called silicosis. Sand blasting is very dangerous and not recommended. If you do sand blasting, **make sure you are properly protected.**

Blasting lead-based paint can be done relatively safely. It requires proper containment, ventilation, and cleanup procedures. It also takes proper work practices, respirators, and protective clothing. Your employer must provide you the type of respirator you need. **When you do blasting, you must work carefully.** OSHA has a separate standard about how to work with blasting safely.

1. **Build work area containment.**
2. **Set up and use ventilation.**
3. **Set up and use a decontamination area.**
4. **Use Type CE, pressure-demand respirators.**
5. **Wear protective gear.**

True story

In March 1988, lead poisoning was diagnosed in workers employed by a contractor to demolish a bridge spanning a river in western Massachusetts. From November 1987 to March 1988, four of the nine workers had used acetylene torches to cut apart large sections of the bridge; one had cut these sections into smaller pieces on a barge moored below the bridge. The other four workers did not work near anyone who was torching. Respirators were sometimes used on the job.

"Lead poisoning in Bridge Demolition Workers in Massachusetts." MMWB 38(40): 692-694

Discussion questions
1. What do you think caused the workers to get lead poisoned?
2. Which workers are at greatest risk of getting lead poisoned?
3. Which workers are at smallest risk of getting lead poisoned?
4. How could lead poisoning have been prevented?
5. How do you think the workers found out they were getting poisoned?

Key facts for Chapter 11

Lead-based paint is removed from steel structures by:
Power tools, chemical stripping, and blasting

All of these methods can be very dangerous.

Whenever you use chemical strippers:
Always use an organic vapor cartridge on your respirator
Wear eye goggles or a face shield.

Avoid burning lead-based paint and sand blasting with silica.

Whenever you blast you must:
1. Contain the work area
2. Set up and use ventilation in the work area.
3. Build a decontamination area.
4. Use a Type CE respirator.
5. Wear protective clothing.

Ventilation can be
Local exhaust ventilation
General ventilation
Negative air ventilation

Local exhaust ventilation on power tools collects lead dust as it is created.

In this chapter you will learn about:

- **Problems with heat**
- **Cuts and bleeding**
- **Eye injuries**
- **Burns**
- **Shock**
- **Chemicals**
- **Electrical shocks**
- **Noise**
- **Fires**
- **Confined spaces**
- **Dangers from ladders and scaffolds**
- **Slips and trips**
- **Back injuries**

Other health and safety problems

Heat, electricity, and chemicals are dangerous on lead jobs

You learned why the buddy system is important whenever anyone is using a respirator. The buddy system helps prevents other types of accidents on any job. **Always use the buddy system**. Lead removal can include demolition work. Demolition is the most dangerous type of construction work. It is important to have someone who knows first aid and CPR on each crew. Your supervisor should have a first aid kit at the job site. Here are some of the short-term dangers on a lead abatement job.

Heat stroke and heat stress

Heat stroke is a medical emergency

Your body tries to cool itself by sweating. On the job, you work in a suit that doesn't let your body heat escape. Your lungs have to work harder to pull air through a respirator. The air conditioning must be shut off. You work very hard. If your body overheats, you can get very sick. Overheating can cause heat stroke (a medical emergency) or heat stress.

Heat stroke happens when your body can't control its temperature. You stop sweating. Sweating is your body's way of cooling itself. Your body overheats. Heat stroke can kill you or cause brain damage.

Signs of heat stroke

• Hot skin	• Headache
• Dry skin	• Dizziness
• Flushed skin	• Nausea (feel sick to stomach)
• Confusion	• Fainting

When a worker has signs of heat stroke, get him or her out of the work room. Take off the suit and respirator. Be sure the person is still breathing. **Cool the body off with water immediately**. You can hold the worker in the shower. Be sure you don't get water in the nose or mouth. You can wet the skin and fan it. Don't give water to a person who has fainted. You could make the person choke.

Unless the worker is treated quickly, he or she could die. Call 911 and tell the operator there is a medical emergency. There are a few places in the country where the 911 system is not available. If you are working in one of these areas, post the number for emergency help. Until the ambulance comes, you need to cool off the body of a person with heat stroke. The body can't do this by itself.

Heat stress is less serious than heat stroke.

Heat stress happens when you lose a lot of water from sweating. Sometimes you lose a lot of salt, too.

Signs of heat stress

• Cool skin	• Headache
• Sweaty skin	• Dizziness
• Pale skin	• Nausea (feel sick to stomach)

Do these sound familiar? The last three signs of heat stress: headache, dizziness, and nausea are also signs of heat stroke. If a worker has hot, dry, flushed skin, he or she probably has heat stroke - cool the person down until an ambulance arrives. If the person has cool, clammy, pale skin, he or she probably has heat stress - cool the body down.

Get the worker out of the work room. Take off the suit and respirator and give the person cool water to drink. If the worker faints, call an ambulance. He or she may have heat stroke. Don't give water to a person who has fainted. You could make the person choke.

Watch out for these warning signs
- Less alert
- Less coordinated
- Gets a headache
- Feels sick to stomach

This could be the beginning of heat stroke or heat stress. If you start to feel like this, let your buddy know. Then, leave the work area. Be sure to take off your booties and wash up. Drink some cool water. If a co-worker shows these signs, get the person out of the work room and have him or her drink cool water.

Heat can make you less coordinated. This can cause other accidents. Heat can also cause muscle cramps or heat rash. These can also be used as warning signals of heat stress or heat stroke. Heat can also make a worker faint.

Take the worker out of the work area. Cool the worker with water or ice. If the worker is conscious, give him or her some water and Gatorade™, or some other thirst quencher. Allow the worker to rest. If the worker feels better in 15 minutes, he or she is probably okay. If the worker is not conscious, call an ambulance.

Preventing heat problems

Take breaks and drink water to prevent problems with heat

Here are some ways to prevent heat problems:

Drink lots of water. Your body loses lots of water when you sweat. It is best to drink every half hour. Make sure you go through the wash station before taking a drink. Drink 8 to 16 ounces of water at every break.

DRINK WATER

Drink orange juice and eat bananas. These will replace special minerals that your body has lost through sweating. You may want to drink a thirst quencher drink like Gatorade™.

Take breaks. Your body handles heat better if it can cool down sometimes. At least two breaks a day and a lunch break will help your body handle heat better. Always exit the work area through the decon. Take off your suit and shower or wash your hands and face every time you leave the work area so that you don't poison yourself with lead. The wash water can help you cool down.

Get used to heat gradually. It takes about two weeks for your body to get used to working in the heat. If you do not work in the heat for even four days, it will take you two weeks to get used to working in the heat again. New workers should only work a half day in the heat for the first few days. They should not work a full shift until the end of their first week.

Cut down on alcohol. Alcohol dries out your body. Even if you only have two beers the night before work, you might have problems with heat. If you drink, do it on the weekend when you don't have to work the next morning. Drink lots of water before going to work.

Start work early in the day. Start work early in the morning so that you are finished before 2 P.M., the heat of the day. Weigh yourself before and after each shift. Make sure you drink enough water.

Cuts and bleeding

Whenever someone has a cut that is bleeding heavily, you should cover the wound with a clean cloth. Press on the cloth to give direct pressure on the wound. Do not remove the cloth. Elevate the wound also. If the wound does not stop bleeding within a few minutes, call 911 for emergency help.

APPLY DIRECT PRESSURE

At the same time you are applying direct pressure on the wound and elevating it, you can put direct pressure on the pressure points. You have two pressure points on each side of your body that can be used to stop bleeding. One is inside the arm under your biceps. The other pressure point is at the top of your leg, just inside your hip. Press hard on the wound and the nearest pressure point, while elevating the wound until emergency personnel arrive.

Eye injuries

An eye injury is the most common injury on a lead abatement job. Eye protection is very important. Wear goggles or a full-face respirator to protect your eyes. Without eye protection, caustic paste, chemicals, dust, and debris can permanently damage your ability to see. Make sure there is an eye wash on site and that you know how to get to it in case you need to. Have your buddy help you.

Burns

Heat guns can operate at over 1,100° F. HUD guidelines say that heat guns should not be operated above 1,100° F. Even 1,100° F is very hot and can cause severe burns. Water boils at 212° F. So a heat gun can be almost five times hotter than boiling water.

If you or one of your co-workers is burned, it is very important to get the person away from the hot object. Then clean, cold water should be run over the burnt skin. Run water over the burn for at least 15 minutes. If the burn is red, or is small, and only has a few blisters, you should clean and cover it with a sterile nonstick gauze pad. Change the dressing twice daily, and check for signs of infection. Never heat a needle and puncture a blister. Never use butter, oil or petroleum jelly for burns.

Call 911 for emergency help if:
- The burned person is going into shock.
- The burned skin covers more than 20% of the body.
- The burn has blisters and is on the hands, feet, face or genitals.
- The burned skin is charred or black.

You can treat the injured person for shock until the emergency personnel arrive, and run cold water over the burned areas. Do not put any covering over the burn.

Shock

Whenever anyone has suffered a serious injury, they can go into shock. People who have been cut badly or have a serious burn may go into shock. Shock happens when some parts of the body have a sudden need for a lot of extra blood. Because blood is flowing to other parts of the body, there is less blood going to the brain and the person goes into shock.

Symptoms of shock are:
- Pale, cold, wet skin
- Rapid heartbeat
- Thready pulse (You may feel blood running under the skin, but no regular heart beat at the wrist.)

Shock is a medical emergency!

Shock can be very serious. People can die from shock. **Whenever someone goes into shock, you should call 911 or the local emergency number for emergency help.**

To treat a person in shock, the person should lie down. Lift their feet up about 6 inches, unless the person has an injury to their legs or back. Cover the person with a light blanket, unless they are sweating heavily. Do not give them anything to eat or drink. It is sometimes hard for people to swallow if they are in shock. Treat the person as best as you can until the emergency personnel arrive.

Chemicals other than lead

There are many dangerous chemicals you might find on a lead abatement job:

- Chemical strippers
- Encapsulants
- Carbon monoxide (from gas motors and air compressors)
- Any other chemicals used in the place you are abating.

You need to know what chemicals are being used. **Your employer must train you about the chemicals you work with.** This is called Right-To-Know training. You need to read the Material Safety Data Sheets (MSDS's) for the chemicals you use. Look at the product information sheets as well, since not all the important information may be included on the MSDS. (See Chapter 4 for more on MSDS's.)

Your employer must use engineering controls to reduce the effects of these hazards. Your employer must make sure there is good ventilation. Whenever possible, use non-hazardous strippers, encapsulants, and other materials. If someone is over-exposed or burned by a chemical, send the MSDS to the hospital with the person.

COMBINATION FILTER

The HEPA filter on your respirator might not protect you from chemicals besides lead. You might need additional filters on top of the HEPA filters. Sometimes you can get combination filters - which are usually HEPA filters combined with an organic vapor filter. You must have the correct filter for the hazard. Depending on the type and level of the contaminant, you may need a Type C supplied-air respirator.

Carbon monoxide

Carbon monoxide is a poisonous gas. It can cause permanent brain damage. It can even kill you. It has no smell, taste, or color. It comes from gas motors, such as air compressors and generators. It can be a problem if you are using Type C respirators.

Signs of carbon monoxide poisoning
- Feeling drunk
- Dizziness
- Swaying back and forth
- Thinking gets foggy
- Begin to act crazy
- Headache
- Sleepiness
- Nausea
- Fainting

Three signs of carbon monoxide poisoning----headache, nausea, and dizziness---are also signs of heat stroke and heat stress. If a worker has these signs, get him or her out of the work room and take off the respirator. If the worker faints, call an ambulance.

If a worker faints because of carbon monoxide, be prepared to give CPR (cardio-pulmonary resuscitation). CPR is a way to get someone's heart and lungs working again. There should always be someone on your crew who has CPR certification. You can get certified by taking CPR classes. They are given at your local Red Cross.

If you are wearing a Type C respirator, and begin to have signs of carbon monoxide poisoning, turn on your escape gear and disconnect your air line. Alert your co-workers and get out of the work area. Help your co-workers to get out, and have the air purification system checked.

Electrical shocks

An electrical shock can stop your heart. Electricity is measured in volts and amps. Even a few amps can kill you, if the electricity goes through your heart. Electricity follows the easiest path to the earth----through you if it has to. It also travels easily through water. If you are wet and you touch electricity, it may travel through your body.

A wire with electricity going through it is called a "live wire." If a tool or an extension cord is broken, it may have a **short**. This means that the electricity doesn't flow through the right wires. It may flow through the tool and into your body.

Electricity is a problem on lead jobs because
- Water is used.
- Power may not be shut off.
- Power tools are used.
- Extension cords are used.
- Metal tools may be used.
- Wires may be exposed when lead paint is removed.

The best way to protect workers from shocks is **prevention**. OSHA has rules designed to prevent shocks. Your employer must follow these rules. Here are some ways to prevent electric shocks.

Use sensitive circuit breakers.
A Ground Fault Interrupter (GFI) is a very sensitive switch. If there is a short, the GFI should shut off the power before it can hurt your heart. A Ground Fault Interrupter is a very good way to prevent shock. **Extension cords should have their own GFI.**

Follow the written safety program. Your employer can also use a written safety program. With a written program, a person is in charge of keeping you safe instead of a piece of equipment. Written programs are not a substitute for a GFI.

Shut off the power. Lock the electrical box. Your employer should have an electrician come in and test the wires. You might think that all the power is shut off, but it may not be. You could be in for a big surprise. **Never use water around outlets or electrical boxes--whether the power is on or off.**

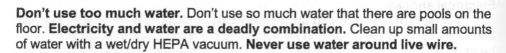

    If you must work around live wires, you need to protect yourself. **You may need: rubber gloves, a hard hat for working with electricity, and rubber boots.**

Don't use too much water. Don't use so much water that there are pools on the floor. **Electricity and water are a deadly combination.** Clean up small amounts of water with a wet/dry HEPA vacuum. **Never use water around live wire.**

Use safe power tools. Power tools should be **double insulated**. This means the outside of the tool doesn't touch the wires in the cord. Tools should also be **grounded**. This means there is an extra wire in the cord. If there is a short, electricity will travel through the extra wire. A grounded tool has three prongs on the plug (instead of two). **Never cut the third prong off a grounded plug. Use an adapter. Attach the wire on the adapter to the plate on the outlet.**

Keep power tools in perfect shape. It is much easier to get a shock from a broken tool. Broken tools should be taken off the job. They should have a DO NOT USE tag on them. Don't try to fix a broken tool unless you have been trained. Always unplug a tool before trying to fix it. Some companies cut the cord of broken tools so no one can use them.

Ways to keep tools in perfect shape:
*   Inspect the tool before you use it.
*   Give broken tools to your supervisor.
*   Be sure the tool is sharp.
*   Don't carry a tool by its cord.
*   Don't unplug a tool by pulling the cord.
*   Store tools where they won't be damaged.

Keep extension cords in perfect shape. There may be a lot of extension cords on the job. Ventilation equipment needs one. So do power tools and lights. Extension cords need to be taped up off the floor. If scaffold runs over the cords, it could cut them.

Never hang extension cords with wire. This could cause a shock. When you attach a tool to an extension cord, put electrical cords together.
Heavy-duty wiring is **not meant** to be used as an extension cord. Your employer must give you extension cords with plugs for power tools. Your employer should give you grounded extension cords.

Use non-metal hand tools or ladders as much as possible. Electricity travels through metal. If you touch a live wire with a metal shovel, you could get a bad shock. Your employer should give you plastic or wooden tools. Metal tools with plastic or rubber handles are safer. Metal ladders are also dangerous. Your employer should give you wood or fiberglass ladders.

Watch out for wires in walls and ceilings. When you abate lead paint on a wall or ceiling, you might uncover wires. It is very important to shut off the electricity and have an electrician test it. **Do not use water near electrical wires.**

Don't touch a worker who has been shocked. You might get a shock yourself. Shut off the power first. Then use a <u>dry</u> wood pole to move him away from anything metal. **Someone on the job should be trained to do CPR.** (CPR stands for Cardio-Pulmonary Resuscitation). A person trained in CPR can keep someone breathing and keep his heart going until an ambulance comes. Do not try CPR unless you have been trained.

Noise

Working in a noisy place can make it more difficult to work. Too much loud noise can also damage your hearing. Hearing loud noises for short periods of time can make it hard for you to hear normal noises temporarily. If you hear loud noises often for long periods of time, your hearing can be damaged forever. Noise can also cause you to have high blood pressure or be irritable. If may upset your sleep temporarily.

Noise is measured in units called decibels (dB). If a noise is increased by 3 dB, it sounds twice as loud. A very soft whisper is 30 dB. A loud rock band may play at 120 dB. OSHA has a law that says your employer must make hearing protection available to you if you work for 8 hours when the noise level is above 90 dB. But many scientists recommend that everyone exposed to 80 dB wears hearing protection. The law requires that you are tested every year to measure your hearing, if you work at noise levels above 90 dB.

Needle guns can cause a noise level of around 80 dB - even higher, if you use them and on metal and other types of building materials. HEPA vacuums also can cause noise levels of around 80 dB. You will be more comfortable if you wear ear plugs or ear muffs while working with a needle gun or HEPA vacuum.

Your employer should help you make sure that your plugs or muffs fit properly.

Fires and explosions

A fire on a lead abatement job is very dangerous. Poly, duct tape, and disposable suits burn fast. Poly will melt and can burn at about 150° F.

The best way to deal with fires is to prevent them. Any fire needs three things: fuel (something that burns), heat (the heat, flame or spark that starts the fire), and oxygen (in the air). **Preventing fires means keeping fuel, heat and oxygen from coming together**.

Fuel	Hea  t	Oxygen
* Poly	• Welding	• Air
* Duct tape	• Cutting torches	• Negative air
* Spray glue	• Electrical wires	machines
* Encapsulant	• Lights	• Fans
* Disposable suits	• Broken tools	
* Wood	• Operating machines	
* Chemical strippers	• Cigarettes	

SCBA

There are a few rare cases where you work around chemicals that can explode. You need to know what you are working around. If there are gases which can explode, you must wear a fire fighter's respirator. This is called a **Self-Contained Breathing Apparatus or SCBA.** You carry a tank of air with you on your back. Methane (a sewer gas) and acetylene (in torches) are two gases that can explode.

If there is a fire or explosion in the work room, GET OUT! The fire will spread very quickly. You may have to cut through the poly to get out of the work room.

The following are ways to prevent fires and explosions:

Be careful of welding and cutting. These work processes are often used in demolition. A worker must stand by with a fire extinguisher in case something catches fire.

Be careful of electrical wires and lights. An ordinary lamp on the floor can start a fire. Never wrap lights in poly. Heat will build up and can set the poly on fire. Your employer must use safety lights. The lights have cages that keep the hot bulb from starting a fire. They are also safe in water.

Keep tools in perfect shape and they will be less likely to start a fire. Protect operating machines during setup.

 No cigarettes on lead abatement job sites. Do not smoke during setup. Poly and spray glue both catch fire very easily.

Use fire resistant products. Some new products can help prevent fires. Fire resistant poly doesn't burn as easily. New spray glues use chemicals that don't burn as easily. Use these when there is known danger of fire hazards.

Have a fire extinguisher on site. Your employer must have fire extinguishers. Fire extinguishers need to be able to put out wood, chemical and electrical fires. These are called ABC-rated fire extinguishers. If there are sprinklers, your employer should try to leave them in service as long as possible. Where is the fire extinguisher? Do you know how to use it?

Look at the escape plan when you start the job. Your employer must have an escape plan. The escape plan includes a map and emergency phone numbers. The plan should be hung in the decon. When you start the job, look at the map.

Figure out how you would get out in an emergency. Do you have to dial "9"? Is there an emergency exit from the work room? Are there arrows made out of tape on the walls to show you how to get out? If the fire started near the decon, you will not be able to get out that way.

Confined spaces

There are sometimes when you might work in a small area that is hard to get out of. You might be removing paint in a small tunnel, manhole, or crawl space. You could be repairing lead mortar inside a tank. It is hard to get out of these **confined spaces**. They may have very little oxygen in them. You can use up all the oxygen in the space very quickly. **Many people die in confined spaces**. OSHA has a special set of rules for working in a confined space. You must get special training before you enter a confined space.

For confined space work, your employer must have	
• Written safety program	• Appropriate safety equipment
• Permit system	• Rescue plan and equipment

Always check the air in a confined space before going in. You need special equipment to do this. **Make sure there is enough oxygen and no toxic or explosive gases**. Never enter a confined space unless you have an outside buddy. You should wear a rescue harness. Your buddy worker outside needs to check on you at least every few minutes. He can pull you out with the harness if something happens to you. He does not leave the confined space entrance until you are outside. The harness is used to pull you out in case of an emergency. No one should go into a confined space to rescue a worker, unless he or she is protected. Many people die going into a confined space and trying to rescue workers.

Ladders

You already know not to use metal ladders. Electricity passes through them, and it can shock you. Also be sure that ladders are in perfect shape. Every time you use a ladder, check for these things:

- Broken steps
- Broken hinges
- Broken feet

- Wobbly ladder
- No rubber safety feet
- Water on the ladder (slippery)

OSHA has a specific set of rules for working with ladders. **Here are some ways to use ladders safely:**

Don't lean a step ladder against a wall. Use a ladder that's made to lean against a wall.

Check the rating on the ladder. How many pounds will it hold?

If you lean a ladder against a wall, set it up so that the top of the ladder is four times higher than the distance from the wall to the base of the ladder.

Only use one side of a step ladder. The other side isn't made to hold a person.

Face the ladder. Don't stand on it backwards.

Don't stand higher than 2 steps from the top of a step ladder. Get a taller ladder.

Don't use a ladder as a platform. Use a piece of wood.

Scaffolds

Scaffolds on wheels are common on large lead abatement jobs. If you use metal scaffolds, remember electricity travels through metal. If you touch a live wire with a metal scaffold, you can get a bad shock.

You can't tell whether a scaffold is safe by looking at it. Scaffolds must be put together by someone with experience. All the parts must fit perfectly. They should be inspected by someone other than the person who built them. **All scaffolds need to have guard rails.**

OSHA has a specific set of rules for working on scaffolds. Here are some rules about scaffolds on wheels:

All scaffolds should have railings. These keep you from falling over the side.

Scaffolds more than 10 feet high must have guardrails.

The scaffold parts must be locked together with pins.

The wheels must be locked at all times.

Scaffolds may not be more than 4 times higher than they are wide. For example, a 6-foot-wide scaffold may not be more than 24 feet high.

Boards may not overlap the ends of the scaffold more than 1 foot. If you step on the end of the board, the board could tip over and you would fall.

It is safer to use scrapers with long handles than to work on a scaffold. If you are using air-supplied respirators, it is easy for the hose to be caught on the scaffold. Be sure that there is enough hose for you to move around. It is even more important not to fall off scaffolding. If you fall, you may be trapped by the hose. It can pull the respirator off your face. The hose could pull other people off the scaffold.

If you are setting up a scaffold outside, do not attach the tarps to the scaffold. Wind can make the tarp act like a sail and pull the scaffold over.

Slips, trips, and falls

When you work, you wear slippery booties on your feet. The floor has plastic on it. There is water on the floor. You may drag a 300-foot-long air hose behind you. It is easy to fall down. You could trip on the hose or it could get tangled. You could fall down and, for example, break your arm. Here are some ways to prevent falls on the job:

Keep the floor dry. Don't use too much water. Use a wet/dry HEPA vacuum to pick up small amounts of water.

Wear boots outside of your booties. You cannot wear these boots outside the work site. **Or** put strips of duct tape along the bottom of the booties to provide traction.

Keep boxes, bags, and other junk out of the way. Tape extension cords up on the walls. Keep air lines from getting tangled.

Use harnesses or safety lines.

Back injuries

Back injuries are very common and very painful. Back injuries are one of the most common injuries to workers in America. They are hard to treat. It is much easier to prevent back problems than to treat them.

Here are some ways to prevent back problems:

Figure out how much you can lift comfortably. Get help to lift heavy bags.

Figure out a way to lift that's comfortable for <u>you</u>. Lift close to your body. Try to keep your back straight when you lift. Use your legs to lift. Make sure your shoulders are in a straight line with your hips. This helps to keep your back straight. Don't lift, twist, and turn at the same time. This is when most back injuries occur.

Key facts for Chapter 12

Short-term dangers on a lead abatement job can be worse than the lead itself.

Heat stroke is a medical emergency---CALL 911!
Symptoms of heat stroke: **hot skin, dry skin, flushed skin**
Get the person out of the work room. Take off the suit and respirator. Cool the body down with water immediately.

Heat stress is a medical alert.
Symptoms of heat stress: cold skin, clammy skin, pale skin
Get the person out of the work room. Take off the suit and respirator. Give the worker a cool drink.

Prevent heat problems.
Drink lots of water.
Get used to heat gradually over 2 weeks. Take breaks.
Always use a buddy system on any lead abatement job.

Apply pressure with a clean cloth to a bleeding cut or wound.
Elevate the wound.
Never use a tourniquet.

Run clean cold water over a burn for at least 15 minutes

You may find dangerous chemicals on a lead abatement job.
You have the right to know what you are working with.
Your employer must train you and make MSDS's available to you.

Make sure your respirator protects you.
HEPA filters may not protect you from dangerous chemicals.
Get the right filters, or use a combination filter or an air-supplied respirator.

Carbon monoxide is a dangerous gas.
Signs of carbon monoxide poisoning: headache, nauseous, dizzy, sleepy, fainting, vomiting.
Get the worker out of the work room and take off the respirator.

An electrical shock can stop your heart. Electricity travels through water. If you are wet and you touch electricity, it will travel through your body. If a worker has been shocked, shut off the power and use a dry wood pole to move the worker.

Prevent electric shocks.
Never use water around live wires.
Shut off the power and lock the electrical box.
Use tools that are double-insulated and grounded.
Never use metal hand tools or ladders.
Use Ground Fault Circuit Interrupters (GFCI's) on all cords.
Wear rubber gloves, hard hat, and rubber boots if you work with live wires.

Working in a noisy place everyday can damage your hearing.
Wear ear plugs or ear muffs to protect your hearing.

In case of fire:
Have a worker stand by with a fire extinguisher when welding or cutting torches are used.
Have an ABC- rated fire extinguisher on the job.

To prevent falls
Inspect ladders every time you use them.
All scaffolds should have railings.
Lock the wheels when people are on the scaffold.
Build scaffolds no more than four times higher than they are wide.

Shock is a medical emergency CALL 911!
Symptoms of shock: pale, moist skin, rapid or irregular heartbeat.

Safety and health exercise
This is not a test. It is **an** exercise. Use it to see for yourself how well you understand the material in the chapter.

1. Why is electricity a hazard on lead abatement jobs?
2. Why do you need Ground Fault Circuit Interrupters for extension cords?
3. What other protection can you use against electrical shocks?
4. Why shouldn't you use metal ladders? What can you use instead?
5. Why are scaffolds on wheels dangerous? How do you protect yourself from these dangers?
6. Name two common tripping hazards on big lead abatement jobs.
7. Why is fire safety a problem on removal jobs?
8. What type of fire extinguisher should be used on a lead abatement job?
9. Why is heat stress a problem on lead abatement jobs?
10. What are the symptoms of heat stress?
11. What should you do if someone cuts themselves on the job?
12. What should you do if one of your co-workers gets a burn on the face from a heat gun?
13. What are the signs and symptoms of shock?

HUD, EPA, OSHA, CPSC, and NPS Lead Paint Rules[1]

EPA-HUD Lead Disclosure Rule

The **Lead Disclosure Rule** (the identical *24 CFR 35, subpart A* and *40 CFR 745, subpart F*) was jointly issued by HUD and the Environmental Protection Agency (EPA) in 1996 (*61 FR 9063-9088, March 6, 1996*) as part of implementing Section 1018 of the Residential Lead-Based Paint Poisoning Lead Hazard Reduction Act of 1992 (commonly referred to as Title X). As of 2011, HUD and EPA had issued three Interpretive Guidance documents about the Lead Disclosure Rule; these are available from both agencies' websites on the Rule. The links from HUD's Lead Disclosure rule web page, *http://portal.hud.gov/hudportal/HUD?src=/program_offices/healthy_homes/enforcement/disclosure*, are at:

+ *Part I, August 21, 1996*

+ *Part II, December 5, 1996*

+ *Part III, August 2, 2000*

Links to the Interpretive Guidance documents are also available at EPA's Residential Lead-Based Paint Disclosure Program web page, *http://www.epa.gov/lead/pubs/leadbase.htm*.

This section of the statute addresses lead hazard disclosure requirements for almost all target housing built before 1978 that is offered for sale or lease. Since Title X focuses on children and pregnant women, target housing is defined as "any housing constructed prior to 1978, except housing for the elderly or persons with disabilities (unless any child who is less than 6 years of age resides or is expected to reside in such housing) or any 0-bedroom dwelling." The rule identifies four exceptions for which it does not apply to certain real estate transactions of certain target housing:

1) sales of target housing at foreclosure;

2) leases of target housing that a certified lead based paint inspector found to be lead based paint free, with suitable documentation;

3) short-term leases of 100 days or less, where no lease renewal or extension can occur; and

4) renewals of existing leases in target housing in which the landlord has previously disclosed all required information and where no new information has come into the possession of the landlord.

---

1 Appendix 6 of the 1995 Guidelines, which was a list of other organizations providing the EPA lead-based paint abatement supervisor and inspector course curriculum, has been deleted. Training providers for these courses are now accredited by EPA-authorized State lead programs or by EPA-operated lead programs. See the website at www.epa.gov/lead/pubs/traincert.htm for a list of EPA-authorized State lead program offices and EPA regional offices. From these offices you can obtain lists of approved training providers in a particular State. [Accessed 7/27/2012; this site may be moved or deleted later.]

The offeror (owners or their agents) and any real estate agents involved in the transaction have responsibilities under Title X. (Buyer's agents paid entirely by the purchaser are not considered "agents" under this rule.) A summary of Title X is provided at the end of this Appendix.

At a minimum, Title X requires the offeror to provide the potential buyer or tenant the following information before signing a written agreement or making an oral agreement:

1) an EPA (or EPA-approved State) brochure on lead hazards for residential properties built before 1978;

2) information regarding the presence of lead-based paint and/or lead-based paint hazards, as well as any other available information, including records and reports on the subject; and,

3) a certification that all the parties sign and date. The certification must indicate that seller or landlord provided:

   a) the required Lead Warning Statement;

   b) disclosure of the information in item 2, above; and

   c) a list of available records or reports (or a statement that no such documents are available).

The brochure, or pamphlet, in item 1 is available in (as of 2011) six languages; the links to these versions are on the EPA website at *http://www.epa.gov/lead/pubs/leadprot.htm*, and on the HUD website at *http://portal.hud.gov/hudportal/HUD?src=/program_offices/healthy_homes/enforcement/disclosure*. HUD recommends that the brochure be provided in the language of the sales or least contract, if that language is one of those for which the brochure is available. (If the language of the contract is not one of those listed, check the EPA or HUD websites to see if it has been translated into that language.) The titles, and the links to the individual adaptations on the EPA web page, are:

+ *Protect Your Family From Lead in Your Home (English)*

+ *Proteja a Su Familia Contra el Plomo en el Hogar (Spanish)*

+ *Hay Bao Ve Gia Dinh Cua Ban Khoi Bi Nhiem Chi O Trong Nha (Vietnamese)*

+ *В Вашем доме: защитите свою семью от свинца (Russian)*

+ ‏حم أسرتك من مخاطر الرصاص الموجود في بيتك‏ *(Arabic)*

+ *Ka Badbaa di Qoyska Halista Leedhka (Somali)*

The certification in item 3 must also indicate that the buyer or tenant received the identified materials. In the case of a sales transaction, the certification must also indicate that the offeror provided the buyer the opportunity to conduct a lead-based paint risk assessment or inspection and whether or not that opportunity was taken. Finally the certificate must include a statement by any real estate agent involved with the seller or landlord that the agent: informed the clients of their obligations under 24 CFR 35, Subpart A, or the identical 40 CFR 745, subpart F, and the agent is aware of his/her duty to ensure compliance.

The agent and the client must retain the certification and acknowledgment for at least three years. Agents who fulfill the required duties are not liable where the client fails to comply with these requirements or for the failure of the buyer's or tenant's agent to transmit materials provided in good faith. The agents should educate potential buyers and sellers about lead hazards and should encourage lead risk assessments or lead-based paint inspections of pre-1978 dwellings.

The Lead Disclosure Rule provides additional information on scope, definitions, recordkeeping requirements, and enforcement.

In the case of a **sale**, the Lead Disclosure Rule requires each contract to sell target housing shall include an attachment containing the following elements, in the language of the contract (e.g., English, Spanish):

1) a Lead Warning Statement that contains specific wording;

2) a statement by the seller disclosing the presence of known lead-based paint and/or lead-based paint hazards in the target housing being sold or indicating no knowledge of the presence of lead-based paint and/or lead-based paint hazards, including any additional known supporting information;

3) a list of any records or reports available to the seller pertaining to lead-based paint and/or lead-based paint hazards in the housing that have been provided to the purchaser, or the absence of any information;

4) a statement by the purchaser affirming receipt of the information in the previous two items;

5) a statement by the purchaser whether or not they availed themselves of the opportunity to conduct the risk assessment or inspection;

6) that any real estate agent involved in the transaction has informed the seller of the seller's obligations and agent is aware of his/her duty to ensure compliance with the requirements of the Lead Disclosure Rule; and

7) the signatures of the sellers, agents, and purchasers, certifying to the accuracy of their statements, to the best of their knowledge, along with the dates of signature.

In the case of a **lease**, the Lead Disclosure Rule requires that each contract to lease target housing shall include, as an attachment or within the contract, the following elements, in the language of the contract (e.g., English, Spanish):

1) a Lead Warning Statement that contains specific wording stated in the Rule;

2) a statement by the landlord disclosing the presence of known lead-based paint and/or lead-based paint hazards in the target housing being sold or indicating no knowledge of the presence of lead-based paint and/or lead-based paint hazards, including any additional known supporting information;

3) a list of any records or reports available to the landlord pertaining to lead-based paint and/or lead-based paint hazards in the housing that have been provided to the tenant, or the absence of any information;

4) a statement by the tenant affirming receipt of the information in the previous two items;

5) that any agent involved in the transaction has informed the tenant of the landlord's obligations and agent is aware of his/her duty to ensure compliance with the requirements of the Lead Disclosure Rule; and

6) the signatures of the landlords, agents, and tenants, certifying to the accuracy of their statements, to the best of their knowledge, along with the dates of signature.

The **preamble to the Lead Disclosure Rule** contains a sample (that is, non-mandatory) one-page disclosure form for sales and one for leases (61 FR 9066, at 9074 and 9075, March 6, 1996); both forms can be downloaded in English or Spanish from the HUD website (**http://portal.hud.gov/hudportal/HUD?src=/program_offices/healthy_homes/enforcement/disclosure**) or EPA website (**http://www.epa.gov/lead/pubs/leadbase.htm**). The titles, and the links to the individual adaptations on the EPA web page, are:

✦ Sample Form: *Lessor's Disclosure of Information on Lead-Based Paint and/or Lead-Based Paint Hazards*

✦ Sample Form: *Declaracion de Informacion por Arrendadores sobre Pintura a Base de Plomo y/o Peligros de la Pintura a Base de Plomo*

✦ Sample Form: *Seller's Disclosure of Information on Lead-Based Paint and/or Lead-Based Paint Hazards*

✦ Sample Form: *Declaracion de Informacion por los Vendedores sobre Pintura a Base de Plomo y/o Peligros de la Pintura a Base de Plomo*

The Lead Disclosure Rule requires that the seller, and any agent, shall retain a copy of the required completed documents for at least three years after the agreements are effective. With respect to enforcement, any person who knowingly fails to comply with any provision of this subpart shall be subject to civil monetary penalties or who knowingly violates the provisions of the Lead Disclosure Rule shall be jointly and severally liable to the purchaser or tenant in an amount equal to 3 times the amount of damages incurred by such individual. Failure or refusal to comply with the Lead Disclosure Rule may result in civil and/or criminal sanctions.[2]

When evaluating hazards as part of a risk assessment, the risk assessor must use either the standards issued by the EPA, as described in Chapter 5, Risk Assessment and Reevaluation, or a state or local standard if it is more protective (e.g., lower). Similarly, when evaluating paint as part of a lead-based paint inspection, the lead-based paint inspector must use either the standards issued by the **EPA**, as described in Chapter 7, Lead-Based Paint Inspection, or a state or local standard if it is more protective (e.g., lower).

For more information about the Lead Disclosure Rule, other lead safety rules, or general information about lead hazards and lead poisoning prevention, contact the National Lead Information Center at 800-424-LEAD or *http://www.epa.gov/lead/pubs/nlic.htm*. If you are a hearing- or speech-impaired person, you may reach the above telephone number through TTY by calling the toll-free Federal Relay Service at 800-877-8339.

The **Lead Safe Housing Rule** (LSHR) (24 CFR Part 35, subparts B-R) was issued by HUD in 1999 as part of implementing Sections 1012 and 1013 of Title X. Title X holds the federal government to a higher standard of care than it does residential property owners in general by requiring most Federally assisted housing to have some specified type of evaluation for the presence of lead-based paint and/or lead-based paint hazards, and controls based on the findings of the evaluation. HUD published the LSHR in the Federal Register (64 FR 50140-50231, September 15, 1999), and later published technical amendments (69 FR 34262-34276, June 21, 2004). The *LSHR as amended June 21, 2004*, and *highlighted changes to Lead Safe Housing Rule reflecting the technical amendments*, are posted on HUD's **LSHR website, *http://portal.hud.gov/hudportal/HUD?src=/ program_offices/healthy_homes/enforcement/lshr***. HUD has issued interpretive guidance on the LSHR, and updated it to reflect the 2004 technical amendments; the updated guidance is posted at **Information and Guidance for HUD's Lead Safe Housing Rule** on HUD's **LSHR website**. HUD has also developed a Lead-Based Paint Compliance Advisor, posted at ***http://portal.hud.gov/CorvidRpt/HUDLBP/welcome.html***. This Advisor presents the requirements of the LSHR, and, by analyzing user responses to a short number of questions, generates a report of project-specific requirements that can be downloaded or printed. Remaining questions about the LSHR may be sent to the HUD Lead Regulations hotline at **Lead.Regulations@HUD.gov** or (202) 402-7698.

---

[2] As of November 2011, the civil money penalties for Lead Disclosure Rule violations were up to $16,000 per violation; each of the 10 elements of a lease transaction, or the 11 elements of a sales transaction may, if violated, result in a penalty being levied up to that dollar amount. In the case of multi-family target housing and/or multiple properties with a single owner or owner's agent, the elements pertain to each real estate transaction on each dwelling unit separately, so the total maximum penalty is multiplied by the number of units and the number of turnovers for which a repeated violation occurred. For example, if a residential property with 9 housing units had each unit rented on two occasions, there were 18 rental transactions. If the property were covered by the rule but there was no compliance with it, there were 18 times 10, or 180 elements of the rule that were violated, and (as of November 2011), the penalty could be as much as 180 times $16,000, or $2.88 million.

The LSHR has a specific subpart (a portion of Part 35) on requirements and definitions, several subparts for different types of housing assistance and activities, and a subpart on methods and standards for the evaluation and reduction of lead-based paint.

The LSHR is implemented in conjunction with other applicable Federal, State and local regulations. For example:

✦ Lead abatement activities in target housing are conducted using certified lead abatement firms and personnel in accordance with the EPA's lead training and certification rule, 40 CFR 745, subpart L, or with a State or Indian Tribal certification program authorized by the EPA under 40 CFR 745, subpart Q.

✦ Renovation, repair, remodeling, weatherization, and painting work in target housing that disturbs more than EPA-specified minimal amounts must be conducted in accordance with the EPA's Renovation, Repair and Painting (RRP) Rule; see the discussion of the RRP Rule below

✦ While the LSHR does not require that firms conducting interim controls be certified, the RRP rule does so (for work more extensive than the RRP rule's threshold for minor repair and maintenance activities). On the other hand, the RRP rule provides that its cleaning verification procedure need not be conducted when work is cleared by a clearance examination under the LSHR or contract requirement, although EPA encourages property owners who include clearance in their renovation contracts also to require renovation firms to perform cleaning verification.

✦ Lead evaluation and control regulations of States, tribes, or localities that are at least as protective as the LSHR are to be followed (24 CFR 35.150(a)). For instance, some localities use a definition of LBP of 0.7 mg/cm², and some States or localities require abatement of paint below a certain height in housing where a young child resides.

✦ The U.S. Department of Labor's Occupational Safety and Health Administration (OSHA) requirements, particularly, its Lead in Construction Rule (29 CFR 1926.1101) and its Lead in General Industry Standard (29 CFR 1910.1025), apply on all projects where employees have the potential for exposure to lead. See the discussion of these standards below.

A summary of the levels of protection under the LSHR, and the basic requirements by subpart follows.

Lead Safe Housing Rule Levels Of Protection

Level of protection	Subpart, section, and type of assistance	Hazard reduction requirements
1	Subpart G, § 35.630, Multi-family mortgage insurance for conversions and major rehabilitations. Subpart L, § 35.1120(a), Public housing being modernized. [a*] Subpart L, § 35.1125, Public housing acquisition and development. [a*]	Abatement of all lead-based paint, and, for the public housing activities shown with *, all lead-based paint hazards. [b]
2	Subpart J, § 35.930(d), Properties receiving more than $25,000 per unit per year in rehabilitation assistance. [c]	Abatement of lead-based paint hazards.
3	Subpart G, § 35.620, Multi-family mortgage insurance for properties constructed before 1960, other than for conversions and major rehabilitations. Subpart H, § 35.715, Project-based assistance for multi-family properties receiving more than $5,000 per unit per year. [a] Subpart I, HUD-owned multi-family property. [ac] Subpart J, § 35.930(c), Properties receiving more than $5,000 and up to $25,000 per unit per year in rehabilitation assistance. [c] Subpart L, § 35.1120(b), Public housing not yet modernized. [a]	Interim controls of lead-based paint hazards, and ongoing lead-based paint maintenance.
4	Subpart F, HUD-owned single family properties. [d] Subpart H, § 35.720, Project-based assistance for multi-family properties receiving up to $5,000 per unit per year and single family properties. [a] Subpart K, Acquisition, leasing, support services, or operation. Subpart M, Tenant-based rental assistance.	Paint stabilization, and ongoing lead-based paint maintenance.
5	Subpart G, § 35.625, Multi-family mortgage insurance for properties constructed after 1959.	Ongoing lead-based paint maintenance.
6	Subpart J, § 35.930(b), Properties receiving up to and including $5,000 in rehabilitation assistance. [c]	Safe work practices during rehabilitation of painted surfaces.

[a] Response of risk assessment, interim controls or abatement of any lead-based paint hazards identified, and notification of building residents required for Environmental Intervention Blood Lead Level (EIBLL) case (§ 35.1130).

[b] Ongoing LBP maintenance required if the abatement uses encapsulation or enclosure.

[c] Ongoing LBP maintenance required for rehabilitation assistance only if HOME funds used for rental unit; ongoing LBP maintenance and reevaluation required for HUD-owned or mortgagee-in-possession multi-family housing only if HUD owns it for over 12 months.

[d] Ongoing LBP maintenance not required for a HUD-owned single family housing after disposition, although HUD recommends it unless the housing has been found to be lead-based paint free.

SUMMARY OF LEAD SAFE HOUSING RULE REQUIREMENTS			
Subpart of Rule/ Type Program	Year Built	Owner/Landlord Requirements[1, 2, 3]	Participant Monitoring Requirements
A Lead Disclosure Rule	Pre-1978	✦ Provide EPA (or State) lead hazard information pamphlet ✦ Disclose knowledge about LBP and its hazards to potential buyers or tenants and seller's agents. ✦ Complete lead disclosure form ✦ Provide opportunity for buyer to conduct evaluation.	Have system in place that documents they ensure Owner/Landlord complies with Lead Disclosure Rule
B General Requirements and Definitions	Pre-1978	✦ Definitions. ✦ Exemptions. [4] ✦ Notice of acceptable evaluation and hazard reduction activities. ✦ Pamphlet.	
C Disposition by Federal Agency Other Than HUD	Pre-1960	✦ LBP inspection and risk assessment. ✦ Abatement of LBP hazards. ✦ Passing clearance exam. ✦ Notice to occupants of LBP inspection, risk assessment, and clearance results.	Agency, or its agent, must document compliance with the Lead Safe Housing Rule unless waived due to insufficient resources.
	1960-1977	✦ LBP inspection and risk assessment. ✦ Notice to occupants of results.	
D Project-Based Assistance by Federal Agency Other Than HUD	Pre-1978	✦ Provision of pamphlet. ✦ Risk assessment. ✦ Interim controls. ✦ Passing clearance exam. ✦ Notice to occupants. ✦ Response to EIBLL child. 5	Have system in place that documents they ensure Owner/Landlord complies with Lead Safe Housing Rule and Lead Disclosure Rule
F HUD-Owned Single Family Sold With a HUD-Insured Mortgage	Pre-1978	✦ Visual assessment. ✦ Paint stabilization. ✦ Passing clearance exam. ✦ Notice to occupants of clearance.	

SUMMARY OF LEAD SAFE HOUSING RULE REQUIREMENTS				
Subpart of Rule/ Type Program	Year Built	Owner/Landlord Requirements[1,2,3]		Participant Monitoring Requirements
G Multi-family Mortgage Insurance:				
1. For prop- erties that are currently residential	Pre-1960	✦ Provision of pamphlet. ✦ Risk assessment. ✦ Interim controls. ✦ Passing clearance exam. ✦ Notice to occupants. ✦ Ongoing LBP maintenance.		Have system in place that documents they ensure Owner/Landlord complies with Lead Safe Housing Rule and Lead Disclosure Rule
	1960-1977	✦ Provision of pamphlet. ✦ Ongoing LBP maintenance.		
2. For conver- sions and major renovations.	Pre-1978	✦ Provision of pamphlet. ✦ LBP inspection. ✦ Abatement of LBP. ✦ Passing clearance exam. ✦ Notice to occupants ✦ Ongoing LBP maintenance if abate using encapsulation or enclosure.		
H HUD Project-Based Assistance:				
For all Multi-family properties	Pre-1978	✦ Provision of pamphlet. ✦ Notice to occupants. ✦ Ongoing LBP maintenance. ✦ Response to EIBLL child. [5]		If no bilateral agreement with owner/Landlord, have system in place that documents they or subre- cipients ensure Owner/ Landlord complies with Lead Safe Housing Rule and Lead Disclosure Rule
1. Property receiving more than $5,000 per unit per year	Pre-1978	✦ Risk assessment. ✦ Interim controls. ✦ Passing clearance exam. ✦ Reevaluation every two years		
2. Property receiving less than or equal to $5,000 per unit per year, and single family properties	Pre-1978	✦ Visual assessment. ✦ Paint stabilization. ✦ Passing clearance exam. ✦ Reevaluation every two years		

SUMMARY OF LEAD SAFE HOUSING RULE REQUIREMENTS			
Subpart of Rule/ Type Program	Year Built	Owner/Landlord Requirements[1,2,3]	Participant Monitoring Requirements
I HUD-Owned Multi-family Property	Pre-1978	✦ Provision of pamphlet. ✦ LBP inspection and risk assessment. ✦ Interim controls. ✦ Passing clearance exam. ✦ Notice to occupants. ✦ Ongoing LBP maintenance and reevaluation if HUD owns property for over 12 months. ✦ Response to EIBLL child. [5]	
J Rehabilitation Assistance:			
For all Properties	Pre-1978	✦ Provision of pamphlet. ✦ Paint testing of surfaces to be disturbed, or presume LBP. ✦ Notice to occupants. ✦ Ongoing LBP maintenance if HOME.	Have system in place that documents they or the subrecipients ensure Owner/Landlord complies with Lead Safe Housing Rule and Lead Disclosure Rule
1. Property receiving less than or equal to $5,000 per unit	Pre-1978	✦ Safe work practices in rehab. ✦ Repair disturbed paint. ✦ Passing clearance exam of the worksite.	
2. Property receiving more than $5,000 and up to $25,000	Pre-1978	✦ Risk assessment. ✦ Interim controls. ✦ Passing clearance exam.	
3. Property receiving more than $25,000 per unit	Pre-1978	✦ Risk assessment. ✦ Abatement of LBP hazards. ✦ Passing clearance exam.	
K Acquisition, Leasing, Support Services, or Operation	Pre-1978	✦ Provision of pamphlet. ✦ Visual assessment. ✦ Paint stabilization. ✦ Passing clearance exam. ✦ Notice to occupants. ✦ Ongoing LBP maintenance.	Have system in place that documents they ensure Owner/Landlord complies with Lead Safe Housing Rule and Lead Disclosure Rule

SUMMARY OF LEAD SAFE HOUSING RULE REQUIREMENTS			
Subpart of Rule/ Type Program	Year Built	Owner/Landlord Requirements[1, 2, 3]	Participant Monitoring Requirements
L Public Housing	Pre-1978	✦ Provision of pamphlet. ✦ LBP inspection. ✦ Risk assessment if LBP not yet abated. ✦ Interim controls if LBP not yet abated. ✦ Abatement of LBP and LBP hazards. ✦ Passing clearance exam. ✦ Notice to occupants. ✦ Ongoing LBP maintenance and reevaluation until abatement. ✦ Ongoing LBP maintenance if abate using encapsulation or enclosure ✦ Response to EIBLL child. [5]	Have system in place that documents they ensure Owner/Landlord complies with Lead Safe Housing Rule and Lead Disclosure Rule
M Tenant-Based Rental Assistance for units already occupied or to be occupied by children under 6 years of age	Pre-1978	✦ Provision of pamphlet. ✦ Visual assessment. ✦ Paint stabilization. ✦ Passing clearance exam. ✦ Notice to occupants. ✦ Ongoing LBP maintenance. ✦ Response to EIBLL child. [5]	Have system in place that documents they ensure Owner/Landlord complies with Lead Safe Housing Rule and Lead Disclosure Rule

[1] Perform and document clearance, lead-safe work practices and occupant protection, which are always required after abatement, interim controls, paint stabilization, or standard treatments, except when the amount of deteriorated paint is below the *de minimis* levels specified in Subpart R of the rule.

[2] Provide and document providing notice to occupants that includes results of evaluations (paint testing, inspection, and risk assessment) and clearance, where applicable.

[3] *Training requirements.* See ***www.hud.gov/offices/lead*** for information. See ***www.epa.gov/lead*** for information and, in particular certification requirements; note that certification is issued by the EPA, or by the EPA-authorized State or Tribe with the authority to implement the certification for the jurisdiction in which the evaluation or hazard control work is to be conducted):

Evaluation and related activities:

Visual assessment: Online HUD visual assessment course, or risk assessment certification.

Inspection: LBP inspection certification.

Risk assessment, lead hazard screen, or re-evaluation: Risk assessment certification.

Clearance: LBP inspection, or risk assessment certification, or, for clearance after renovation, repair or painting work (but not abatement), sampling technician certification.

Hazard Control (other than small (*de minimis*) amounts of paint disturbance – see 24 CFR 35.1350(d)):

Repair of paint, paint stabilization, or interim control: Project supervisor being a certified renovator, and all additional workers being either certified renovators or having passed a HUD-approved lead-safe work practices course.

Abatement: Project supervisor being a certified abatement supervisor, and all additional workers being certified abatement workers.

[4] See 24 CFR 35.115 for exemptions.

[5] Environmental Intervention Blood Lead Level: A confirmed concentration of lead in whole blood of a child under age 6 of at least 20 micrograms of lead per deciliter (µg/dL) for a single test, or 15-19 µg/dL in two tests taken at least 3 months apart. (While the term and its definition were based on guidance from the Centers for Disease Control and Prevention, in 2012 CDC revised its guidance, and it is anticipated that the EIBLL provisions of Lead Safe Housing Rule may be reconsidered at some point. See Chapter 16.)

[6] Field Office monitoring areas of interest: covered program responsibility, partnerships, information management (monitoring, data processing, tracking), reporting and responding, and resources.

EPA's Lead-based Paint Activities Training and Certification Rule (40 CFR 745, subpart L)

On August 29, 1996, the EPA published a rule for the certification and training of lead-based paint profession-als (61 FR 45778). Lead-based paint professionals include abatement personnel, project designers, lead-based paint inspectors and lead-based paint risk assessors. Lead-based paint activities include abatement, inspection and risk assessment. This rule contains the requirements for certification of lead-based paint abatement and evaluation firms and individuals, requirements for training providers, and work practice standards. As of July 2012, 39 States, the District of Columbia, Puerto Rico, and three Indian tribes have applied for and received authorization to run their own EPA-approved lead-based paint certification programs that are at least as protec-tive of public health and the environment as the model program that EPA provided and uses for operating its certification program directly.

After the federal program became effective in non-authorized states and tribal areas on August 29, 1998, the rule also provided for an additional phase-in period there for the requirements for training program accredi-tation, individual and firm certification, and work practice standards. After March 1, 1999, training programs could no longer provide, offer, or claim to provide training or refresher training for lead-based paint activi-ties defined at 40 CFR 745.223 there without being accredited by EPA according to the requirements of section (§) 745.225. In addition, after August 30, 1999, no individuals or firms could perform, offer, or claim to perform lead-based paint activities as defined at § 745.223 there without certification from EPA under § 745.226 to conduct those activities. (More information on training and the certification/accreditation process is available at: *http://www.epa.gov/lead/pubs/traincert.htm*.)

EPA's Lead Renovation, Repair and Painting Rule (40 CFR 745, primarily in Subpart E, Residential Property Renovation, with some provisions in Subparts L and Q)

The Renovation, Repair, and Painting (RRP) Rule was issued by the EPA under sections 402 and 406 of the Toxic Substances Control Act (15 U.S.C. §§ 2682 and 2686). It applies to most renovation, repair and paint-ing projects (for brevity, EPA calls these projects "renovations") performed for compensation that disturb paint that is known or presumed to be lead-based paint in target housing and child-occupied facilities first constructed before 1978. In general, the RRP Rule requires that RRP work in these homes and facilities be conducted by certified renovation firms and supervised by a certified renovator assigned to the project, with occupants (or the families/guardians of children at the child-occupied facilities) being notified of the work, with the certified renovator on the job site at least when specified critical steps are taken, with the work being done using lead-safe work practices, and with the project completion determined by the certified renovator conducting a specific "cleaning verification" protocol that the work area has to pass. The cleaning verifica-tion protocol involves a visual inspection for residue, and, if none is observed, wiping the windowsills, coun-tertops, and uncarpeted floors in the work area with disposable cleaning cloths, and comparing color of the wipes to a specified level of grayness on an EPA standard cleaning verification card.

The RRP Rule changed several subparts of 40 CFR 745, especially subpart E, Residential Property Renovation, when it was issued (73 FR 21692-21769, April 22, 2008). The RRP rule has been amended several times since (through the publication of this edition of these *Guidelines*, amendments had been published at 74 FR 34257-34262, July 15, 2009; 75 FR 24802-24819, May 6, 2010; and 76 FR 47918-47946, August 5, 2011). For further details on the RRP Rule's development, see the EPA's Renovation, Repair and Painting page, *http://www.epa.gov/lead/pubs/renovation.htm*. For the annual edition of 40 CFR 745, reflecting all amendments up to the time of publication of the latest edition, see the General Printing Office's Federal Digital System website, *http://www.fdsys.gov* or *http://www.gpo.gov/fdsys/*. (As of 2012, the search involves clicking on the right column's Featured Collection of the Code of Federal Regulations, then, within that collection, searching for the current year, then Title 40, then Chapter 1, then Subchapter R, then Part 745.)

The purpose of the RRP Rule is to ensure the following:

+ Owners and occupants of target housing and child-occupied facilities receive information on lead-based paint hazards before these renovations begin; and

+ Individuals performing renovations regulated in accordance with §745.82 are properly trained; renovators and firms performing these renovations are certified; and the work practices in §745.85 are followed during these renovations.

The RRP Rule requires that contractors performing most renovation, repair or painting projects that disturb paint in target housing of child-occupied facilities that is known or presumed to be lead-based paint provide to owners and occupants of the target housing and child-occupied facilities built before 1978, and to parents and guardians of children under age six that attend these facilities the lead hazard information pamphlet. As of 2011, the pamphlet for renovations is available from EPA and HUD in English, as **Renovate Right: Important Lead Hazard Information for Families, Child Care Providers, and Schools**, and in Spanish, as **Remodelar Correctamente: Guía de Prácticas Acreditadas Seguras para Trabajar con el Plomo para Remodelar Correctamente**. The rule affects paid workers who do RRP work in pre-1978 housing and child-occupied facilities, including:

+ Renovation contractors;

+ Maintenance workers in multi-family housing; and

+ Painters and other specialty trades; among others;

and the firms that hire them or otherwise contract or subcontract for their RRP services.

Under the rule, child-occupied facilities are defined as residential, public or commercial buildings where children under age six are present on a regular basis. The requirements apply to renovation, repair or painting activities. The RRP rule does not apply to minor repair and maintenance activities where up to six square feet of lead-based paint is disturbed in a room, or up to 20 square feet of lead-based paint is disturbed on the exterior, where none of the work practices prohibited or restricted by the rule (at 40 CFR 745.85(a)(3)) are used and where the work does not involve window replacement. Property owners and contractors who perform these projects in pre-1978 rental housing or space rented by child-care facilities must be certified and follow the lead-safe work practices required by the RRP Rule. (Property owners who work on the homes in which they reside are exempt from the rule. If this housing in which the owner reside has additional dwelling units the owner rents out, the owners are covered by the rule for work on the rental units or those units' exteriors, to the same extent as contractors they would hire to do that work.) To become certified, property owners and contractors must submit an **application for firm certification** and fee payment to EPA or, if the State or Tribe is authorized by EPA to operate the RRP certification program, to the State or Tribe directly. As of July 2012, 12 states had this authority. The EPA or EPA-authorized State or Tribe has up to 90 days after receiving a complete request for certification to approve or disapprove the application.

Differences between HUD's LSHR and EPA's RRP Rule

A description of requirements under HUD's LSHR as it was in place before the EPA RRP Rule went into effect, and the corresponding requirements of EPA's RRP Rule, and the changes for HUD LSHR projects resulting from the implementation of the RRP Rule, are summarized in the following table and explained in the narrative following the table:

Differences between HUD LSHR and EPA RRP regulations

Stage of Job	Requirement	HUD LSHR before EPA RRP Rule went into effect	EPA RRP Rule	Changes to LSHR projects to incorporate RRP Rule.
Planning and Set-Up	Determination that lead-based paint (LBP) is present.	Only a certified LBP inspector or risk assessor may determine whether LBP is present. EPA-recognized test kits cannot be used to determine that paint is not LBP.	Certified renovators use an EPA-recognized test kit, or a certified LBP inspector or risk assessor makes a determination of whether LBP is present.	No change.
	Training	HUD does not certify renovators or firms. HUD generally requires all workers and supervisors to successfully complete a HUD-approved curriculum in lead-safe work practices, such as the EPA/HUD initial RRP curriculum, except that uncertified workers supervised by a certified LBP abatement supervisor need only project-specific on-the-job training. The EPA/HUD initial RRP curriculum is approved by HUD under the LSHR, as are others listed at **www.hud.gov/ offices/lead/training/ hudtraining.pdf.**	EPA or EPA-authorized States certify renovation firms and accredit training providers that certify renovators. Only the certified renovator is required to have classroom training. Workers must receive on-the-job training from the certified renovator. Workers who passed one of the lead-safe work practices listed at **www.epa. gov/lead/pubs/trainerinstructions. htm** (including a certified LBP abatement supervisors) before October 4, 2011 may become certified renovators by taking either the 4-hour RRP refresher or the 8-hour initial RRP course. Certified LBP inspectors and risk assessors may act as certified dust sampling technicians without further training. People who passed an accredited LBP inspector or risk assessor course before October 4, 2011, but are not certified in those disciplines, may become a certified dust sampling technician by taking either the dust sampling technician refresher or the initial training.	Renovation firms must be certified. At least one certified renovator must be at the job or available when work is being done. Not all workers need to be certified renovators.

Stage of Job	Requirement	HUD LSHR before EPA RRP Rule went into effect	EPA RRP Rule	Changes to LSHR projects to incorporate RRP Rule.
Planning and Set-Up (cont.)	Pre-Renovation Education	HUD requires conformance with EPA (and other agencies') regulations, including EPA's Pre-Renovation Education Rule. Before December 22, 2008, EPA and HUD had required renovators to hand out the EPA / HUD / CPSC *Protect Your Family from Lead in Your Home* (Lead Disclosure Rule) pamphlet.	Renovators must hand out the EPA / HUD *Renovate Right: Important Lead Hazard Information for Families, Child Care Providers and Schools* pamphlet. (This requirement went into effect on December 22, 2008.)	LSHR requires *Renovate Right* to be handed out.
During the Job	Treating LBP hazards	Depending on type and amount of HUD assistance, HUD requires that lead hazards be treated using "interim controls," "ongoing lead-based paint maintenance," or abatement.	EPA does not require that LBP hazards be treated, only how they are treated when this is done. In general, EPA requires that renovations in target housing be performed using lead-safe work practices by certified renovation firms and certified renovators (with exceptions, such as for minor repair and maintenance projects [see below] and projects that do not disturb known or presumed LBP). When the intent of work is to eliminate the hazards or the LBP for reasons of lead safety, the work is abatement, and certified abatement contractors, certified supervisors and certified workers must be used.	Certified renovation firms and certified renovators must be used for most interim control and ongoing LBP maintenance projects. (The requirements for abatement projects are unchanged.)

Stage of Job	Requirement	HUD LSHR before EPA RRP Rule went into effect	EPA RRP Rule	Changes to LSHR projects to incorporate RRP Rule.
During the Job (cont.)	Prohibited Work Practices	HUD prohibits 6 work practices. These include EPA's 3 prohibited work practices plus: heat guns that char paint, dry scraping or sanding farther than 1 ft. of electrical outlets, and use of a volatile stripper in poorly ventilated space.	EPA prohibits 3 work practices (open flame burning or torching, heat guns above 1100 degrees F, machine removal without HEPA vacuum attachment).	None.
	Threshold minimum amounts of interior paint disturbance which trigger lead activities.	HUD has a smaller interior "de minimis" threshold (2 sq. ft. per room, or 10% of a small component type) than EPA for lead-safe work practices. HUD also uses this smaller threshold for clearance and occupant notification.	EPA's interior threshold (6 sq. ft. per room) for **minor repair and maintenance** activities is larger than HUD's *de minimis* threshold.	None.
End of Job	Confirmatory Testing	HUD requires a clearance examination done by an independent party instead of the certified renovator's cleaning verification procedure.	EPA allows cleaning verification by the renovator or clearance examination if required by regulation or contract. The cleaning verification does not involve sampling and laboratory analysis of the dust.	None.
	Notification to Occupants	HUD requires the designated party to distribute notices to occupants' units or by posting in centrally located common areas, within 15 days after lead hazard evaluation (or presumption) and control activities in their unit or common areas they access).	EPA has no requirement to notify residents after the renovation, unless they contracted for the renovation, in which case they get the clearance results within 30 days after the renovation is completed.	None.

A. Responsibilities Shifted from the Renovator to the Designated Party under HUD's LSHR:

1. Under the LSHR, the designated party is generally responsible to either have the paint tested by a certified lead inspector or risk assessor or presume the presence of lead-based paint. Therefore, when HUD's rule applies, the Certified Renovator may **not** use a paint test kit to determine that the paint is **not** lead-based paint. Note: Some states may have conflict-of-interest regulations prohibiting renovators from testing paint on which they will be working.

2. When the HUD LSHR applies, the designated party must have a qualified person, independent of the renovation firm, conduct a lead clearance examination. The Certified Renovator does not conduct a cleaning verification. See below for more information on clearance testing.

B. Additional HUD Requirements for the Renovator:

1. **Training requirements for workers and supervisors performing interim controls.** To meet the requirements of both rules:

   a. If the supervisor (in HUD terms) was certified before October 4, 2011 as a lead-based paint abatement supervisor or had successfully completed an accredited abatement supervision or abatement worker course before that date, that person must complete a 4-hour RRP refresher course to become a Certified Renovator.

   b. For workers who are not themselves supervisors / Certified Renovators:

      ✦ If their supervisor on this project is a certified lead-based paint abatement supervisor who has completed a 4-hour RRP refresher course, thereby becoming a Certified Renovator, the workers must obtain on-the-job training in lead-safe work practices from the supervisor; unless,

      ✦ The workers must successfully complete either a one-day RRP course, or another lead-safe work practices course approved by HUD for this purpose after consultation with the EPA. HUD has approved the one-day RRP course, the previously-published HUD/EPA one-day Renovation, Remodeling and Repair course, and other one-day courses listed on HUD's website, at *www.hud.gov/offices/lead/training/hudtraining.pdf*. Note that if the workers had completed some of these courses, the ones listed at *www.epa.gov/lead/pubs/trainerinstructions.htm* before October 4, 2011, they may become certified renovators by taking either the 4-hour RRP refresher or the 8-hour initial RRP course.

   c. Where the work is being done in a State or Tribal jurisdiction that has been authorized by the EPA to operate an RRP training and certification program, the one-day RRP course and half-day RRP refresher course must be accredited by the State or Tribe. HUD will approve all one-day RRP courses accredited by EPA-authorized States or Tribes.

   d. The 4-hour RRP refresher course is not sufficient on its own to meet either the EPA or HUD training requirements.

2. **The certified renovation firm and the certified renovator must take additional precautions to protect residents from lead poisoning beyond those in EPA's RRP Rule.**

   a. Renovators must use lead-safe work practices in work exempt from the RRP Rule that:

      ✦ Disturbs between 2 and 6 square feet of paint per room, and so is above the LSHR's *de minimis* threshold but below the RRP's minor repair and maintenance activities threshold.

      Note: Window replacement, window sash replacement, and demolition of painted surface areas disturb more paint than the LSHR's de minimis threshold, even without a calculation of the paint area disturbed.

      ✦ Disturbs more than 10% of a component type with a small surface area (such as window sills, baseboards, and trim).

   b. **Not using HUD's three additional prohibited work practices**, in addition to not using EPA's three prohibited work practices (open flame burning or torching, heat guns above 1100 degrees F, and machine removal without HEPA vacuum attachment):

      ✦ Heat guns that char the paint even if operating at below 1100 degrees F.

      ✦ Dry sanding or dry scraping, except dry scraping in conjunction with heat guns or within 1 ft of electrical outlets.

      ✦ Paint stripping using a volatile stripper in a poorly ventilated space.

   c. **Taking additional measures to protect occupants** during longer interior hazard reduction activities: Temporarily relocating the occupants before and during longer interior hazard reduction activities to a suitable, decent, safe, and similarly accessible dwelling unit that does not have lead-based paint hazards. Temporary relocation is not required for shorter projects, where:

      ✦ The work is contained, completed in one period of 8-daytime hours, and does not create other safety, health or environmental hazards; or

      ✦ The work is completed within 5 calendar days, after each work day, the worksite and the area within 10 feet of the containment area are cleaned of visible dust and debris, and occupants have safe access to sleeping areas, and bathroom and kitchen facilities.

C. Additional Designated Party Responsibilities that may Affect the Renovator

On jobs covered by the HUD LSHR, the certified renovation firm and the certified renovator should know other requirements for the designated party that may affect their role on the project.

1. **Designated party must provide occupants with two notices, if the amount of work is above HUD's *de minimis* threshold:**

   a. NOTICE OF EVALUATION OR PRESUMPTION: This notice informs the occupants that paint has been evaluated to determine if it is LBP or that paint has been presumed to be LBP. The designated party must notify the occupants within 15 calendar days of receiving the evaluation report or making the presumption. The renovator should ask the client if he/she has made this notice. The owner may provide a copy of this notice to the renovator so the renovator knows where LBP is located.

b.   NOTICE OF HAZARD REDUCTION ACTIVITY: This notice describes the hazard reduction work that was completed, information on the location of any remaining LBP, the date of the notice, and the contact for occupants to get more information. The designated party must notify the occupants within 15 calendar days of completing the hazard reduction work. The renovator may be given a copy of this notice, or may be asked to prepare or distribute the notice for the owner as part of the renovator's work for the owner.

2.   **Depending on the type and amount of housing assistance provided, HUD generally requires that identified LBP hazards be treated.**

Treatments may include LBP hazard abatement, interim controls or ongoing LBP maintenance. Renovators should inquire if their contract with the owner requires them to perform lead hazard treatment tasks listed below. If so, all workers and supervisors must have the proper training and qualifications. Generally, interim controls include the following activities, which are required if the amount of work is above HUD's *de minimis* threshold; for work below the *de minimis* threshold, any deteriorated paint must be repaired, but the work need not be done using lead-safe work practices, although HUD strongly encourages their use:

a.   Deteriorated LBP must be stabilized. This means that physical defects in the substrate of a paint surface or component that is causing the deterioration of the surface or component must also be repaired.

b.   Friction surfaces that are abraded must be treated if there are lead dust hazards nearby.

c.   Friction points must be either eliminated or treated so the LBP is not subject to abrasion.

d.   Impact surfaces must be treated if the paint on an impact surface is damaged or otherwise deteriorated and the damage is caused by impact from a related building component (such as a door knob that knocks the wall or a door that rubs against its door frame).

e.   LBP must be protected from impact.

f.   Chewable LBP surfaces must be made inaccessible for chewing by children of less than six years of age if there is evidence that such a child has chewed on the painted surface.

g.   Horizontal surfaces that are rough, pitted, or porous must be covered with a smooth, cleanable covering or coating.

3.   **For certain types of HUD assistance, when a child known to have an environmental intervention blood lead level is present, the designated party must take additional steps to assess the situation and respond to potential lead hazards.**

An environmental intervention blood lead level (as of the publication if this edition of these *Guidelines*) is a confirmed reading in a child under 6 years old of 20 micrograms per deciliter of blood (20 µg/dL), or two readings of 15 to 19 µg/dL at least 3 months apart. For certain types of HUD assistance (tenant-based rental assistance, project-based rental assistance, public housing, and HUD-owned multi-family housing), the owner or designated party may ask the renovator to perform work in the unit to address specific lead hazards identified by an environmental investigation risk assessment. All persons participating in such work should have appropriate training and qualifications.

4. **The designated party must arrange for someone independent of the renovator to conduct a clearance examination, if the amount of work is above HUD's *de minimis* threshold:**

   a. A clearance examination includes a visual assessment at the end of the renovation work for deteriorated paint, dust, debris, paint chips or other residue; sampling of dust on interior floors, window sills and window troughs; submitting the dust samples to a laboratory for analysis for lead; interpreting the lab results, and preparing a clearance report. EPA also allows a clearance examination to be used instead of the post-cleaning verification, if the clearance examination is required by federal, state or local regulations or by the contract. The unit – or, where work is contained, just the work area and an area just outside the containment – must pass clearance, and must not have any remaining lead hazards. If clearance fails at either the visual assessment step or the dust testing step, cleaning has to be redone in the failed part of the work area. The failed part of the work area is the specific area that was tested, as well as any areas that were not tested, and any other areas that are being represented by the sampled area. For example:

      ✦ Just one bedroom was tested, because it was to represent all bedrooms in the housing unit; it failed. Therefore, all of the bedrooms in the unit have to be re-cleaned and re-cleared.

      ✦ In a large multi-family apartment building, if a percentage of units are tested in accordance with the HUD Guidelines, if any fail, all of the units except those that passed clearance have to be re-cleaned and re-cleared. (If there are patterns of just certain component types failing, just those component types need to be re-cleaned and re-cleared in the failed and untested units.)

   b. The person conducting the clearance examination must be both:

      ✦ A certified lead-based paint inspector, risk assessor, clearance examiner, or dust sampling technician, depending on the type of activity being performed. (Either the State or the EPA certifies this person, depending on whether or not the State the housing is in is authorized by EPA to certify people in the lead discipline.)

      ✦ Independent of the organization performing hazard reduction or maintenance activities. There is one exception, which is that designated party may use a qualified in-house employee to conduct clearance even if other in-house employees did the renovation work, but an in-house employee may not do both renovation and clearance.

D. **How to Find Out About Lead-Based Paint Requirements that Apply to Planned Work in Properties Receiving HUD Housing Assistance, such as Rehabilitation or Acquisition Assistance:**

Finding out whether the work is receiving federal housing assistance is important because failing to meet lead-based paint requirements could affect the continuation of the assistance. For each job, the renovation firm should find out whether:

✦ The housing receives financial assistance; and

✦ Any lead-based paint requirements apply to the work because of the assistance provided.

The renovation firm should take the following steps:

1. Ask the property owner if the property or the family receives any type of housing assistance, including low-interest loans, from a local, State, or Federal agency. If so:

    ✦ Find out the name of the agency, contact person, address and phone number. (See the list of types of agencies below.)

    ✦ Get a basic description of the type of assistance the property receives.

Note: You should be able to explain to the owner that there will be information about the work that you will need, and that you also need to check if there are any special requirements.

2. If you have any questions about the Federal or State lead-based paint requirements that apply to the work, contact the public agency administering the assistance and discuss the project with the program specialist or rehabilitation specialist working with the property. For example:

    ✦ Some types of public agencies administering housing assistance, such as rehabilitation or acquisition assistance, include:

        — State Housing Agency, Corporation or Authority

        — State Community Development Agency, Corporation or Authority

        — State Housing Finance Agency

        — City or County Housing Authority, Corporation or Authority

        — City or County Community Development Agency, Corporation or Authority

        — USDA Service Center – Rural Housing Programs

    ✦ Is the project considered lead abatement?

        — If so, what are the agency's abatement requirements?

        — If the project is not abatement, what are the agency's lead-based paint requirements for the project, and how should they be incorporated into the work write-up?

EPA's **Pre-Renovation Education (PRE) Regulation** (40 CFR 745, subpart E)

EPA's PRE home page can be accessed at: *http://www.epa.gov/lead/pubs/leadrenf.htm*. Section 406 of TSCA directed EPA to develop requirements for renovators to distribute a lead hazard information pamphlet to housing owners and occupants before conducting renovations in pre-1978 housing. The Lead Renovation, Repair and Painting (RRP) rule amends and supplements the 1999 PRE rule.

Since June 23, 2008, renovators have been required to distribute a lead hazard information pamphlet to the owners and administrators of child-occupied facilities before beginning renovations in these facilities. Renovators must also make renovation information available to the parents or guardians of children under age six that attend these facilities. As defined in the rule, child-occupied facilities are residential, public or commercial buildings built before 1978 where children under age six are present on a regular basis. Child care facilities and kindergarten and pre-kindergarten classrooms are examples of child-occupied facilities. Since December 22, 2008, contractors have had to use the new renovation-specific lead hazard information pamphlet, entitled *Renovate Right: Important Lead Hazard Information for Families, Child Care Providers and Schools*, to comply with these requirements. For more information, visit EPA's ***Renovation, Repair, and Painting web page***, or contact the **National Lead Information Center (NLIC)** at 1-800-424-LEAD [5323] to speak with an information specialist. If you are a hearing- or speech-impaired person, you may reach the above telephone number through TTY by calling the toll-free Federal Relay Service at 800-877-8339.

OSHA's Lead Regulations (29 CFR 1910.1025 and 29 CFR 1926.62)

OSHA's lead regulations are described at OSHA's main lead regulation web page at: ***http://www.osha.gov/SLTC/lead/***. **Note:** As of July 2012, 25 states, Puerto Rico and the Virgin Islands had **OSHA-approved State Plans** and had adopted their own standards and enforcement policies. For the most part, these States adopted standards to Federal OSHA's. However, some States have adopted different standards or have different enforcement policies.

OSHA has two lead standards, one for construction and one for general industry. The two standards complement each other; the first covers construction work (construction, alteration, repair, painting and/or decorating (29 CFR 1926.10, (a))), while the second covers work that is not construction work (such as maintenance work not related to construction) and that is not maritime work (i.e., shipyard, marine terminal, or longshoring work). Employers are responsible for determining which standard applies to their workers on a particular project. See Chapter 9, Worker Protection, for information on how the OSHA standards relate to the HUD and EPA lead regulations, and for HUD's recommendations on worker protection even for activities not covered by HUD or EPA regulations.

OSHA's **Lead in General Industry Standard** (29 CFR 1910.1025) covers the use of lead in general industry. This industry includes non-construction-related maintenance work, as well as lead smelting, manufacturing and the use of lead-based pigments contained in inks, paints and other solvents in addition to the manufacturing and recycling of lead batteries. A compliance advisor is available for the Lead in General Industry Standard at ***http://www.osha.gov/dts/osta/oshasoft/gilead.html***.

Maintenance work associated with construction, alteration or repair activities is covered by the Construction Standard (29 CFR 1926.62, subsection (a), as discussed below). Non-construction-related maintenance work (such as maintenance activities associated with operations, or if lead is a component of any product that workers make or use) is covered by the General Industry Standard (29 CFR 1910.1025(e)(3)(ii)(A)).Construction activities do not include routine cleaning and repainting (for example, minor surface preparation and repainting of rental apartments between tenants or at scheduled intervals) where there is insignificant damage, wear, or corrosion of existing lead-containing paint and coating or substrates. Maintenance activities covered by the General Industry Standard are those which involve making or keeping a structure, fixture, or foundation in proper condition in a routine, scheduled, or anticipated fashion.

OSHA's **Lead in Construction Standard** (29 CFR 1926.62) applies to all construction work where an employee may be occupationally exposed to lead. OSHA has published a 332-page booklet on this regulation (OSHA 3142-09R 2003), posted at ***http://www.osha.gov/Publications/osha3142.pdf***. OSHA has also posted an on-line interactive expert system (compliance advisor) on the Lead in Construction Standard at *http://www.dol.gov/elaws/oshalead.htm*.

The Lead in Construction Standard applies to any source or concentration of lead to which workers may be exposed as a result of construction work. OSHA standards are not limited to lead-based paint as defined by

HUD or EPA, or lead-containing paint as defined by or the Consumer Product Safety Commission (CPSC). Several letters of interpretation are accessible from OSHA's lead home page (*http://www.osha.gov/SLTC/lead/index.html#standards*) including a letter of interpretation dated July 18, 2003, posted at *http://www.osha.gov/pls/oshaweb/owadisp.show_document?p_table=INTERPRETATIONS&p_id=24601*, which states that Lead Check and Lead Alert spot test kits are not sufficient for an employer to rule out the possibility of employee exposure to lead.

OSHA's lead in construction standard applies to all construction work where an employee may be exposed to lead. All work related to construction, alteration, or repair, including painting and decorating, is included. Under this standard, construction includes, but is not limited to:

+ Demolition or salvage of structures where lead or materials containing lead are present;

+ Removal or encapsulation of materials containing lead;

+ New construction, alteration, repair, or renovation of structures, substrates, or portions or materials containing lead;

+ Installation of products containing lead;

+ Lead contamination from emergency cleanup;

+ Transportation, disposal, storage, or containment of lead or materials containing lead where construction activities are performed; and

+ Maintenance operations associated with these construction activities.

Construction work is defined as work for construction, alteration and/or repair, including painting and decorating. All construction work with the potential for lead exposures excluded from coverage in the general industry standard for lead by 29 CFR 1910.1025(a)(2) is covered by the lead in construction standard. The construction standard establishes maximum limits of exposure to lead for all workers covered, including a permissible exposure limit (PEL) and action level (AL). The PEL sets the maximum worker exposure to lead: 50 micrograms of lead per cubic meter of air (50 $\mu g/m^3$) averaged over an eight-hour period. If employees are exposed to lead for more than eight hours in a workday, their allowable exposure as a TWA for that day must be reduced according to this formula:

Employee exposure (in $\mu g/m^3$) = 400 divided by the hours worked in the day.

The Action Level, regardless of respirator use, is an airborne concentration of 30 $\mu g/m^3$, averaged over an eight-hour period. The Action Level is the level at which an employer must begin specific compliance activities outlined in the standard. Additional compliance activities are required when the exposure exceeds the PEL.

Employers of construction workers are responsible for developing and implementing a worker protection program. At a minimum, the employer's worker protection program for employees exposed to lead must address those requirements that apply no matter what lead exposure is. As noted by OSHA in its 2003 informational booklet "Lead in Construction" (OSHA Publication 3142-09R; *http://www.osha.gov/Publications/osha3142.html* and *http://www.osha.gov/Publications/osha3142.pdf*.)

+ The employer must maintain any employee exposure and medical records to document ongoing employee exposure, medical monitoring, and medical removal of workers. This data provides a baseline to evaluate the employee's health properly. Employees or former employees, their designated representatives, and OSHA must have access to exposure and medical records in accordance with 29 CFR 1910.1020. Rules of agency practice and procedure governing OSHA access to employee medical records are found in 29 CFR 1913.10.

✦ If the initial assessment indicates that no employee is exposed above the AL, the employer may discontinue monitoring. Further exposure testing is not required unless there is a change in processes or controls that may result in additional employees being exposed to lead at or above the AL, or may result in employees already exposed at or above the AL being exposed above the PEL. The employer must keep a written record of the determination, including the date, location within the work site, and the name and social security number of each monitored employee.

In regard to an employee's exposure to lead in air being at or above the AL, certain compliance activities are required, including:

✦ For an employee exposed to lead on the job at or above the AL on any one day per year, the employer must make available, at no cost to the employee, initial medical surveillance.

✦ For an employee exposed to lead on the job at or above the AL for more than 30 days in any consecutive 12 months, the employer must make available, at no cost to the employee:

— A medical surveillance program with biological monitoring and provisions for medical removal:

✦ At least every two months for the first six months and every six months thereafter;

✦ At least every two months for employees whose last blood sampling and analysis indicated a blood lead level (BLL) at or above 40 µg/dL; and

✦ At least monthly while an employee is removed from exposure due an elevated BLL.

— An immediate medical consultation when the employee notifies the employer that the employee:

✦ Has developed signs or symptoms commonly associated with lead-related disease;

✦ Has demonstrated difficulty in breathing during respirator use or a fit test;

✦ Desires medical advice concerning the effects of past or current lead exposure on the employee's ability to have a healthy child; and

✦ Is under medical removal and has a medically appropriate need.

— Medical removal from work with an exposure at or above the AL when:

✦ A periodic and a follow-up blood sampling test indicate that the employee's BLL is at or above 50 µg/dL; or

✦ A final medical determination has been made that the employee has a detected medical condition which places the employee at increased risk of material impairment to health from exposure to lead.

The worker protection program must address additional requirements if the lead exposure to lead in air is above the PEL, including:

✦ Hazard determination, including exposure assessment, and notifying employees of results.

✦ Medical surveillance and provisions for medical removal.

✦ Job-specific compliance programs.

✦ Engineering and work practice controls.

✦ Respiratory protection.

✦ Protective clothing and equipment.

✦ Housekeeping.

✦ Hygiene facilities and practices.

✦ Signs.

✦ Employee information and training (Note: This training is different than HUD or EPA training. For more information, contact your OSHA regional office (*http://www.osha.gov/html/RAmap.html*).

✦ Recordkeeping.

For each job where employee exposure exceeds the PEL, the employer must establish and implement a written compliance program to reduce employee exposure to the PEL or below. The compliance program must provide for frequent and regular inspections of job sites, materials, and equipment by a competent person. Written programs, which must be reviewed and updated at least every six months, must include:

✦ A description of each activity in which lead is emitted (such as equipment used, material involved, controls in place, crew size, employee job responsibilities, operating procedures, and maintenance practices);

✦ The means to be used to achieve compliance and engineering plans and studies used to determine the engineering controls selected, where they are required;

✦ Information on the technology considered to meet the PEL;

✦ Air monitoring data that document the source of lead emissions;

✦ A detailed schedule for implementing the program, including copies of documentation (such as purchase orders for equipment, construction contracts);

✦ A work practice program;

✦ An administrative control schedule, if applicable; and

✦ Arrangements made among contractors on multi-contractor sites to inform employees of potential lead exposure.

Consumer Product Safety Commission Ban of Lead-Containing Paint and Lead in Consumer Products Used by Children (16 CFR Part 1303)

In 1978, the U.S. Consumer Product Safety Commission lowered the legal maximum lead content in most kinds of paint to 0.06% of the weight of the total nonvolatile content of the paint or the weight of the dried paint film (which paint and similar surface-coating materials are referred to as "lead-containing paint"). The Commission issued the 1978 ban because it found that there was an unreasonable risk of lead poisoning in children associated with lead content of over 0.06% in paints and coatings to which children have access and that no feasible consumer product safety standard under the Consumer Product Safety Act would adequately protect the public from this risk.

Under section 101(f) of the Consumer Product Safety Improvement Act of 2008 (Pub. L. 110–314; see 15 U.S.C. 2051 note, via the U.S. Code search website, *http://uscode.house.gov/search/criteria.shtml*), this amount was reduced to 0.009% (90 parts per million) in consumer products.

The CPSC also bans:

✦ Toys and other articles intended for use by children that bear "lead-containing paint".

✦ Furniture articles for consumer use that bear "lead-containing paint".

The CPSC lead regulation is posted at: *http://www.gpo.gov/fdsys/pkg/CFR-2011-title16-vol2/xml/ CFR-2011-title16-vol2-part1303.xml*.

For additional CPSC lead-related information, use the Find CPSC Product Safety Standards or Guidance search engine at: *http://www.cpsc.gov/cgi-bin/regs.aspx*.

National Park Service's regulations on Protection of Historic Properties (36 CFR Part 800)

The *National Historic Preservation Act of 1966 (NHPA)* requires Federal agencies to take into account the effects of their undertakings on historic properties, and give the *Advisory Council on Historic Preservation* a reasonable opportunity to comment. The historic preservation review process mandated by Section 106 of the Act is outlined in regulations issued by ACHP. Revised regulations, *"Protection of Historic Properties,"* became effective January 11, 2001, with amendments effective August 5, 2004; the current regulations, at 36 CFR Part 800, are posted at *http://www.gpo.gov/fdsys/pkg/CFR-2011-title36-vol3/ xml/CFR-2011-title36-vol3-part800.xml*, and summarized on the ACHP's web page at: *http://www.achp. gov/106summary.html*.

See Chapter 18, Lead Hazard and Historic Preservation, of these *Guidelines*, and the National Park Service's Preservation Brief 37, *Appropriate Methods for Reducing Lead-Paint Hazards in Historic Housing*, posted at *http://www.nps.gov/history/hps/tps/briefs/brief37.htm*, for further information and guidance on lead hazard evaluation and control considerations in historic properties.

In this chapter you will learn the following:

- Identify the rules governing contract and tort liability.
- Explain the relationship between the standard of reasonable care and applicable regulatory standards.
- Describe the nature of vicarious liability and the circumstances under which it may arise in lead abatement.
- Identify the elements of property damage and personal injury awards and their potential amounts.
- Compare/contrast the types of insurance applicable to lead abatement.

As a supervisor/contractor of a lead-abatement project, this section is important to you because you should understand:

- The dangers associated with a lead abatement project and the legal liability resulting from improper abatement;
- The importance of the contract documents as a guide to the conduct of a safe abatement project.

I. LEGAL LIABILITY

The material that follows is intended to introduce lead abatement contractors and consultants to the potential for legal liability arising out of abatement operations, and to suggest some precautions that may help reduce that potential.

Types of Potential Liability

"Liability" does not mean only one kind of financial obligation; it may refer to any of three different kinds:
- Criminal liability
- Regulatory liability, or
- Civil liability

Criminal liability would arise from violation of a statute, such as the National Emission Standards for Hazardous Air Pollutants (NESHAPS) standards of the Clean Air Act. Statutes impose criminal punishments for actions that disobey its provisions, such as intentionally discharging visible quantities of lead particulates into the atmosphere. Such statutes may impose fines or imprisonment or both. Public prosecutors enforce them through trials, usually involving juries, in which the guilt of the defendant must be proven beyond a reasonable doubt.

Regulatory liability is imposed through the operations of governmental regulatory agencies. Some regulatory agencies have very limited powers. Their authority may extend only to suspending or revoking a license they have previously granted. Others have broader powers and may be authorized to impose monetary penalties for violation of their regulations. Both EPA and OSHA have such authority. They can charge an offender with a violation of administrative regulations, hold a hearing before an agency hearing officer, and impose an administrative fine directly.

Civil liability differs from the other two in that it primarily arises out of controversies between private parties, and is imposed through lawsuits brought by private parties. Most of the rules that govern civil liability do not come from statutes passed by legislatures. They are, instead, derived from the written opinions of judges in previous cases--judicial precedents--that we call "The Common Law," a body of customs (some very ancient), that govern most of our interactions with one another. Sometimes, as we will see, a legislature will enact a statute that will modify an existing Common Law rule.

Civil liability arising out of lead abatement is most likely to arise under two sets of Common Law rules, those governing contracts and torts.

Contract Liability

A contract is a legally enforceable agreement. Typically, a contract involves a promise from one party to provide goods or services, and a promise by the other to pay a specified amount of money for them. If either party fails to live up to the promise, the other is entitled to recover the sum of money that will put him/her where he/she would have been if the defaulter had lived up to the promise. In the lead abatement context, that means if an abatement contractor fails to perform at the contract price, the building owner is entitled to hire another contractor of comparable skills at the lowest price reasonably obtainable (presumably higher than the contract price or there wouldn't be any controversy), and sue the nonperforming contractor for the difference between the contract price and the price actually paid.

The cost of the work may not be the only consequence of the first contractor's failure to perform. The contract may have specified when the work was to be done and failure to do it on time may cause problems. For example, a tenant might not be able to use rented space at a critical time. The defaulting contractor also would be liable for such consequential damages as the cost of renting other space for the tenant, or the loss of profits from business interruption.

Losses resulting from delays in completion are sometimes hard to prove with any precision. As a result, building owners sometimes require provisions in their lead abatement contracts specifying that the contractor who fails to meet a contractual deadline will pay an agreed sum of money for each day of delay—so called- "liquidated damages." If the sum named is a reasonable approximation of the actual losses the default would cause the building owner, the courts will enforce it. If, however, the amount named is grossly disproportionate to potential losses from the delay, the courts will deem it a "penalty" provision and refuse to enforce it.

Some contract controversies result from outright, intentional failure to perform. Most, however, result from disagreements between the parties about what the contract's terms mean. Such disputes arise either because the contract's words can be read to have two or more different meanings or because an important term has been left out.

Such problems can be reduced by careful reading and written clarification of the proposed contract before signing. Contractors should also include a standard set of clarifying "standard terms and conditions" in their bid proposals to eliminate the causes of the most common ambiguities. Arbitration clauses, binding the parties to a contract to accept quick, informal procedures for settling contract disputes if they arise, can greatly reduce the cost of resolving them.

Tort Liability

"Tort" comes from the French word meaning "wrong." In English, it is defined as a "civil wrong for which the law provides a remedy of money damages." Judicial precedents have established that a tort consists of three elements, all of which must be present, before there is a tort:

- First, the courts must previously have defined a "duty" or rule of conduct;
- Second, there must have been breach of the duty; and,
- Third, the breach must have caused an injury or damage to the person bringing the complaint.

The duty that underlies tort liability in connection with lead abatement is called the "duty of reasonable care" or of "due care." The courts say that each of us owes others a duty to conduct him or herself as a reasonable person would, under the circumstances, to avoid accidental injury to others. Breach of that duty is called "negligence."

The important words are "reasonable" and "under the circumstances." Remember that the first test is what a <u>reasonable</u> person would do, not what an average person or the majority of all people would do. And, second, remember that as the circumstances change, the duty changes.

The answer to that question is a disappointing "usually." The Common Law rule is that compliance with a regulatory standard equals reasonable care under normal circumstances. When there are unusual circumstances, the standard of care may require behavior that is more restrictive, more careful, than what the regulation would normally require. For example, a motorist driving along an uncongested highway under normal conditions of dry road and unrestricted visibility, who complies with the posted speed limit (the regulatory standard) is exercising reasonable care. Unusual conditions, such as bad weather or an accident blocking the road, may require the motorist exercising reasonable care to go at a much lower speed.

State-of-the-Art Defense

Whether an action was reasonable under particular circumstances is normally a question of fact to be decided by the jury. However, once a defendant has proven that he relied on a particular precaution based on the most advanced technical knowledge available at a given time or used the most advanced technology available at that time to create a safe condition, the defendant can assert as a matter of law, outside the jury's consideration, that he was not negligent. This is called the "state-of-the-art defense."

In some circumstances, different levels of precaution may be permissible under the regulations (as when air samples indicate a low enough level of air-borne contamination to allow a choice among alternative types of respirators), even though there is a threat of higher levels to come. However, there is some chance reasonable people might differ about which level of protection was appropriate under those circumstances. The possibility of being able to invoke the state-of-the-art defense in future litigation may be a strong argument in favor of using more extensive protection that the regulations might otherwise require.

Anticipatory Injury

Recall that the third necessary element of a tort is that failure to exercise reasonable care must cause **injury**. Differences have developed among the states as to what constitutes injury when a slow-acting toxic or hazardous material is involved.

When a pedestrian walks down the sidewalk, he or she is under a legal duty to exercise the care of a reasonable pedestrian, so as not to heedlessly knock others down. At the end of the block, when that pedestrian gets into an automobile and drives away, the same person comes under a new set of obligations to exercise the care of a reasonable automobile driver, knowing and obeying all the rules of the road and using the skills necessary to operate the controls.

As the foregoing suggests, different categories of people, such as building owners, lead abatement contractors, and lead abatement consultants, will be held to different standards of care under the Common Law. Normally we would expect the Common Law to impose the least onerous standard on the building owner (a layman); a higher standard on the contractor because he/she is a specialist, being paid for his/her specialized services; and a higher standard still on the consultant, because he/she sells advice based on his/her specialized knowledge. This is an area, however, where a legislature has modified the Common Law.

Several States provide that building owners will be held liable for injuries resulting from lead paint in buildings where young children reside, whether or not they are aware that lead is present. This is a form of strict liability, that is, liability imposed even though the building owner's conduct may have been reasonable under the circumstances. The Massachusetts law goes even further. It provides that if the building owner did know that lead paint was present and failed to take the required remedial action, that owner will be liable for three times the amount of any compensatory damages awarded.

Regulatory Standards and the Standard of Due Care

Consider the relationship between the standard of behavior that is imposed by the standard of reasonable care, and the standards that are mandated by applicable administrative regulations. Put the question: when a contractor or inspector has lived up to all of the regulations imposed on lead abatement by federal, state, and municipal regulations, has he/she, by doing so, automatically exercised reasonable care?

Some states, such as Massachusetts, take the position that there is no "injury" until there are sufficient symptoms to enable a physician to diagnose damage or disease. In those states, there is, therefore, no tort until the diagnosis can be made.

In California, Mississippi, Louisiana, Texas, and Maine the courts have taken the position that the injury and the tort take place at the moment the human cell is exposed to the harmful substance (even though it may take decades for the symptoms to appear), if there is a high probability persons exposed will eventually become sick (especially where the exposed person suffers mental distress from fear of the high probability of the impending illness). New Jersey formerly took this position, but later changed to the Massachusetts view. Most states have not yet ruled on the question.

Vicarious Liability

Our discussion, up to this point, has concerned an individual's liability for his own torts. Next, consider the circumstances in which a person, or organization, that has done nothing wrong may be liable for someone else's torts because of the nature of the relationship with the wrongdoer. This liability for the actions of others is called "vicarious liability."

In its simplest form it is expressed in two parts. The first is: "The master is liable for the torts of the servants provided these torts take place in the course of the servants' duties." Notice two things about this first part. The master is liable no matter how careful he/she has been in the selection, training, and supervision of the servant, for torts in the line of duty. However, the master is not liable for actions taken by the servant when the servant was off-duty, engaged in his/her own amusements.

The second part of the rule is: "The master is not liable for torts of his/her independent contractors provided that the master has exercised reasonable care in the selection of the contractors." Notice that the two parts of the rule are not symmetrical. Reasonable care in choosing whose services to use protects the master against liability for the independent contractor's tort but not for the servant's.

Subcontractors and other suppliers of services to a lead abatement contractor or consultant (such as test laboratories) normally would be considered independent contractors within the meaning of this rule. For that reason, before deciding to use the services of a possible subcontractor or supplier, ask others about the company's reputation and check out references, emphasizing the issue of safety. **Keep records** of whom you spoke to and what was said so that at some time in the remote future you would be able to show that you used reasonable care in the selection process.

Damages

"Damages" is the legal term for the amount of money the plaintiff is seeking to recover. They may be awarded for damage to property or for personal injury. They may be "compensatory" or "punitive." Consider first compensatory damages.

Property damage during lead abatement may be the result of such traditional problems as leakage or water damage caused by the work. The damages unique to lead abatement will be those for contamination of property by the abatement process itself because of accidental failure of containment enclosures, decontamination procedures, or the like.

The measure of damages for property damage claims is the difference in value of the property before and after the damage. Usually the court will consider the cost of repairing or cleaning up contamination as the best indication of the loss in value.

Damages for **personal injury** consist of payments for medical bills, lost earnings, and an amount representing the dollar value of pain and suffering. The claimant must collect all damages for a single tort from a single wrongdoer at one time. Therefore, the recovery will include not only damages up to the time of trial, but also for the estimated future duration of the injury.

Punitive damages are allowed under the Common Law of most states when the damages have resulted not from an accidental failure to exercise reasonable care, but from conduct that was grossly negligent, wanton, or reckless. Massachusetts has been foremost among the states that have not allowed punitive damages (but review the earlier discussion of the Massachusetts statutory provision imposing treble (triple) damages on property owners who are aware of the presence of lead but fail to abate it).

Punitive damage awards are supposed to punish the wrongdoer for egregious behavior or deter him/her or others from repeating such conduct. As of the writing of these materials, the United States Supreme Court was considering whether punitive damages should be prohibited as an unconstitutional taking of property.

Recent damage awards in personal injury cases may be a guide to possible future recoveries. A successful plaintiff in an anticipatory injury jurisdiction, having no symptoms of injury or disease but a high probability of developing future asbestos-related considers, has recovered in excess of $1 million. Persons badly injured, resulting in total disability and severe pain and suffering, routinely recover between $6 million and $10 million. Punitive damage awards against major corporations have reached $100 million several times.

Likely Sources of Liability

Building owners, seeking to recover the cost of lead removal, have sued lead pigment manufacturers for failure to warn of the products' hazards. Tenants, alleging injury, have sued building owners for negligent failure to remove lead. So far, lead removal contractors and consultants have not been the targets of large-scale civil litigation. However, the following are a few of the circumstances most likely to give rise to future litigation involving them.

Contractor:

- Allowing workers to leave the work space without decontaminating themselves;
- Failure to maintain containment enclosure integrity;
- Inadequate attention to completion-of-work criteria on jobs where building owners do not have professional representatives to work;
- Worker misconduct arising out of abuse of alcohol or drugs on the job.

Consultants:

- Failing to identify lead paint during inspection; failing to inspect portions of the building because of misunderstanding or

231

inaccessibility at time of inspection; failure to maintain state-of-the-art knowledge of changing scientific information, testing technology or regulatory standards; failure to exercise due care in assisting the building owner to select deleading contractors; failure to exercise stop-work authority in the presence of defective contractor performance when serving as building owner's representative.

II. INSURANCE CONSIDERATIONS

Liability insurance is typically a job requirement for performance of lead abatement work on federal, state, municipal, and public school projects. Also, in nearly every state, the law requires virtually all employers to carry Workers' Compensation insurance to cover possible injury claims by their employees. Even in the absence of these requirements, prudent business judgment suggests that liability insurance is an important safeguard for any business in which there is a significant risk of very large personal injury claims.

The material that follows is intended as a guide to help understand the forms of liability insurance that are available for contractors and consultants engaged in lead abatement, to help obtain such insurance, and to help understand the language of insurance requirements as they appear in abatement project specifications.

Disclaimer

The information about insurers and insurance that follows is provided subject to three qualifications. First, by describing these insurance programs and the considerations to bear in mind when evaluating them, the author and the sponsors of any training program in which these course materials may be used do not mean to endorse the insurers or brokers named or to recommend any one of them over the others. Different insurers will present different advantages and disadvantages, including different levels of financial reliability, and choosing among them will be a business decision in which the buyer must exercise an independent judgment. Second, these programs are in the process of evolving. Their conditions, prices and organizational framework are likely to change from those summarized in these materials. Third, the information is presented as it was furnished by the insurance programs themselves and has not been independently verified.

Types of Liability Insurance

Contractors must carry workers' compensation insurance and need to consider comprehensive general liability insurance. Consultants will have these same concerns as well as an interest in professional errors and omissions liability insurance. Contractors carrying out very large-scale deleading projects may be asked to provide "Builders' Risk" insurance. Each type is discussed below.

a)   Workers' Compensation Insurance

Every state now has some form of statutory administrative compensation system replacing the tort-based liability system previously discussed. These systems provide no-fault compensation to employees injured in the course of their work, without requiring them to prove that they were hurt as a result of their employer's negligence. Typically, they pay for medical expenses and lost wages, but do not provide compensation for pain and suffering. They are designed to provide faster and more certain payments than the tort system. In many states, the remedy they provide is exclusive. In others, employees may be allowed to elect a tort recovery under prescribed circumstances.

In all states, employers are required to take part in the system by carrying workers' compensation insurance. Generally, the policy wording and the amount of coverage to be carried are prescribed by regulation. Premiums are set by a quasi-regulatory process. In addition, all insurance companies wishing to sell workers' compensation to employers are obliged to take part in an insurance pool that will make workers' compensation insurance available to every employer at a regulated price.

b)   Comprehensive General Liability Insurance

This insurance may also be called "commercial general liability" or just "general liability" insurance or even by the initials "CGL." It is the standard insurance for protecting the policyholder-company against any claims against it for personal injury or property damage caused, by accident, to persons outside the company. Typically, it will defend the policyholder from claims by "third-parties" (persons other than the policyholder or the policyholder's employees) and pay any judgment in favor of a third party subject to the terms and conditions of the policy and its deductible. The maximum amount the insurer will pay is governed by the "limits" set forth in the policy.

Since 1973, nearly all CGL policies have contained exclusions for liability from gradually released pollution or contamination. Since 1983, the pollution exclusion has typically included all coverage for pollution-related claims. Lead particulates released in the course of lead abatement would come within this pollution exclusion and therefore not be covered by a standard CGL policy.

Persons engaged in lead abatement share a concern that they may become liable to claims arising out of negligence resulting in the release of lead-containing materials that later cause injury to building occupants. They have sought insurance that would protect against this risk. The appendix of this section, titled "Insurance Carriers for the Lead Abatement Industry", identifies a number of insurance programs that currently provide specialized CGL policies that are designed to meet this need. They extend coverage to include pollution-related claims resulting from lead abatement activities by partially or totally eliminating the pollution exclusion.

Nearly all CGL policies contain another standard exclusion for liability for claims arising out of errors or omissions in providing "professional services" the so-called "E & O" exclusion. Professional services are those services provided by specialists who are qualified to provide them by extensive training usually, but not always, academic training. Doctors, lawyers, architects, and engineers are examples of persons whose services are considered "professional" within the meaning of the E & O exclusion. Lead abatement consultants, such as industrial hygienists, inspectors, designers, and project monitors, also come within it.

Note that the E & O exclusion is narrow. It only excludes the professional act itself, usually the giving of advice or the preparation of designs. It means that although an inspector who drops a flashlight on a passing tenant will be covered by the CGL policy, the inspector who fails to identify lead-containing materials, or the architect who designs a defective containment scaffold that collapses, will not be. From the viewpoint of the lead abatement contractor, the important thing to remember is that the CGL policy will protect from accidents that arise during the performance of the contract but will not protect from claims that result from his/her giving advice on lead abatement.

c) Professional Liability Errors and Omissions Insurance

Tort law imposes a higher standard of care on experts than it does on laymen. Insurance companies, therefore, treat expert professionals as a separate category for insurance purposes. Persons who make a profession of giving advice based on specialized knowledge are insured under policies called "professional liability errors and omissions insurance." Such coverage exists in more or less specialized forms for physicians, lawyers, architects and engineers, and consultants carrying out inspection, design, and project monitoring on lead abatement projects.

Specialized E & O coverage for lead abatement professionals is provided by approximately half of the companies identified in the appendix "Insurance Carriers for the Lead Abatement Industry."

d) Builders' Risk Insurance

Builders' Risk insurance is described here because, very rarely, it will be required of lead abatement contractors by building owners.

It is a specialized form of property insurance designed for insuring large buildings while they are under construction and under the control of a general contractor. It is intended to cover such risks as loss by fire before the building owner takes possession. Once the building owner takes possession, the owner normally insures the building against damage through conventional property insurance.

In some cases, the basic Builders' Risk policy is augmented by a very narrow additional coverage. This is specialized liability insurance covering only damage to other property caused by the insured building. An example is damage to automobiles parked on a neighbor's parking lot caused by a collapsing structure. In such cases the augmented insurance is called "All Builders' Risk" insurance.

It is not well adapted for lead abatement applications, because in most lead abatement projects the building owner never gives up over-all control of the building to the contractor and the building owner's property insurance stays in effect. Requiring the contractor to carry Builders' Risk insurance under such circumstances is only paying twice for the same coverage. Furthermore, if the lead abatement activity accidentally causes damage to either the structure or adjacent property, in nearly every case the contractor's CGL insurance would cover such damage. Finally, standard Builder's Risk and All Builders' Risk policies include pollution exclusions that would eliminate coverage for damage caused by lead particulates. Obtaining a one-of-a-kind, custom-built policy that includes lead pollution coverage, if possible, would be extremely expensive.

Considerations When Purchasing Insurance

- Policy Form: Occurrence-Based or Claims-Made?

Liability insurance is written in two different ways, using so-called "occurrence-based" or "claims-made" forms. Recent insurance practices have blurred some of the differences between the two standard forms; we will consider them first in their pure states, and then discuss the ways in which the distinctions are being blurred.

In modern insurance terminology, an accident is called an "occurrence." An occurrence-based policy is one that covers claims resulting from an occurrence that happens during the term of the policy (the usual policy term is one year), regardless of how long it takes for the claims to be made. On a pure occurrence-based policy, it does not matter that the policy may have expired decades before the claim finally arises so long as the accident on which the claim is based happened during the policy term.

A claims-made policy, on the other hand, is not concerned with when the accident happened. It covers any claim that is made during the policy term without regard to when the occurrence that led to the claim took place. It will cover even a claim that results from an accident that took place before the policyholder had any insurance. Its main drawback is that the policyholder must have a claims-made policy in effect when the claim arrives to have coverage. If the policy has been canceled or been allowed to expire sometime after the accident but before the claim comes in, the policyholder has no insurance.

As suggested above, current trends have blurred the differences between the two-traditional forms. Many, but not all, occurrence-based forms today include "sunset" clauses. A sunset clause says that the policy will respond only if the claim is made within a specified time after the policy's expiration date (usually five years but sometimes shorter). A corresponding provision on nearly all claims-made policies, called a "retroactive' or "retro-date," says that the policy will not cover claims resulting from occurrences that happened more than a specified number of years before the inception date of the policy, or even before the inception date itself.

Persons buying insurance should be aware that insurance companies may be willing to modify policy wording to make a sale. Don't be afraid to negotiate. Some occurrence-based insurers will usually be willing to push a policy's retro-date back to a date before the policyholder started lead abatement work, so as to make sure there will be coverage for all claims arising out of the insured's lead abatement activities.

One recent change is helpful to policyholders. Some claims-made insurers now offer so-called "extended discovery periods." These allow a policyholder who is retiring or ceasing to do lead abatement work to purchase, for a modest additional premium, an extension of time in which to file claims that would have been covered by the expiring policy but for the fact they came in after it had expired. Extended discovery periods of one year are common; five-year and even ten-year periods have been offered but are not common.

- Financial Reliability of Insurers

Purchasers of insurance need to take into account the possibility that the company offering to sell insurance might go out of business or be unable to pay a future claim because of insolvency. In evaluating the financial reliability of an insurance company, consider three major classifications:

companies closely regulated by state insurance commissioners,

companies unregulated but annually evaluated by commercial financial evaluation services, and unregulated organizations offering forms of collective self-insurance that are not evaluated by the commercial services.

A closely regulated insurance company that:

- submits its policy wording and price schedules for approval by a state's insurance commissioner,
- maintains the high financial reserves specified by the insurance commissioner, and
- allows the insurance commissioner to audit the company's financial records to confirm that the reserves meet the standard,

is called an "admitted" insurance company. Most states have laws providing that, if any admitted company cannot pay its policy holders for lack of funds, the other admitted insurance companies have to help pay the policyholders of the insolvent company. Only one of the insurance companies active in providing pollution liability coverage to contractors and consultants doing lead abatement work has become an admitted company.

Most of the companies offering lead abatement liability insurance are in a second category known as "approved but not admitted" or "excess and surplus lines" insurance companies. They are essentially unregulated. Companies in this category range from very large (larger than most admitted companies), to very small, new undercapitalized companies with little experience, or with known financial troubles.
Persons considering purchasing from companies in this latter category should first consult one of the various commercial evaluation services that publish annual reports on all insurance companies selling to the public, and have been in business for more than five years. These services, of which:

- A.M. Best,
- Dun & Bradstreet, and
- Moody's

are the most widely known, are subscribed to by insurance brokers and, through them are free to potential policyholders. These services report on the balance sheet, profit and loss statement, reserves, claims-history, and management of each listed company and describe the relative financial strength of listed companies through a letter code. In the case of Best's, for example, the code is A+, A, A-, B+, . . . etc.

The third category of insurers is insurance programs in which the financial reserves have been provided by the policyholders themselves. Called "risk retention groups" or "group captive insurance," these are various forms of collective self-insurance, in which policyholders have organized an insurance program, perhaps making capital contributions at the time of joining, and rely on these and the accumulated annual premiums to pay potential claims. Group self-insurance is encouraged under the laws of some states like Kentucky, Colorado, and Vermont. It is prohibited under the laws of others, like Connecticut. A federal law, the Federal Risk Retention Act, provides that a policyholder may participate in such a program, even if prohibited in the policyholder's own state, so long as the program is legal under the laws of the state in which it is organized. Group captive insurance programs are not regulated by the states in which they operate, nor evaluated by the commercial rating services. Applicants of such programs receive information from financial data provided by the programs themselves.

As the above information indicates, potential policyholders should be aware of the distinctions among the three categories of insurers. Policyholders may reduce the likelihood of using an unreliable insurance company by buying from an admitted carrier, by checking the financial strength of an approved but not admitted carrier through one of the commercial evaluating service directories, or by themselves evaluating financial data from, and reputations of participants in, a risk retention group.

- Limits

Insurance policies state under the "limits" heading the amount of coverage they provide. Most define limits in two ways: the amount to be paid for any one claim and the total amount to be paid for multiple smaller claims. Sometimes the per-claim limit and the multiple-claim limit will be two or three times greater than the per claim limit, e.g., "$1 million per claim, $2 million aggregate in any one year for multiple claims." Some of the existing programs have arranged for $5 million to $10 million of optional additional coverage through other insurance companies. This will be described as available "excess limits" or "umbrella" coverage.

If you are considering participating in a group captive program, be aware that such programs' limits may be administered in two different ways. Some are organized so that their full stated limits are available to each member. Others, however, are set up so that the state limits apply to the group as a whole. They are administered on a first-come, first-served basis, so the policy holder who does not make a claim until after an earlier claim has been paid may find the group's limits already have been exhausted before reaching his claim.

- Price and Minimum Premium

Commercial liability insurance premiums are usually paid at the beginning of the policy year and priced as a percentage of the insured's estimated gross annual lead abatement revenues. At the end of the year, if the insured has grossed more than originally estimated, an additional payment must be made, at the agreed rate, to cover the excess of actual, over estimate, revenues. Conversely, if actual revenues are below the estimate, the insurance company will refund the agreed percentage of the shortfall. However, the insurer limits the extent of such a refund by specifying a minimum premium for each policyholder.

In recent years, the rates for large policyholders with annual sales in excess of $1 million have been around three percent, with minimums around $27,000. Smaller firms, with sales of $200,000 or less, may pay eight to twelve percent but receive minimums as low as $5,000. Group captive programs tend to charge lower rates but may require large initial capital contributions of their members, and may make members liable for an additional assessment equal to the annual premium if the group's funds are ever inadequate to pay a member's claim.

- Policy Term

The typical policy extends for a one-year term. Companies sometimes offer longer terms of up to three years. Occasionally, a company may offer a policy only for the duration of the job. This is undesirable with claims-made policies but acceptable with occurrence-based ones. Other companies may insure for one-year terms, but require the insured to list all projects to be covered and to notify the insurer before adding each job.

Insurance companies typically require the insured to pay the first portion of any claim (the "deductible" or "self-insured retention") in order to motivate policyholders to operate effective loss-prevention programs. The insurance company will charge lower premiums for higher deductibles, but will not wish a policyholder to assume so large a deductible that the insured would be unable to afford a loss prevention program if it had to pay its full deductible.

Bonding

The term "bonding" is used to describe three kinds of security procedures used in connection with construction-related projects such as abatement:

- bid bonds,
- payment bonds, and
- performance bonds.

All three involve promises by bonding companies to pay sums of money to, or do something for, an "obligee" in the event the company buying the bond, "the obligor," fails to live up to an agreement.

A **bid bond** accompanies a promise by a bidder to pay some percentage of the cost of the job to the building owner if the low bidder decides, after winning the bid, not to accept the work.

A **payment bond** accompanies a prime contractor's promise to pay the subcontractors and will pay them if he/she fails to do so after being paid by the building owner.

A **performance bond** is a promise to complete, or arrange for completion of, a job if the contractor has not performed all the terms of the contract to the satisfaction of the building owner. Most public agencies, including school districts, are required by law to buy performance bonds in order to protect themselves from the possibility that their contractors on a deleading project will be financially unable to complete the project, or that a dispute will arise whether all the terms of the contract have been satisfied.

Unlike an insurance company, a bonding company is not in business to assume risk. It charges a modest percentage of the value of a project for its services, 2%-3%, for example. It provides an administrative convenience for the obligee. The bonding company will not issue the bond until it has satisfied itself that if the bond is called, the bonding company will be able to foreclose on easily available assets to reimburse itself for its costs. For a large contracting company, just indicating what bank handles its payroll account will be adequate security for the bonding company. For small contractors, satisfying the bonding company may be more difficult. It may be necessary to post collateral in order to obtain a bond. Like liability insurers, bonding companies must be admitted to write in each state by its insurance commissioner. Most companies are admitted in some states but not in others.

Brokers
Most insurance brokers deal in standard forms of insurance coverage such as:

- life insurance,
- homeowners insurance, and
- automobile insurance.

When they need specialized forms of insurance for their customers they obtain it through brokers who are in the business of handling such coverage. These are called "excess and surplus lines" or "E & S" brokers.

Chapter 15 - PROJECT MANAGEMENT

In this chapter you will learn about:

- Management Overview
- Contract Specifications
- Supervisory Skills
- Record Keeping Books

OBJECTIVES AND LEARNING TASKS

Are presented on separate pages at the beginning of each sub-section.

THE ABATEMENT PROCESS

A lead-abatement project (paint, dust, or soil abatement) is a complex task because of the hazards associated with handling a toxic material. It is made more complex if the work is performed within the residential community. The material being abated is often near to occupied residences; or, in many cases, within the homes. Because of this, there is the potential to:

- Disrupt the lives of individuals and families;
- Contaminate the environment with lead;
- Raise the exposure level higher than that which existed prior to the abatement.

The risk is of greater concern if children are present, because children are more likely to ingest lead-contaminated dust and their developing bodies are more susceptible to effects of lead. (The relative risk of children vs. adults is covered in other sections of this manual.)

Additionally, if soil abatement is carried out in the residential community, the residents of that community have the potential for increased exposure during the abatement activities or, at a minimum, are somewhat inconvenienced by the abatement activities. These factors make it necessary to inform and advise the residents of the nature of the work and the necessary precautions.

It is necessary for those who perform or are associated with lead abatement to take special precautions and to plan adequately. In order to ensure that this process is safe with the least amount of disruption, a diverse group of individuals and organizations may be involved depending on the size and scope of the project.

PARTICIPANTS

One individual may serve in several of these roles depending on the size of the project. The abatement process in a large project may require the involvements of the following individuals and groups:

1. The Project Owner

The owner has the ultimate responsibility for the abatement process. This includes not only the initiation and the completion of the abatement, but also any resultant liability from increased exposure to lead or injuries which may occur during the abatement process. Because of this responsibility, the owner must be involved in the abatement process. This involvement must include the periodic monitoring of the abatement. The owner is also responsible for the cost of the abatement and must provide funding for the entire project.

2. The Project Manager

The project manager has the responsibility for the abatement process. This begins with the planning of the project, continues with the abatement process, and finally the successful conclusion of the abatement. Because of this responsibility, the project manager must have access to all parties involved in the abatement, including the owner. The manager must also have the authority to shut down the project.

3. The Project Consultant, Designer, Architect or Engineer

The consultant, designer, architect, or engineer has the responsibility for planning the details of the abatement project and providing technical guidance through the execution of the abatement plan. This member of the team must be familiar with all aspects of lead abatement to recommend the most cost-effective method of abatement. The consultant, designer, architect, or engineer must also have the authority to shut down the project.

4. The Abatement Contractor

The abatement contractor has the responsibility for the successful execution of the abatement plan. This includes providing material, supplies, and labor to successfully complete the project. The contractor must have access to enough well-trained abatement workers to complete the project on schedule.

5. The Abatement Supervisor

The abatement supervisor is the individual who has the responsibility for the conduct of the activities on the abatement site including the scheduling of workers and material. The abatement supervisor should be able to read and

implement an abatement plan designed by the project consultant, architect, or engineer. He/she should be able to understand applicable federal, state and local regulations. This person may sometimes be called the superintendent.

6. The Abatement Workers

The abatement workers are responsible for accomplishing the work designated by others on the abatement site. Workers must be well-trained in abatement techniques and be knowledgeable of routes of exposure.

7. Legal Counsel

Legal counsel has the responsibility for addressing the legal issues associated with the abatement process including liability issues along with guidance regarding the abatement contracts. In order to meet this responsibility, the legal counsel must be familiar with issues and regulations relevant to lead abatement. Legal counsel must keep the owner informed about legal aspects of the project. Legal counsel is often needed for cases involving a child with an elevated blood lead.

8. Environmental Consultant/Inspector

The environmental consultant and/or the inspector have the responsibility for maintaining a safe environment for both workers and any others who come into contact with the abatement process. The environmental consultant and/or the inspector also have responsibility for the inspections and making sure that clearance criteria have been met. Environmental consultant and inspectors may be part of an environmental consulting firm or they may be employed by a public agency.

9. Regulatory Authority and OSHA

The regulatory authority is that branch of the local, state, or federal government associated with licensing abatement contractors, abatement workers, or environmental consultants where such legislation exists. OSHA is the legal authority responsible for worker safety. As the agency responsible for worker safety, OSHA has the authority to levy fines and use other means to force compliance with regulations.

10. The Occupational Health Facility

The occupational health facility is the health organization responsible for worker health. Because blood monitoring or medical monitoring is a part of the project, it is the occupational health facility that is responsible for this section of the

abatement plan. The physicians and staff of the occupational health facility should be familiar with lead issues and exposure.

11. Environmental Testing Lab

The environmental testing lab is the facility responsible for providing the analysis of wipe tests and other environmental samples taken during the abatement project. These environmental samples (air, wipes, etc.) are tested for lead content.

12. The Disposal Facility

The disposal facility is that entity responsible for accepting the hazardous and/or non hazardous waste generated by the abatement process.

11. Occupants

The owners and the residents of an abatement site must be considered as participants in the abatement process. It is necessary to have both the participation and cooperation of the occupants in order to achieve a successful abatement. This is a complex process for large multi-family projects. For single-family abatement projects, the process is much easier, but just as important.

ABATEMENT STEPS

Just as there are many participants, there are also many steps required to complete the abatement process. Clearly, the size of the project, whether it is a single family swelling or a multi-unit complex, will impact the process. Those steps are as follows:

1.   The Environmental Survey

The abatement process begins with the environmental survey. An environmental survey must be completed in order to determine the extent of the problem. This survey is done by a qualified lead inspector or by a team or teams of individuals who collect data on the location and quantity of lead on painted surfaces, in soil and dust, or in drinking water within the residential community or single-family home. Knowledge of the quantities of lead on surfaces and in the environment will provide the necessary information for other participants in the abatement project to proceed with adequate planning.

2. Assembling The Team

Following the environmental survey, the next step is to assemble the team. After adequate analysis of the extent of the lead problem, it is necessary for the owner to assemble the abatement team. The key member in the abatement process is the project manager. Because this individual must work with all of the other abatement team participants, it is necessary for the abatement manager to be brought on board early.

A successful abatement project requires the lines of authority and communication to be established and understood by all participants. In a single-family dwelling abatement, the team is more easily assembled. The owner would most likely hire a competent abatement contractor to handle the project.

3. Preparing An Abatement Plan

The next important step in the abatement process is the preparation of an abatement plan and the health and safety plan (see chapter on PPE). It is during this step that decisions are made about the bidding process, the selection of the contractor, the extent of abatement, the time line for abatement, the worker training needed, how the abatement will be accomplished, and the type and quantity of waste that may be generated. Care should be taken that the abatement plan is complete, and that it has some flexibility for altering direction if necessary during the abatement process.

4. Preparing The Community Relations Plan

Once the abatement plan has been completed and the contractor has been selected, the community relations plan should be established by staff whom are trained and skilled in this area. This is the plan by which the residents in the community are informed and brought into the abatement process. If working in a single-family home, the supervisor/contractor or owner may serve as the person who interacts with the residents and their neighbors, so it is important to understand the essential nature of this process. This part of the abatement process is covered separately in another section of this course. (Residents and organizations of the community should be informed of the lead abatement plans as soon as possible in the abatement processes.)

5.   Critical Path Planning

Those who are familiar with planning construction projects are also familiar with critical path planning. This is the planning process through which individual tasks necessary to complete a project are assessed to determine where and at

what time they fit into the overall time line of the project. Some parts of the project may require completion prior to the initiation of other parts of a project. Some tasks can go on concurrently with other tasks. It is necessary to determine where each task fits in relation to other tasks required in an abatement project. It is this assessment of the time of the individual tasks which determines the overall time line of a project.

6.   Site Characterization

Prior to beginning the actual abatement, each site would be surveyed in order to determine if unusual conditions exist;

- Develop a clear understanding of the abatement required;
- Establish necessary requirements for public safety and
    employee protection.

7.   Begin Abatement

Once personnel have been selected and adequately trained, the abatement plan has been completed, and the medical monitoring program has been put into effect, abatement can begin. It is during this time that the reliability of the plan and the participants are and, that changes can be readily made in the abatement process in order to successfully complete the project.

8.   Daily Cleanup

At the end of every workday, sufficient time should be set aside for cleanup. This cleanup should include dampening the debris with a garden sprayer and a gentle sweeping or vacuuming the floors. Removed components should be wrapped and stored appropriately. This daily cleanup reduces risk to workers and improves the possibility of passing final clearance.

9.   Initial Cleanup, Replacement, & Final Cleanup

Once the lead abatement activities have been completed, clean-up of dust and other debris should take place. After this initial clean up has been completed, the replacement of material removed during abatement such as trim, doors, windows, or soil (during a soil abatement project) takes place. Final clean-up occurs after the replacement, re-cleaning, and painting. Separation of the lead abatement, initial clean-up, and replacement phases allows the worker protection practices to be more specifically tailored to the expected exposures. For example, airborne lead concentrations during the replacement of doors, in a relatively clean environment, may be only slightly above outside air concentrations and are not expected to require respiratory protection.

This is the final step in the abatement process. Once abatement has been completed, either in a group of units or on a portion of a project, the technical success of the project can be tested by the wipe tests or other means of environmental sampling. It is not possible for an individual or families to return to their residences or homes until the clearance criteria for the project have been achieved. The clearance test is an important technical assessment of the success of the abatement project.

As stated earlier, a successful abatement project requires the complete participation of a variety of entities. It is necessary for all of those entities and individuals to work through a series of steps in order to complete the technical and social responsibilities of an abatement project.

CONTRACT SPECIFICATIONS

OBJECTIVE:

To present a comprehensive description of the nature of contract specifications.

LEARNING TASKS:

Supervisors/contractors should be able to:

- Explain the purpose of contract specifications.

- Name and describe at least three contract documents

- List three ways in which a contract protects the parties involved.

As a supervisor/contractor of a lead-abatement project, this section is important to you because:

- You may be required to read and interpret specifications of the job site;

- You should understand the nature of different types of

specifications so they may be interpreted appropriately;

- **You should understand that specifications are part of a legal document.**

CONTRACT SPECIFICATIONS

A contract can be defined as a legally enforceable agreement between two or more competent persons or parties.

Individuals make contracts every day. When trainees sign up for a training course at a university, those individuals are making a contract with the university. In that example, the party seeking the training agrees to pay a specified amount of money for a defined amount of training. The university, the other party in the contract, agrees to provide a specified amount of training for a fixed amount of money.

When a customer goes into a restaurant for lunch, he/she will enter into a contract with the restaurant for food service. The customer will agree to exchange money, in most cases, for food. In such a contract, which is established when purchasing food at a restaurant, the specifications are

always implied. The purchaser, when ordering the food implies that the cost of the food will be paid prior to receiving the food, at the time it is received, or after it has been consumed. The other party, the restaurant, agrees to provide a fixed amount of food and implies that the food is prepared properly and is safe to eat.

When entering into a contract involving larger amounts of money or value, implied contracts are generally not adequate and the parties involved often want to be more specific about the terms of the contract. In such a situation, the parties entering into the contract may choose to agree upon the terms of the contract in writing. This type of contract is called an *expressed contract* rather than an implied contract.

Expressed contracts can become very complex documents consisting of many parts. Most construction-type contracts will consist of the actual contract, along with other documents required by the contract such as a bid guarantee and contract bond, the general conditions of the contract, the general project specifications, and the construction drawings. All of these items are part of a package called the contract documents, defined as follows:

1. The formal contract identifies the parties involved, the time of the contract, the time and amount of payments, the penalties for breach of contract, the items which constitute breach of contract, and other minor issues.

2. The general conditions and specifications define the scope and performance criteria of the work.

3. The bid guarantee and contract bond specify the penalties imposed upon the bidder if he/she is the lowest qualified bidder and fails to enter into a contract or fails to complete the contract according to the agreed-upon terms.

What do contract documents accomplish?

- **Contract documents define the work.**

The contract documents define what, how much, when, and where the work will be performed. The contract documents also define responsibility. This includes responsibility for not only the contractor but also the owner and any other parties referred to in the contract. The contract documents define the sequence of work; i.e., where the contractor will begin, at what time the contractor will begin, the work which will be performed during the time specified in the contract, and when the work specified in the contract will be completed.

The contract also defines who the workers will be, what kind of training the workers will have, and the materials which will be used in the project.

- **Contract documents define standards.**

Some standards for lead abatement are set by Local, State, or Federal regulations. These are the minimum standards which apply. Often a project owner or architect will specify more-stringent standards.

The contract documents also define the standards to be used in the abatement project. Those standards could be in the form of minimum training for workers. Some construction contracts require all workers to be union workers, which implies that those workers will have completed an apprenticeship or some kind of training program and presumably are better qualified than other workers. Standards are also important for the materials which are used in the project. There are inexpensive materials which are not durable and expensive materials which generally are more durable than the cheap materials. The "standards" section of the contract defines the quality and quantity of materials going into a project.

In some cases, the contract specifications may omit or not reference one or more standards. If such a standard exists in the form of a regulatory standard or industry standard, the contractor should abide by that standard.

- **Contract documents define completion.**

The contract documents define when the work will end, not with a defined date, but with what is required to fulfill the requirements specified in the contract. For example, a person could enter into an agreement with another person to sand a new floor. The owner, or person contracting to have the floor sanded, could specify the work must be done within one day and the contractor could send a person to sand the floor for one day. But that effort might not achieve the goal desired or specified in the contract. The desired objective of the person hiring the contract, or might be, to have the floor sanded until the floor is ready for stain or varnish. A worker could easily sand the floor for eight hours with 400 grit sandpaper and achieve none of the desired results, yet could fulfill the requirement for completing the work within one day. If the objective is to have a smooth floor ready to stain or varnish, the specification in the contract might read that the floor must be sanded until the surface is uniform and ready for stain or varnish. It would then be up to the contractor to sand the floor, first with a rough grade of sandpaper and then with a medium or fine grade of sandpaper within the specified one-day time period.

- **Contract documents define costs and payments.**

The contract documents define the time and amount of the payments, one of the major purposes of those documents.

- **Contract documents are used for bidding.**

The contract documents are used for bidding purposes. For the purpose of competitive bidding, all bidders on a project must have a clear understanding of the scope and nature of the proposed work.

- **Contract documents are for protection.**

Contract documents function as a vehicle to protect the owner. This is achieved in two ways:

1. The contract documents provide for the enforcement of the contract. Without the specifications and general conditions, it would be very difficult to enforce the contract.

2. The protection afforded the owner, by the contract documents, includes protection from the errors, mistakes, and omissions of others.

The contract documents protect the workers, especially if there is a safety and health plan included as part of the contract documents.

- Contract documents also provide protection for the residents and the public.

- Contract documents provide information for permits.

- Lastly, the contract documents provide the ability for the contractor to obtain permits, if necessary, to accomplish the work specified in the contract.

What is the purpose of the contract as art of the contract documents?

The contract essentially drives the specifications. Without the contract there is no enforcement of the specifications. A contract could contain the most complete set of specifications in the world and yet be unenforceable because of flaws and inconsistencies in the contract.

What is the purpose of the specifications in a contract?

The specifications support the contract. Without adequate specifications, no one would know when the contract was completed, or when payments were to be made, or when there was a violation of the contract.

There are three types of specifications which are used in construction contracts:

1. Performance
2. Means and methods
3. A combination of means and methods and performance

Performance driven specifications are generally concerned with the end product. An example of this type of specification could be seen in a painting contract which specifies that the painter prep and coat the walls of a room with two coats of paint; the final product should be free of sags and bare spots and imperfections; and the color is to be Robin's Egg Blue.

In a performance-driven abatement contract, a contract specification might require the contractor to come in and remove some trash, clean the floors, and dispose of the trash.

From these two examples, it is obvious that with the performance-driven specification, the purchaser or owner is not as concerned about the way in which a job is completed, but only in the end product. This kind of specification works well in a construction project, where the owner has little concern over

how a building might be built or how a hole is dug, as long as the process doesn't provide additional liability to the owner and the end product is satisfactory to the owner. Because of the owner liability, performance-driven specifications are almost always inappropriate for work involving hazardous substances.

The second type of specification, though driven by means and methods are probably more commonly used on abatement projects. This type specifies how the work is to be accomplished, by whom, and under what conditions.
A soil abatement project is one in which the means and methods specification would be preferred. In such a situation, the owner is not only very concerned about the end product, but also concerned with how that end product is achieved. It is not enough to instruct a contractor to remove six inches of soil and replace it with clean soil. The method in which that goal is accomplished is also important. The owner certainly doesn't want to have the clean soil contaminated with whatever toxic or hazardous material is in the soil being removed. Because of this, it is necessary for the owner to specify precisely how the process of abatement occurs.

Abatement projects are sometimes driven by combination specs whereby the method of achieving the goal is clearly specified and described; but also some limited parts of the path necessary to achieve the goal are left up to the contractor involved.

Since there is some variation in the area of worker protection regulations and recommendations relative to lead abatement, the contract specifications should include the standards to be followed on the specified project. This accomplishes several things:

- It defines worker safety issues.

- It levels the playing field for all contractors bidding a project. Contractors who always show concern for worker safety should not be penalized by losing jobs to contractors who bid low and save money by placing workers, their families, and the public at risk.

The most important parts of the contract documents for the contractor are the contract specs and the general conditions. It is the detail specified in this section of the contract documents which will either make it a mutually-satisfactory contract or a disaster. This is true for both the owner and the contractor. If the specifications are not written clearly and concisely, it is very likely that the owner may not achieve his or her required goal.

On the other hand, if the specifications are not totally understood during the bidding process or during the execution of the work specified in the contract, the contractor could very well suffer significant losses.

PROJECT MANAGEMENT

SUPERVISORY SKILLS

OBJECTIVE:

To present skills which will be useful in supervising abatement workers.

LEARNING TASKS:

Supervisors/contractors should be able to:

- Name and explain two methods used in teambuilding.

- Compare and contrast communication and expectations as they are used in supervision.

As a supervisor/contractor of a lead-abatement project, this section is important to you because: You will be responsible for supervising other abatement workers;

- **Your success as a supervisor will depend upon your team's ability to complete an abatement project.**

- **You are responsible for ensuring safe work practices**

are used. This is critical in protecting the health and safety of the workers and the building occupants.

It is believed that employees want to do their best because of pride and personal achievement.

There is probably some truth in both views. It depends greatly upon the individual employee as well as the supervisor's ability to interact with and motivate them. The quality of work performed by an individual depends upon the basic attitudes held by that individual, his/her values, and beliefs.

Some workers will very likely perform well regardless of the circumstances. Other workers require more supervision.

Regardless of the basic attitudes held by the worker, <u>no employee will perform well unless he/she is given the correct information and the supervisor performs his/her appropriate function.</u> An effective supervisor will provide the necessary information through the following actions:

- Communicating

- Establishing clear expectations;

- Giving positive reinforcement; and

- Taking corrective action when necessary

Supervisors who take these actions will have a more efficient team.

Communicating

An effective supervisor is an effective communicator; very little will be accomplished without communication. Supervisors must communicate a variety of information effectively with their workers. Tasks, duties, job descriptions, etc., must be explained clearly for the workers. All employees must know and understand the what, when, and how their jobs are to be done.

Communication is not a one-way street. Supervisors must listen to the other members of the team, the workers, to make certain they understand the nature of the job. The supervisor must listen to the concerns of the workers. Employees often have some valid concerns about issues such as safety or other important matters. The workers also have good ideas about how a task could be better accomplished.

SUPERVISORY SKILLS

One of the principal responsibilities of the lead-abatement supervisor is that of supervising the activities of the abatement workers. This activity may in fact be the most important role of the supervisor. Effective supervision is one method of ensuring that the workers will perform all of their tasks correctly. Correct performance of tasks in a residential abatement project is important because it:

- Is vital to the safety of the community;
- Helps ensure the personal safety of the workers;

- Protects the environment from contamination; and
- Makes the abatement project successful.

If the workers are not performing their tasks correctly, there is the possibility of:

- Injury to themselves;
- Injury to their co-workers;
- Injury to their families;
- Property damage;
- Injury to a community resident; and
- The work having to be redone.

If the workers are not performing their tasks correctly, some parts of the abatement may not meet the minimum clearance criteria. This would result in additional expense for the contractor.

There are two opposing views to supervision, Theory X and Theory Y. One view (X) holds that workers require constant supervision. They will not perform all tasks in a correct manner unless someone is watching all of the time. The other view (Y) is that workers will do their best with a minimum of interference. What do these statements mean?

Develop Cooperative Goals

All studies on achievement in groups have demonstrated that when people work cooperatively they accomplish much more than when they work competitively. When individuals work cooperatively, they come to depend on each other and work better together. A supervisor could develop cooperative goals by demonstrating that he/she wants to contribute whatever possible to achieve a mutual goal. The supervisor will have to do his/her part. That could consist of making sure equipment and supplies are present when needed by the workers. It could mean listening to their ideas about performing the assigned tasks. It could also mean giving that extra boost to workers' morale.

Cooperative goals are established when workers believe in the importance of the project. They also have to believe they can do the job and what they are doing will make a difference. It is up to the supervisor to communicate these ideas to the workers.

Develop Trust

Followers will not follow if they do not trust the leader. Honesty is essential for a supervisor to develop the trust of the workers. Part of honesty is following through on commitments.

Develop a Team Spirit

Developing a positive team spirit is related to the way in which the supervisor interacts with other team members.

- When speaking, use "we," not "I" or "you."
- Create interactions. When you arrive on the job site, interact with the other team members. Don't just come and go without some kind of interaction, even if it is a simple, "Hello! How are you?"
- Be positive. Focus on the gains made. Make comments about what has been accomplished.

Establishing Clear Expectations

Workers need to know what is expected of them. If they do not know and understand what is expected of them, they do not perform as expected. Workers must understand the expectations regarding such issues as tardiness, attention to detail on the job, performance standards, personal hygiene requirements designed to minimize lead exposure, attitudes regarding fellow employees, resident relations, etc.

Workers also have their own expectations on the job site. A supervisor should know and understand the workers' expectations.

Giving Positive Reinforcement

When a worker has accomplished a task, he/she should know if that task was performed adequately. If the worker does not know if the task was done correctly, will the worker perform the same way the next time? Will it be

performed as well or will it be performed poorly? Additionally, if you tell someone a job was performed correctly, that tells the worker you care about how it was done. It tells the worker that you noticed what he/she did.

Taking Corrective Action

Just as it is important to inform workers when they do something correctly, they should also know when they do something incorrectly. It may have been done incorrectly because of lack of understanding, carelessness, or whatever. The worker should know the implications of his/her actions. If a worker's actions jeopardize his/her safety, the safety of others, or the success of the project, that information should be made clear to the employee.

Perhaps more important than communication, is the concept of leadership. A good supervisor will be a good leader. How does a supervisor become a leader? There are three important ways to acquire leadership:

- Develop cooperative goals
- Develop trust
- Develop a team spirit

PROJECT MANAGEMENT

RECORD KEEPING/LOG BOOKS

OBJECTIVE:

To present the record keeping requirements of an abatement project.

LEARNING TASKS:

Supervisors/contractors should be able to:

Differentiate between the types of records recommended and required to be kept by abatement contractors

Describe the concept of "cradle to grave" as defined by the Resource Conservation and Recovery Act

As a supervisor/contractor of a lead-abatement project, this section is important to you because:

As the person responsible for the records, you must understand the importance of those records.

Do not focus on the negative. Try not to arrive on the job site and complain every day. This will accomplish nothing but having people tune you out before you say anything.

As the agent on the job, you will have the responsibility for maintaining the appropriate records

If you must criticize a team member, do not do it in front of the group. Express criticism in private.

Meet with team members on a one-to-one basis. Do this on different occasions; not just when there is criticism to be given. When you meet with team members on a one-to-one basis, it indicates that you find the other person important enough to devote the time.

Lead abatement has its own set of challenges. These challenges are in the areas of safety, working conditions, community relations, and other concerns. One of the greater challenges for the supervisor is dealing successfully with a broad range of individuals in the work force.

RECORD KEEPING/LOG BOOK

Contractors involved in residential lead-abatement projects must be aware of the extensive record keeping responsibilities. Record keeping falls into three categories:

- Legally mandated records;

- Records to support other legal requirements;

- Recommended record keeping

Those record classifications are described in the following sections.

Legally Required Records

- Hazardous Waste Records

The only abatement projects which carry a legal requirement for record keeping for waste materials are those where hazardous wastes will be generated. There are minimum requirements for record keeping associated with the handling of hazardous wastes. Those requirements were established by the United States Environmental Protection Agency (U.S. EPA). The U.S. EPA regulations control the disposal of hazardous waste under the Resource Conservation and Recovery Act (RCRA) .The lead being abated or the material used to remove lead-based paint have the potential to be hazardous waste, depending on the characteristics of the lead and its matrix and the chemicals in the paint remover. Some paint strippers contain hazardous chemicals and thus the strippers are also considered to be hazardous materials.

Unless the generator of the hazardous waste is considered to be a *conditionally exempt small generator* (individuals and institutions which generate no more that 100 kilograms of hazardous waste per month), all hazardous waste shipments should be accompanied by a document called the Uniform Hazardous Waste Manifest (see Appendix A to this chapter). This is essentially a shipping document, which is signed by the generator, the transporter, and the waste treatment and/or disposal facility. The purpose of this document is to track the hazardous waste from the point at which it is generated to the point at which it is permanently disposed.

This is in keeping with the "cradle to the grave" philosophy instituted by the RCRA legislation and implemented by the U.S. EPA.

•   When the hazardous material is transported from the abatement or storage site, this document is signed by the transporter

•   When the material is received by the disposal facility, the copy is again signed by the receiver of the material.

Once the operator of the disposal facility signs the manifest, a signed copy of the manifest is returned to the generator. This copy must be received within thirty-five (35) days of the shipment of the waste. If the generator does not receive a signed copy of the document, he or she must then contact the operator of the disposal facility to determine the status of the shipment. If a copy is not received within forty-five (45) days of the shipment, the generator must contact the regional administrator of the U.S. EPA and send a copy of the signed manifest to that office with an explanation of efforts undertaken to find the lost material.

These records must be maintained by individuals and institutions generating such wastes, including any Public Housing Authority (PHA), lead-abatement contractor, or other entity generating or disposing of hazardous waste, for a minimum period of three years. These records include copies of the manifest and any other exception reports required during the course of abatement and the results of testing of wastes for hazardous status. (Records should also be maintained of shipments of waste to sanitary landfills - See Appendix B for an example.)

The U.S. EPA is in the process of preparing a report on waste classification of debris from lead abatement projects. EPA is also directing research into the feasibility of sending contaminated waste from lead-abatement projects to smelters for reprocessing. This might involve intermediate agents who would accept the waste products and forward it to the smelters.

. Soil and dust are not adequately addressed in most areas. Lead in the soil can contaminate an abated residence.

Construction Drawing

HUD requires as-built drawings to be completed on abatement sites where encapsulation was used as an abatement strategy. These drawings are intended to be a permanent record of where lead was left in place. This record will serve to warn contractors and others during future remodeling efforts and maintenance activities.

Recommended Record Keeping Private Property Records

Many abatement projects require the contractor to be responsible for the moving and storage of private property or work on private property. Records describing the condition and status of that property are important. Photographs and/or videotapes are extremely useful records of the

condition of private property. Access permission records for entering and working on private property should also be maintained. Communications with residents and property owners should also be handled in a methodical

manner using multi-copy forms that track the message from origination to conclusion (see Appendix C).

Site Access

Records should be maintained regarding worker access to abatement sites. The OSHA Lead Standard does not apply to construction sites (abatement sites are considered to be construction projects). Therefore, it is not mandatory to keep records regarding the amount of time workers spend in environments where there is a potential for exposure to lead. It is, however, advisable for contractors to maintain these records for their own protection.

Records to Support Legal Requirements

Worker Training and Safety Inspections

Chapter 15 - PROJECT MANAGEMENT

Some worker training is mandated by the HUD Interim Guidelines and the OSHA Hazard Communication Standard (HAZ COM). It is required to maintain records of the training under the HAZ COM Standard. The form of the record is left up to the company. The form should be sufficient to provide proof of the training at a later date. Besides providing proof that required training was completed, there are other reasons for the contractor to keep track of times and dates of worker training and safety inspections of abatement sites.

- This can be an additional layer of protection for the contractor in the event of worker injury and illness resulting from exposure to toxic materials.

- If there is a record of adequate worker training, accidents resulting in injuries or environmental damage can be attributed to other factors besides poorly trained workers. If respirator use is legally required, the requirement will also include record keeping of the overall program and fit testing.

Clearance Testing

Records of the times and dates of clearance tests, along with the environmental lab results for those tests, should be maintained as a part of the permanent record for the abatement project. This is a requirement on abatement projects in Public and Indian Housing. In other abatement projects, a contractor should maintain records of clearance tests because of the possibility that the property may become contaminated at a future time.

- Some state regulations do not require complete abatement. Significant amounts of lead-based paint, which may deteriorate in the future, can remain after the abatement is completed.

Site Log

A record of the daily activities on the abatement site should be maintained. This record would include such items as:

- Visitors to site;
- Violation of safety rules;
- Equipment failures;
- Workers on site;
- Visits by supervisors;
- Tools and equipment used;
- Documentation of work accomplished;
- Frequency of clean-up activities;
- Unusual conditions.

This information may be very helpful for a variety of reasons, such as the modification of practices for future projects, the assessment of equipment performance and for potential legal actions resulting from the abatement activities.

Material Log

This log would record the delivery of supplies and material to the abatement site.

Respirator Use

If respirators are used on the project, it is important that there be a written respirator use plan and that records be maintained of worker training and respirator fit-testing. (These records may be legally required in some circumstances).

Other Testing Results

Records of other environmental testing such as the testing of replacement soil should also be maintained for future protection.

THE COMMUNITY RELATIONS PROCESS

OBJECTIVE:

To present the phases necessary to implement, maintain, and manage an effective community relations plan before and during a lead abatement project.

LEARNING TASKS:

Supervisors/contractors should be able to:

- List and define the phases necessary to have a successful community relations plan.

- Describe three major tasks a community relations coordinator must complete.

- Determine the role of the supervisor in implementing the community relations plan.

As a supervisor/contractor on a lead-abatement project, this section is important to you because you will be interacting with persons of the community and organizations involved. Dealing with the concerns of the community goes a long way in helping the project go as smoothly as possible. You should be aware of the existence and nature of the community relations plan.

THE COMMUNITY RELATIONS PROCESS

The community relations plan will provide the community* with specific guidelines, which will enable the lead abatement project to proceed with the least amount of inconvenience and disruption to persons within the community, as well as the organizations involved. Such a tool assures favorable resident, owner, and media interaction.

This community relations plan can best be executed in a four-phase process:
- The planning and development phase,
- The implementation phase,
- The maintenance phase, and
- The evaluation phase.

  *The term community, as presented here, refers to the residents, property owners(s), local government, business groups, community action organizations, and the abatement contractor/consultant who will be directly impacted by this abatement.

PHASE I:

Planning and Development of the Community Relations Plan

In Phase one, it is important to address three major tasks:

- Appointment of the community relations coordinator,

- Development of the individual community relations plan,

- Defining contractor/resident needs.

The Coordinator:

- Interacts with local, state, and federal agencies, other contractors, the residents, and the news media.

- Establishes a jobsite office.

- Maintains honest, open, and frank communication with all involved parties.

The community relations coordinator must be familiar with community groups and their interests.   A listing of the tenant association, community council, action groups, and building managers including names, addresses and phone numbers are needed to gain an awareness of what is happening and who is in the community.   This listing will be used in future mailings. Information on residents directly affected by the abatement process is also needed.

In the development of a community relations plan (the second step in the planning and development phase), it is essential to address six major areas:

- Knowledge of the community and its components,

- Selection of an information distribution process,

- Formulation of a resident relocation plan,

- Identification of areas of inconvenience to residents, business, and other neighborhood activities,

- Development of a process that addresses problems and complaints, and

- Generation of a master schedule and forms.

-

Selection of an information distribution process is key in the development of the community relations plan. A timely area-wide press release announcing the abatement project and information sheets to residents via a general mailing are needed. A residential meeting for additional abatement questions (have a sign-in sheet) or door-to-door personal contact may also be needed. Also have a general "fact sheet" available to give to residents.

Formulation of a resident relocation plan is a critical part of the community relations plan. This includes:

- Identifying the units scheduled for abatement

- Locating alternative housing and storage (other public housing units or motels),

- Estimating the time needed for abatement, and

- Identifying requirements for contingency housing, arranging for residents timely use of it.

Providing packing boxes for residents will help ensure they will be ready to vacate premises on the appointed date. Coordinating and confirming the moving contractor's schedule are also critical to the success of the abatement process.

Identification of possible inconveniences caused by the abatement project is another part of the community relations plan. If a trailer is used for the abatement office, will resident parking spaces be lost? Will barricades hamper local business trade? What daily disruptions are like to cause community concern?

Development of a process that addresses problems, concerns, and complaints is part of the community relations plan. Providing residents access to the coordinator is valuable. The coordinator must daily set aside time to respond to and resolve resident problems. Documentation of problems/complaints is necessary. For example, an "in-house" form allows for the abatement team to be aware of problems/complaints.

The final task in the development of the community relations plan is the generation of a **master community relations schedule** and creation of any associated forms. The master schedule includes date assignment for major mailings, new media releases, resident moving and unit re-entry dates, and community meeting times and places.

The third step in the planning and development phase is to define contractor and resident needs. The coordinator makes sure that the community relations plan works in harmony with the abatement workplan. For example, news media announcements and resident notification are linked to the abatement work schedule. Abatement workers must be sensitive to resident concerns which can impact the success of a contractor in an abatement project and influence the awarding of future contracts. Abatement workers must also be aware of contractor liability for residents' personal property and containment of leaded materials (particularly if only part of a unit is being abated). Consider pre- and post-abatement video taping.

Likewise, the resident must understand the contractor's need to complete the abatement process in a timely, cost-effective manner.

Phase II: Implementation of the Community Relations Plan

The second phase in the community relations process is to implement the plan. Implementation begins by meeting and presenting the community relations plan to the abatement project manager for approval. The presentation includes discussion of general community make-up supported by mailing lists, media procedures, sample resident letters and information sheets, as well as dates and times for mailings and publicity.

A comprehensive resident relocation plan is also presented to the project manager to verify compatibility with the abatement workplan. Does the abatement timetable work well with the community relations timetable? Make appropriate changes and implement relocation plan.

After the community relations plan has been approved by the project manager, the community relations coordinator begins to **publicize** and **promote** the abatement process through news media releases which outline the benefits of abatement and the steps to be taken for the health and safety for residents, workers, and the community-at-large. Inform area groups and organizations of the abatement workplan and solicit their support. General mailings and information sheets are then mailed to all area residents. Notify abatement residents of relocation dates and times. Timely release of unit abatement dates also occurs during the implementation step. Flyers mailed and hand-delivered to each resident scheduled for abatement are essential. Residents in surrounding units should also receive a flyer with general abatement information and dates.

Instruction of office support staff is an essential part of a successfully implemented community relations plan. Directing callers seeking project information and obtaining accurate telephone information for coordinator callbacks adds to the success of the community relations plan. Support staff assistance will be needed for mailings and distribution of flyers. Make arrangements for ample support staff during peak work periods as necessary.

Adherence to the community relations schedule is critically important. Daily meetings with the project manager are needed as the abatement process begins in order to ensure a smooth, cost-effective process. As the project proceeds, adjust meeting times as needed.

Checklists for:

- News media dates and announcements, if needed,

- Resident relocation information, (e.g. abatement start date, packing box delivery date), and

- Unit re-entry dates,

are important tools to help maintain the project timetable. (Sample forms are included at the end of this section.)

A brief resident survey, distributed at the end of the project to families both directly and indirectly involved in abatement, provides important feedback to the Community Relations Coordinator. Questions about the benefits of abatement, staff courtesy and resident comments should be included in the survey.

Several questions to be asked during the evaluation step are:

1. Did the information provided to all parties throughout the abatement process work well?

2. Did the resident relocation plan work well?

3. Were contractor, community, and resident needs met?

In summary, the four phases of the community relations plan are the planning and development phase, the implementation phase, the maintenance phase, and the evaluation phase. The success of the project depends upon the understanding and active support of the community. With a well-constructed Community Relations Plan, this is possible.

Phase III: Maintenance of Community Relations Plan

Maintaining the Community Relations Plan is the third phase in the community relations process. At this time, there is a need to:

- Maintain weekly meetings with the project manager to review project and community relations plan timeliness,

-

- Address resident problems and suggested solutions to problems, and

- Re-evaluate the overall community relations plans and make necessary adjustments based on current needs.

Send resident reminder flyers to all abatement residents one week before the abatement relocation date. Verify moving dates with the moving contractor. A project representative must be on the abatement site as each family is relocated to address any areas of concern.

Phase IV: Evaluation of the Community Relations Plan

The fourth and final phase for an effective community relations plan is the evaluation of the plan. There are two times the plan is evaluated:

1. During the abatement process, and

2. At the abatement project's completion.

Consideration for needed changes during abatement should be evaluated and changes should be made to fit both contractor and resident needs. For example, it may be more cost-effective and practical to evacuate an entire building at one time versus a unit by unit approach. If so, implement the change during the abatement process.

ABC CONSTRUCTION, INC
555-1234

PLEASE MARK YOUR CALENDAR

Dear _____

Your home is scheduled for lead paint removal soon. The moving van will be at your home on:

Day:

_____

Date:

_____

Time:

_____

Please be at home so you can tell the mover what things are to be moved.

Reminder:

1.   If you need your telephone transferred call _____

2. Complete your mail transfer card and place the card in your mailbox.

Your new temporary address is: _____
   Apt #_____
   Zip_____

ABC CONSTRUCTION COMPANY
555-1234

REMINDER

Dear _____

Your home is scheduled for lead paint removal soon. The moving van will be at your home on:

        Day: _____

        Date: _____

        Time: _____

Please be at home so you can tell the mover what things re to be moved.

Reminder:
1. If you need your telephone transferred, call _____
2. Complete your mail transfer card and place the card in your mailbox.

Your new temporary address is: _____

        Apt # _____

        Zip _____

RESIDENT/PROPERTY COMMUNICATION

AREA: _____

PROPERTY ADDRESS _____**APT #**_____

RESIDENT _____

TELEPHONE NO. _____ **CONTACT NO.** _____

 CONTACT NAME _____**RELATIONSHIP**_____

MESSAGE

DATE_____**TIME**_____**RECORDED BY**_____

ACTION TAKEN

DATE_____**TIME**_____**RECORDED BY**_____

RESOLUTION checked by _____**Date**_____
COMMENTS:

DATE: _____ **SIGNATURE** _____

ADDITIONAL COMMENTS:

NOTE: *Refer to Appendix A – EPA's Renovation, Repair and Painting Program Final Rule (40 CFR Part 745)* April 22, 2008

Chapter 17 – Cost Estimation

Cost Estimation

OBJECTIVE :

To present the major cost consideration in the lead abatement project.

LEARNING TASKS:

Supervisors / Contractors should be able to:

- List at least five cost considerations in the lead abatement project

- Differentiate between the relative costs of waste disposal associated with encapsulation and stripping.

- Assess abatement project progress relative to the project budget

As a supervisor/contractor of a lead-abatement project this section is important to you because:

- You may be responsible for monitoring project costs for your employer;

- You should be aware of the relative costs of the parts of an abatement project so that you can use resources wisely;

- During an abatement a property owner may ask for a substitution, e.g., gravel instead of topsoil and sod. In such a situation you may be asked to calculate the cost difference.

COST ESTIMATION

Cost estimation in a lead abatement project can be a difficult task for a variety of reasons. Those reasons stem from the nature of the abatement process. When performing an interior dust or paint abatement project, the contractor will be working within the confines of individual residences. Exterior dust and soil abatement projects sometimes require the work to be performed on both public and private property. Requirements for abatement work in theses two environments may differ considerably.

With both interior and exterior abatement, the opportunity for unexpected contingencies is frequent. These contingencies can have a significant effect on the overall cost of the project. They often can be very costly, thus making it difficult to calculate the overall cost of abatement projects while trying to remain competitive.

These contingencies can impact the various participants in an abatement project in different ways. An owner, who may have a fixed budget for an abatement project, must be able to consider all of the contingencies at an early stage in the planning process in order to make certain sufficient funds will be available to complete the project. If the owner has adequate information about the total cost of abatement during the planning stage, decisions about the extent and type of abatement can be made early enough for changes to made to accommodate a limited project budget.

The bidding process is the best time to quantify all costs for the contractor. At that time, he must be aware of all-potential contingencies or problems which may occur in an abatement project. If all costs are known during the bidding process, there will be fewer disagreements about who pays those costs at the end of the project.

Additionally, the architect and engineer should be aware of what may go wrong in an abatement project in order to be able to write specifications, which address as many unforeseen problems as possible. This will also help assure that there will be sufficient funds to complete the project.

Interior dust and paint abatements may be bid on a per-square-foot basis. Contractors are expected to be familiar with the costs for removal or encapsulation of lead-based paint, or the unit costs associated with vacuuming and other cleaning operations specified in a dust abatement project.

Chapter 17 – Cost Estimation

The unexpected and more difficult aspects of an interior dust or paint abatement project are those costs associated with the families living within the abatement site. Some families may be neat and tidy while other families are not so-oriented. Some families

have very few personal belongings, while other families have literally tons of material to be moved and stored during the abatement process. These conditions are very difficult for the abatement contractor to bid, and for the owner to anticipate when planning the abatement project budget.

It can be very discouraging for abatement workers to enter a residence and see an almost never ending supply of toys; clothes and other personal belongings unpacked and scattered on every imaginable surface. Some residents can be very helpful in packing and organizing prior to an abatement project where other families are very uncooperative in this regard. When workers are faced with an overwhelming job, they quickly become discouraged. This attitude is often reflected in lower productivity.

Resident cooperation can be enhanced and costs thereby reduced, through a good community relations plan, which is partly directed toward preparing the families for abatement.

It is also difficult for a contractor prior to the start of an abatement project to anticipate the extent of damage costs, resulting from abatement activities. For example, personal belongings a contractor thinks are junk, the family may consider irreplaceable heirlooms. If an heirloom is damaged during the course of abatement, there can be some disagreement as to the exact value of the item in question.

Careful planning in establishing the responsibility for liability and a fair methodology for assessing the damages are helpful in the cost estimation of an abatement project. It is impossible or impractical for all abatement project bidders to physically view every site in the project. It is incumbent upon the owner to provide the abatement contractor with sufficient detail for the contractor/bidder to make a fair assessment of expected costs.

In a soil or exterior dust abatement project, the contractor or bidders for a project may be able to view most, if not all, of the abatement sites(s) prior to submitting a bid. These may, however, be items of consequence not visible during a site visit. Some of these invisible items may include utility lines not buried adequately or undetected cisterns or sanitary facilities. Additionally, sites may change from the time they were viewed for the bidding process and the beginning of the abatement. It is not unusual for frequent and spontaneous trash dumping on inner city vacant lots and alleys to occur. Consequently, quantities and types of materials to be removed can change drastically in short periods of time.

The important items to be considered in cost estimations for an abatement project include:

Chapter 17 – Cost Estimation

1. The unit costs associated with an abatement project.

Paint and interior dust lead abatement cost estimates contained in the HUD "Comprehensive and workable Plan for the Abatement of Lead-Based Paint in Private Housing" are presented in Tables 1 and 2.

Unit costs for interior dust abatement could be determined by the time required to vacuum bare floors or carpeted surfaces and the associated damp mopping which could go along with the vacuuming. Unit costs for sealing cracks in the flooring may also have to be included. Paint abatement unit costs are determined by the type and quantity of surface requiring abatement and the technique(s) required for the abatement, whether chemical stripping, encapsulation, or replacement of the painted material. Establishing the unit costs for abatement activities are the first costs for the 172 units in the HUD Demonstration Project are presented in Table 3 according to component type and abatement method.

For soil abatement, this is the unit cost for removing and replacing one cubic yard of soil along with the cost of ground cover for the area which, most commonly, is either seeding or sod.

For exterior dust abatement, the unit cost is the cost to vacuum or sweep paved surfaces along with the cost of removing bulk debris prior to cleaning. This could vary depending upon the texture of the paved surface. Some smoother surfaces can be more easily cleaned than rough surfaces like cobblestones or rough concrete. Additionally, the size of the area to be cleaned can impact costs. Small inaccessible areas may require cleaning with a HEPA equipped vacuum while large areas such as streets and parking lots may be amenable to sweeping with large vacuum street sweepers.

2. Disposal costs

The disposal of the material resulting from the abatement activities may represent significant cost for an abatement project. This cost is determined by calculating the amount of materials to be disposed of and the disposal cost of that amount of material at a disposal site. Disposal costs for material will vary significantly, depending upon whether the material is considered to be solid or hazardous, the applicable tipping charges and the transportation cost. Disposal and transportation costs may be an important consideration when considering the type of abatement to be used. Hazardous waste disposal costs from the HUD Lead-Based Paint Demonstration (FHA) are presented in the Chapter on Waste Disposal.

Chapter 17 – Cost Estimation

3. Worker Training.

OSHA 29CFR1926.134 requires training of all employees who work with Lead-Based Paint. Worker training cost is important. EPA requires all lead-based paint workers and some states have adopted stiffer requirements for the

licensing of abatement contractors and require that the workers successfully complete an approved training program. The costs of utilizing such workers must be incorporated into the estimation of the abatement costs. Contractors could lose their contractor licenses for failure to train their employees under these regulations.

Workers who have concerns about their health because of exposure in the work place may be less enthusiastic about performing the work. Health concerns also could cause higher worker turnover impacting the success or the final cost of a project. Consequently, worker training could be a cost-effective part of the abatement process. The cost of the worker training does, however, have to be included in the cost estimation process.

4. Safety and health costs

The cost of the safety and health program also must be considered when estimating the abatement project costs. Providing personal protection equipment, blood-lead monitoring and medical monitoring are all costs to be considered when estimating the cost.

5. Moving and other relocation costs

Moving families, office personnel, and other occupants and their belongings is a very important cost consideration when estimating the abatement project cost. The costs depend upon many factors such as the family size and composition, the length of time required to move each family, and the amount and type of material to be moved.

6. Bonding and liability insurance

Bonding and liability insurance are critical cost items to be calculated during the cost estimation phase of an abatement project.

7. Clearance testing

In addition to the costs associated with the collection of clearance samples and environmental monitoring samples, there are the additional costs for the analysis of those samples. Since the chemical sampling processes can be expensive, it is very important for those calculating the cost of abatement to consider the cost of those processes.

8. Damages

Resolution of disputes resulting from abatement can be expensive. A procedure must be established for making decisions about disputes regarding damage and /or losses suffered by individuals during the abatement process. This procedure must be established before beginning the abatement project. The cost of settling disputes and anticipated damage costs must be estimated during the planning stages for an abatement project and figured into the overall cost estimate for the abatement project.

9. Site inspection

The cost of site inspection for an abatement project should also be calculated in the overall cost. The environmental consultant may be asked to provide site inspectors for an abatement project to ensure that the process is completed according to the specifications written by the architect or engineer for the project.

The foregoing items are the major expenses to be considered when developing an abatement budget or calculating a bid to be submitted for an abatement project. All abatement projects will have their own unique set of requirements and considerations to be included in the cost estimate. This means care must be taken with the estimating process.

Chapter 17 – Cost Estimation

TABLE I

ESTIMATED AVERAGE COST OF ABATEMENT PER DWELLING UNIT BY
LOCATION OF PAINT AND ABATEMENT STRATEGY

Strategy	Units w exterior LBP only	Units Interior LBP only	Units both Exterior and Interior	All Units
Removal	$	$	$	$
Encapsulation	$	$	$	$

TABLE 2

ESTIMATED COST PER HOUSING UNITO OF A DUST LEAD ABATEMENT

	Activity	*high*	*Low*
1	Initial sampling and testing	$	
2	Initial cleanup	$	
3	Clearance sampling and testing	$	
	Sub-Total w/o interative cleanup	$	
4	Iterative cleanup, if needed	$	
	Sub-total with interative	$	
5	six month sampling and testing	$	
	Sub-total: w/o six month cleanup	$	
6	Six month cleanup	$	
	Subtotal with 6 month cleanup	$	
7	twelve month sampling & and testing	$	
		$	
8	Twelve month cleanup	$	
	Potontial one-year cost	$	

NOTE: *Refer to Appendix A - EPAs Renovation, Repair and Painting Program Final Rule (40 CFR Part 745)* April 22, 2008

Chapter 18 - Employee Information & Training

<u>OBJECTIVE</u>:

To present the legal and recommended requirements and recommendations for lead-abatement worker training.

<u>LEARNING TASKS:</u>

Supervisors/ should be able to:

- Know local, state and federal regulations pertaining to Lead based paint

- Explain topics which should be included in a worker-training program.

- List reasons and explain why the OSHA Hazard Communication Standard (HAZ COM) will apply to lead-based-paint abatement projects.

As a supervisor/contractor of a lead-abatement project, this section is important to you because:

- **you must make sure that the employees are trained in lead;**

- **you may be responsible for implementing HAZ COM on the job site;**

- **You should be aware of the training recommendations and requirements.**

- **Understand the role and responsibilities of everyone on an abatement project**

- **Know the resources available to you on the abatement project**

- **Understand your responsibilities on tn abatement project**

EMPLOYEE INFORMATION & WORKER TRAINING

Employee information and worker training are important aspects of a lead abatement project and should not be overlooked or treated lightly. Worker training falls into four categories:

- Training required on Federal housing (HUD) projects;

- Training required by state and local lead regulations.

- Training required by other Federal regulations;

- Recommended training or training required as a prudent action.

"Right to Know" legislation requires employers to provide workers with information about hazards in the workplace. This could be used as part of a worker-training program.

This section of the manual covers the current requirements for worker training. The regulations section of this manual includes all applicable regulations as we know them. Training regulations can change frequently. Current regulations should always be checked. This section of the manual also includes recommendations for training in those regions where no lead abatement regulations currently exist. EPA is developing a worker course and accreditation requirements.

Training Requirements under HUD

The "Lead-Based Paint: Interim Guidelines for Hazard Identification and Abatement in Public and Indian Housing," recently released by the Department of Housing and Urban Development, include a requirement for mandatory worker education and training (Section 5.7). Additionally, those states, which presently have lead standards, also require worker education and training, generally modeled after the HUD guidelines. The HUD guidelines state:

"Employers of deleading workers, either abatement contractors or PHAs using force account labor, must provide worker education and training. The employer may train workers either in an array of abatement methods or only for the methods specified in the particular abatement plan. All education and training should include information on the following topics:

- Possible routes of exposure to lead.

- The known health effects associated with exposure.

- The importance of good personal hygiene.

- The specific methods of abatement to be used.

- The proper use and maintenance of protective clothing and equipment.

Chapter 18 - Employee Information & Training

- OSHA: Hazard Communication Standard (29 CFR 1910.1200).

- The correct use of engineering controls and implementation of good work practices.

These are the minimum requirements for worker training specified in the HUD guidelines.

<u>Training Requirements Under OSHA (29 CFR 1926.62)</u>

The OSHA Lead in Construction final standand (29 CFR 1926.62, this standard, like the OSHA General Industry Lead Standard (29 CFR 1910.1025) requires training of workers.

<u>Training Requirements Under OSHA (29 CFR 1910.1200)</u>

There are other Federal regulations which apply to all lead abatement projects, including those completed outside of federally owned (HUD) housing. Since soil and paint abatement work is considered to be a construction process, the requirements of the OSHA Hazard Communication Standard (29 CFR 1910.1200), HAZ COM, will apply. This legislation states that workers have the right to know about:

- hazards associated with their work;

- what protective measures can be taken;

- where to go for information.

Additionally, HAZ COM requires employers have:

- a written hazard communication program;

- an Information and training program.

Most soil and dust abatement projects would expose workers to the hazard of particulate lead. For a lead-based paint abatement project, the hazard would not only include lead but there might also be exposure to the paint strippers. Some of these strippers contain chemicals that are considered to be hazardous and would be covered by the HAZ COM standard.

<u>Training Requirements for States & Local Areas</u>

Chapter 18 - Employee Information & Training

Several States had passed their own lead standards prior to the release of the regulations governing lead-based paint abatement in Federal and Indian housing. The State regulations, like the Federal regulations, generally contain a requirement for worker training. Those requirements range from very specific training in Massachusetts to almost non-specific in Minnesota.

Local lead regulations generally do not specify training except for "right to know." Training requirements exist for the private sector abatement in some states and on Federal projects. Similar legislation is currently being proposed in other states. These current and proposed regulations indicate there is some concern about worker safety in various states. Hopefully other states will show concern for worker safety by passing adequate legislation in the area of lead abatement.

Training Requirements Under OSHA (29 CFR 1910.1025)

The OSHA Lead Standard (29 CFR 1910.1025) does not presently apply to residential lead abatement projects. Residential lead abatement is considered to be a construction process and as such is not covered by 29 CFR 1910.1025. Both agriculture and construction are exempt from that Standard. Some specifications require these contractors to abide by the OSHA Lead Standard. There is the possibility that construction will soon be covered. The training requirements are presented in this manual.

Under OSHA's Lead Standard, worker training must be provided:

- when employees are exposed to airborne lead at or above the action level.

- when skin or eye irritation exists.

- annually,

- by 180 days from exposure to level at or above the PEL.

Worker training must include the content of OSHA's Lead Standard including appendices A and B. Detailed content descriptions of appendices A and B are as follows:

Appendix A

- lead as a substance

- lead compounds covered by the Standard

- uses of lead

- permissible exposure limits

- action levels

- health effects related to lead exposure

Appendix B

This appendix summarizes key provisions of the Lead Standard with which workers should become familiar. Included are:

- PEL'S

- exposure monitoring

- methods of compliance

- respiratory protection

- protective work clothing and equipment

- housekeeping

- medical surveillance

- medical removal protection

- signs

- observation of monitoring

Recommended Worker Training Program

Training

A precedent for mandated worker training has been set by the Federal Government and some state governments. Worker training is an integral part of any well-designed project, and contractors considering an abatement project should incorporate worker training as part of the overall abatement plan. Owners and contractors providing voluntary worker training would facilitate the work being accomplished in a safe, efficient and appropriate manner.

Chapter 18 - Employee Information & Training

Training also provides a degree of self-protection for the owner and the contractor performing the abatement work. Failure to adequately train workers could present significant liability for the owner and the contractor performing the abatement work. Failure to adequately train workers could present significant liability for the owner and contractor in the event of an injury to a worker or a member of the worker's family resulting from lead exposure from the abatement process. There is also the possibility for contamination of the environment from the actions of a worker who did not understand the risks associated with sub-standard work practices. Any contractor who performs lead abatement in a manner which results in injury to others would likely be considered negligent in a court of law.

Abatement means any measure or set of measures designed to permanently eliminate lead-based paint haz Abatement includes, but is not limited to: the removal of paint and dust, the permanent enclosure or encapsulation of lead-based paint, the replacement of painted surfaces or fixtures, or the removal or permanent covering of soil, when lead-based paint hazards are present in such paint, dust or soil; and all preparation, cleanup, disposal, and post-abatement clearance testing activities associated with such measures.

Agent means any party who enters into a contract with a seller or lessor, including any party who enters into a contract with a representative of the seller or lessor, for the purpose of selling or leasing target housing. This term does not apply to purchasers or any purchaser's representative who receives all compensation from the purchaser.

Available means in the possession of or reasonably obtainable by the seller or lessor at the time of the disclosure.

Arithmetic mean means the algebraic sum of data values divided by the number of data values (e.g., the sum of the concentration of lead in several soil samples divided by the number of samples).

Adequate quality control means a plan or design which ensures the authenticity, integrity, and accuracy of samples, including dust, soil, and paint chip or paint film samples. Adequate quality control also includes provisions for representative sampling.

Binder: Solid ingredients in a coating that hold the pigment particles in suspension and attach them to the substrate. Consists of resins (e.g., oils, alkyd, latex). The nature and amount of binder determine many of the paint's performance properties--washability, toughness, adhesion, color retention, etc.

Blistering: Formation of dome-shaped projections in paints or varnish films resulting from local loss of adhesion and lifting of the film from the underlying surface.

Chewable surface means an interior or exterior surface painted with lead-based paint that a young child can mouth or chew. A chewable surface is the same as an "accessible surface" as defined in 42 U.S.C. 4851b(2)). Hard metal substrates and other materials that cannot be dented by the bite of a young child are not considered chewable.

Chalking: Formation of a powder on the surface of a paint film caused by disintegration of the binder during weathering. Can be affected by the choice of pigment or binder.

Child-occupied facility means a building, or portion of a building, constructed prior to 1978, visited regularly by the same child, under 6 years of age, on at least two different days within any week (Sunday through Saturday period), provided that each day's visit lasts at least 3 hours and the combined weekly visits last at least 6 hours, and the combined annual visits last at least 60 hours. Child-occupied facilities may include, but are not limited to, day care centers, preschools and kindergarten classrooms. Child-occupied facilities may be located in target housing or in public or commercial buildings. With respect to common areas in public or commercial buildings that contain child-occupied facilities, the child-occupied facility encompasses only those common areas that are routinely used by children under age 6, such as restrooms and cafeterias. Common areas that children under age 6 only pass through, such as hallways, stairways, and garages are not included. In addition, with respect to exteriors of public or commercial buildings that contain child-occupied facilities, the child-occupied facility encompasses only the exterior sides of the building that are immediately adjacent to the child-occupied facility or the common areas routinely used by children under age 6.

Cleaning verification card means a card developed and distributed, or otherwise approved, by EPA for the purpose of determining, through comparison of wet and dry disposable cleaning cloths with the card, whether post-renovation cleaning has been properly completed.

Common area means a portion of a building generally accessible to all residents/users including, but not limited to, hallways, stairways, laundry and recreational rooms, playgrounds, community centers, and boundary fences.

Contract for the purchase and sale of residential real property means any contract or agreement in which one party agrees to purchase an interest in real property on which there is situated one or more residential dwellings used or occupied, or intended to be used or occupied, in whole or in part, as the home or residence of one or more persons

Common area group means a group of common areas that are similar in design, construction, and function. Common area groups include, but are not limited to hallways, stairwells, and laundry rooms.

Concentration means the relative content of a specific substance contained within a larger mass, such as the amount of lead (in micrograms per gram or parts per million by weight) in a sample of dust or soil. **Dry disposable cleaning cloth** means a commercially available dry, electrostatically charged, white disposable cloth designed to be used for cleaning hard surfaces such as uncarpeted floors or counter tops. **Certified firm** means a company, partnership, corporation, sole proprietorship, association, or other business entity that performs lead-based paint activities to which EPA has issued a certificate of approval pursuant to §745.226(f).

Clearance levels are values that indicate the maximum amount of lead permitted in dust on a surface following completion of an abatement activity.

Component or building component means specific design or structural elements or fixtures of a building, residential dwelling, or child-occupied facility that are distinguished from each other by form, function, and location. These include, but are not limited to, interior components such as: ceilings, crown molding, walls, chair rails, doors, door trim, floors, fireplaces, radiators and other heating units, shelves, shelf supports, stair treads, stair risers, stair stringers, newel posts, railing caps, balustrades, windows and trim (including sashes, window heads, jambs, sills or stools and troughs), built in cabinets, columns, beams, bathroom vanities, counter tops, and air conditioners; and exterior components such as: painted roofing, chimneys, flashing, gutters and downspouts, ceilings, soffits, fascias, rake boards, corner boards, bulkheads, doors and door trim, fences, floors, joists, lattice work, railings and railing caps, siding, handrails, stair risers and treads, stair stringers, columns, balustrades, window sills or stools and troughs, casings, sashes and wells, and air conditioners.

Containment means a process to protect workers and the environment by controlling exposures to the lead-contaminated dust and debris created during an abatement.

Deteriorated paint means paint that is cracking, flaking, chipping, peeling, or otherwise separating from the substrate of a building component.

Diluent: A liquid used in coatings to reduce the consistency and make a coating flow more easily. The water in latex coatings is a diluent. A diluent may also be called a "Reducer," "Thinner," "Reducing Agent" or "Reducing Solvent."

Distinct painting history means the application history, as indicated by its visual appearance or a record of application, over time, of paint or other surface coatings to a component or room.

Documented methodologies are methods or protocols used to sample for the presence of lead in paint, dust, and soil.

Dripline means the area within 3 feet surrounding the perimeter of a building.

Dust-lead hazard. A dust-lead hazard is surface dust in a residential dwelling or child-occupied facility that contains a mass-per-area concentration of lead equal to or exceeding 40 $\mu g/ft^2$ on floors or 250 $\mu g/ft^2$ on interior window sills based on wipe samples.

EPA means the Environmental Protection Agency.

Evaluation means a risk assessment and/or inspection.

Encapsulant means a substance that forms a barrier between lead-based paint and the environment using a liquid-applied coating (with or without reinforcement materials) or an adhesively bonded covering material.

Encapsulation means the application of an encapsulant.

Enclosure means the use of rigid, durable construction materials that are mechanically fastened to the substrate in order to act as a barrier between lead-based paint and the environment.

Fire Retardant: A coating which will (1) reduce flame spread, (2) resist ignition when exposed to high temperature or (3) insulate the substrate and delay damage to the substrate.

Friction surface means an interior or exterior surface that is subject to abrasion or friction, including, but not limited to, certain window, floor, and stair surfaces.

Housing for the elderly means retirement communities or similar types of housing reserved for households composed of one or more persons 62 years of age or more at the time of initial occupancy.

HUD means the U.S. Department of Housing and Urban Development.

HEPA vacuum means a vacuum cleaner which has been designed with a high-efficiency particulate air (HEPA) filter as the last filtration stage. A HEPA filter is a filter that is capable of capturing particles of 0.3 microns with 99.97% efficiency. The vacuum cleaner must be designed so that all the air drawn into the machine is expelled through the HEPA filter with none of the air leaking past it. **Indian Country** means (1) all land within the limits of any American Indian reservation under the jurisdiction of the U.S. government, notwithstanding the issuance of any patent, and including rights-of-way running throughout the reservation; (2) all dependent Indian communities within the borders of the United States whether within the original or subsequently acquired territory thereof, and whether within or outside the limits of a State; and (3) all Indian allotments, the Indian titles which have not been extinguished, including rights-of-way running through the same.

Indian Tribe means any Indian Tribe, band, nation, or community recognized by the Secretary of the Interior and exercising substantial governmental duties and powers.

Impact surface means an interior or exterior surface that is subject to damage by repeated sudden force such as certain parts of door frames.

Hands-on skills assessment means an evaluation which tests the trainees' ability to satisfactorily perform the work practices and procedures identified in §745.225(d), as well as any other skill taught in a training course.

Hazardous waste means any waste as defined in 40 CFR 261.3.

Hazardous Air Pollutant: Pollutants that are known or suspected to cause cancer or other serious health effects, such as reproductive effects or birth defects, or adverse environmental effects.

HEPA Vacuum: High-efficiency particulate air-filtered vacuum designed to remove lead- contaminated dust.

Inspection means a surface-by-surface investigation to determine the presence of lead-based paint and the provision of a report explaining the results of the investigation.

Interim controls means a set of measures designed to temporarily reduce human exposure or likely exposure to lead-based paint hazards, including specialized cleaning, repairs, maintenance, painting, temporary containment, ongoing monitoring of lead-based paint hazards or potential hazards, and the establishment and operation of management and resident education programs.

Interior window sill means the portion of the horizontal window ledge that protrudes into the interior of the room.

Lead-based paint means paint or other surface coatings that contain lead equal to or in excess of 1.0 milligram per square centimeter or 0.5 percent by weight.

Lead-based paint free housing means target housing that has been found to be free of paint or other surface coatings that contain lead equal to or in excess of 1.0 milligram per square centimeter or 0.5 percent by weight.

Lead Certified inspector means an individual who has been trained by an accredited training program, as defined by this section, and certified by EPA pursuant to §745.226 to conduct inspections. A certified inspector also samples for the presence of lead in dust and soil for the purposes of abatement clearance testing.

Lead-based paint means paint or other surface coatings that contain lead equal to or in excess of 1.0 *Paint-lead hazard.* milligrams per square centimeter or more than 0.5 percent by weight.

paint-lead hazard is any of the following: 1 - Any lead-based paint on a friction surface that is subject to abrasion and where the lead dust levels on the nearest horizontal surface underneath the friction surface (e.g., the window sill, or floor) are equal to or greater than the dust-lead hazard levels identified in paragraph (b) of this section. 2 - Any damaged or otherwise deteriorated lead-based paint on an impact surface that is caused by impact from a related building component (such as a door knob that knocks into a wall or a door that knocks against its door frame. 3 - Any chewable lead-based painted surface on which there is evidence of teeth marks. 4 - Any other deteriorated lead-based paint in any residential building or child-occupied facility or on the exterior of any residential building or child-occupied facility.

Lead-based paint activities means, in the case of target housing and child-occupied facilities, inspection, risk assessment, and abatement, as defined in this subpart.

Lead-based paint hazard means any condition that causes exposure to lead from lead-contaminated dust, lead-contaminated soil, or lead-contaminated paint that is deteriorated or present in accessible surfaces, friction surfaces, or impact surfaces that would result in adverse human health effects as identified by the Administrator pursuant to TSCA section 403.

Lead-hazard screen is a limited risk assessment activity that involves limited paint and dust sampling as described in §745.227(c).

Living area means any area of a residential dwelling used by one or more children age 6 and under, including, but not limited to, living rooms, kitchen areas, dens, play rooms, and children's bedrooms.

Lead Certified abatement worker means an individual who has been trained by an accredited training program, as defined by this section, and certified by EPA pursuant to §745.226 to perform abatements.

Lead Certified project designer means an individual who has been trained by an accredited training program, as defined by this section, and certified by EPA pursuant to §745.226 to prepare abatement project designs, occupant protection plans, and abatement reports.

Lead Risk assessment means an on-site investigation to determine and report the existence, nature, severity, and location of lead-based paint hazards in residential dwellings, including: Information gathering regarding the age and history of the housing and occupancy by children under age 6; Visual inspection;

Limited wipe sampling or other environmental sampling techniques; Other activity as may be appropriate; and Provision of a report explaining the results of the investigation.

Lead Certified risk assessor means an individual who has been trained by an accredited training program, as defined by this section, and certified by EPA pursuant to §745.226 to conduct risk assessments. A risk assessor also samples for the presence of lead in dust and soil for the purposes of abatement clearance testing.

Lead Certified supervisor means an individual who has been trained by an accredited training program, as defined by this section, and certified by EPA pursuant to §745.226 to supervise and conduct abatements, and to prepare occupant protection plans and abatement reports.

Lead Inspection means: A surface-by-surface investigation to determine the presence of lead-based paint as provided in section 302(c) of the Lead-Based Paint Poisoning and Prevention Act [42 U.S.C. 4822], and the provision of a report explaining the results of the investigation.

Paint in poor condition means more than 10 square feet of deteriorated paint on exterior components with large surface areas; or more than 2 square feet of deteriorated paint on interior components with large surface areas (e.g., walls, ceilings, floors, doors); or more than 10 percent of the total surface area of the component is deteriorated on interior or exterior components with small surface areas (window sills, baseboards, soffits, trim).

Permanently covered soil means soil which has been separated from human contact by the placement of a barrier consisting of solid, relatively impermeable materials, such as pavement or concrete. Grass, mulch, and other landscaping materials are not considered permanent covering.

Owner means any entity that has legal title to target housing, including but not limited to individuals, partnerships, corporations, trusts, government agencies, housing agencies, Indian tribes, and nonprofit organizations, except where a mortgagee holds legal title to property serving as collateral for a mortgage loan, in which case the owner would be the mortgagor.

Purchaser means an entity that enters into an agreement to purchase an interest in target housing, including but not limited to individuals, partnerships, corporations, trusts, government agencies, housing agencies, Indian tribes, and nonprofit organizations.

Loading means the quantity of a specific substance present per unit of surface area, such as the amount of lead in micrograms contained in the dust collected from a certain surface area divided by the surface area in square feet or square meters.

Material Safety Data Sheet (MSDS): Information sheet that lists any hazardous substance that comprises one percent or more of the product's total volume. Also lists procedures to follow in the event of fire, explosion, leak or exposure to hazardous substance by inhalation, ingestion or contact with skin or eyes. Coatings manufacturers are required to provide retailers with an MSDS for every product they sell to the retailer. Sales clerks should make MSDSs available to retail customers.

Mid-yard means an area of a residential yard approximately midway between the dripline of a residential building and the nearest property boundary or between the driplines of a residential building and another building on the same property.

Pamphlet means the EPA pamphlet titled Renovate Right: Important Lead Hazard Information for Families, Child Care Providers and Schools developed under section 406(a) of TSCA for use in complying with section 406(b) of TSCA, or any State or Tribal pamphlet approved by EPA pursuant to 40 CFR 745.326 that is developed for the same purpose. This includes reproductions of the pamphlet when copied in full and without revision or deletion of material from the pamphlet (except for the addition or revision of State or local sources of information). Before December 22, 2008, the term "pamphlet" also means any pamphlet developed by EPA under section 406(a) of TSCA or any State or Tribal pamphlet approved by EPA pursuant to §745.326.

Pigment: Insoluble, finely ground materials that give paint its properties of color and hide. Titanium dioxide is the most important pigment used to provide hiding in paint. Other pigments include anatase titanium, barium metaborate, barium sulphate, burnt sienna, burnt umber, carbon black, China clay, chromium oxide, iron oxide, lead carbonate, strontium chromate, Tuscan red, zinc oxide, zinc phosphate and zinc sulfide.

Play area means an area of frequent soil contact by children of less than 6 years of age as indicated by, but not limited to, such factors including the following: the presence of play equipment (e.g., sandboxes, swing sets, and sliding boards), toys, or other children's possessions, observations of play patterns, or information provided by parents, residents, care givers, or property owners.

Recognized test kit means a commercially available kit recognized by EPA under §745.88 as being capable of allowing a user to determine the presence of lead at levels equal to or in excess of 1.0 milligrams per square centimeter, or more than 0.5% lead by weight, in a paint chip, paint powder, or painted surface.

Renovation means the modification of any existing structure, or portion thereof, that results in the disturbance of painted surfaces, unless that activity is performed as part of an abatement as defined by this part (40 CFR 745.223). The term renovation includes (but is not limited to): The removal, modification or repair of painted surfaces or painted components (e.g., modification of painted doors, surface restoration, window repair, surface preparation activity (such as sanding, scraping, or other such activities that may generate paint dust)); the removal of building components (e.g., walls, ceilings, plumbing, windows); weatherization projects (e.g., cutting holes in painted surfaces to install blown-in insulation or to gain access to attics, planing thresholds to install weather-stripping), and interim controls that disturb painted surfaces. A renovation performed for the purpose of converting a building, or part of a building, into target housing or a child-occupied facility is a renovation under this subpart. The term renovation does not include minor repair and maintenance activities.

Residential building means a building containing one or more residential dwellings.

Room means a separate part of the inside of a building, such as a bedroom, living room, dining room, kitchen, bathroom, laundry room, or utility room. To be considered a separate room, the room must be separated from adjoining rooms by built-in walls or archways that extend at least 6 inches from an intersecting wall. Half walls or bookcases count as room separators if built-in. Movable or collapsible partitions or partitions consisting solely of shelves or cabinets are not considered built-in walls. A screened in porch that is used as a living area is a room.

Renovator means an individual who either performs or directs workers who perform renovations. A certified renovator is a renovator who has successfully completed a renovator course accredited by EPA or an EPA-authorized State or Tribal program. **Reduction** means measures designed to reduce or eliminate human exposure to lead-based paint hazards through methods including interim controls and abatement. **Recognized laboratory** means an environmental laboratory recognized by EPA pursuant to TSCA section 405(b) as being capable of performing an analysis for lead compounds in paint, soil, and dust.

Reduction means measures designed to reduce or eliminate human exposure to lead-based paint hazards through methods including interim controls and abatement.

Residential dwelling means (1) a detached single family dwelling unit, including attached structures such as porches and stoops; or (2) a single family dwelling unit in a structure that contains more than one separate residential dwelling unit, which is used or occupied, or intended to be used or occupied, in whole or in part, as the home or residence of one or more persons.

Risk assessment means (1) an on-site investigation to determine the existence, nature, severity, and location of lead-based paint hazards, and (2) the provision of a report by the individual or the firm conducting the risk assessment, explaining the results of the investigation and options for reducing lead-based paint hazards.

Start date means the first day of any lead-based paint activities training course or lead-based paint abatement activity.

Start date provided to EPA means the start date included in the original notification or the most recent start date provided to EPA in an updated notification.

State means any State of the United States, the District of Columbia, the Commonwealth of Puerto Rico, the Virgin Islands, Guam, the Canal Zone, American Samoa, the Northern Mariana Islands, or any other territory or possession of the United States.

Residential dwelling means: A single-family dwelling, including attached structures such as porches and stoops; or a single-family dwelling unit in a structure that contains more than one separate residential dwelling unit, and in which each such unit is used or occupied, or intended to be used or occupied, in whole or in part, as the residence of one or more persons.

Target housing means any housing constructed prior to 1978, except housing for the elderly or persons with disabilities (unless any child who is less than 6 years of age resides or is expected to reside in such housing) or any 0-bedroom dwelling.

TSCA means the Toxic Substances Control Act, 15 U.S.C. 2601.

Chapter 19 -Glossary of terms

0-bedroom dwelling means any residential dwelling in which the living area is not separated from the sleeping area. The term includes efficiencies, studio apartments, dormitory housing, military barracks, and rentals of individual rooms in residential dwellings

Soil sample means a sample collected in a representative location using ASTM E1727, "Standard Practice for Field Collection of Soil Samples for Lead Determination by Atomic Spectrometry Techniques," or equivalent method.

Soil-lead hazard. A soil-lead hazard is bare soil on residential real property or on the property of a child-occupied facility that contains total lead equal to or exceeding 400 parts per million (μg/g) in a play area or average of 1,200 parts per million of bare soil in the rest of the yard based on soil samples.

Target housing means any housing constructed prior to 1978, except housing for the elderly or persons with disabilities (unless any one or more children age 6 years or under resides or is expected to reside in such housing for the elderly or persons with disabilities) or any 0-bedroom dwelling.

Visual inspection for clearance testing means the visual examination of a residential dwelling or a child-occupied facility following an abatement to determine whether or not the abatement has been successfully completed.

Visual inspection for risk assessment means the visual examination of a residential dwelling or a child-occupied facility to determine the existence of deteriorated lead-based paint or other potential sources of lead-based paint hazards.

Weighted arithmetic mean means the arithmetic mean of sample results weighted by the number of subsamples in each sample. Its purpose is to give influence to a sample relative to the surface area it represents. A single surface sample is comprised of a single subsample. A composite sample may contain from two to four subsamples of the same area as each other and of each single surface sample in the composite.

The weighted arithmetic mean is obtained by summing, for all samples, the product of the sample's result multiplied by the number of subsamples in the sample, and dividing the sum by the total number of subsamples contained in all samples. For example, the weighted arithmetic mean of a single surface sample containing 60 μg/ft^2 , a composite sample (three subsamples) containing 100 μg/ft^2 , and a composite sample (4 subsamples) containing 110 μg/ft^2 is 100 μg/ft^2 . This result is based on the equation [60+(3*100)+(4*110)]/(1+3+4).

Window trough means, for a typical double-hung window, the portion of the exterior window sill between the interior window sill (or stool) and the frame of the storm window. If there is no storm window, the window trough is the area that receives both the upper and lower window sashes when they are both lowered. The window trough is sometimes referred to as the window "well."

Wipe sample means a sample collected by wiping a representative surface of known area, as determined by ASTM E1728, "Standard Practice for Field Collection of Settled Dust Samples Using Wipe Sampling Methods for Lead Determination by Atomic Spectrometry Techniques, or equivalent method, with an acceptable wipe material as defined in ASTM E 1792, "Standard Specification for Wipe Sampling Materials for Lead in Surface Dust."

Wet disposable cleaning cloth means a commercially available, pre-moistened white disposable cloth designed to be used for cleaning hard surfaces such as uncarpeted floors or counter tops.

Wet mopping system means a device with the following characteristics: A long handle, a mop head designed to be used with disposable absorbent cleaning pads, a reservoir for cleaning solution, and a built-in mechanism for distributing or spraying the cleaning solution onto a floor, or a method of equivalent efficacy.

Work area means the area that the certified renovator establishes to contain the dust and debris generated by a renovation.

TPS 131712